PALESTINE IS THROWING
A PARTY AND THE WHOLE
WORLD IS INVITED

PALESTINE IS
THROWING
A PARTY
AND THE
WHOLE
WORLD
IS INVITED

CAPITAL
AND STATE
BUILDING
IN THE
WEST
BANK

KAREEM RABIE

DUKE UNIVERSITY PRESS
DURHAM AND LONDON   2021

Project editor: Lisa Lawley
Designed by Aimee C. Harrison
Typeset in Minion Pro and Trade Gothic LT Std by
Copperline Book Services

Library of Congress Cataloging-in-Publication Data
Names: Rabie, Kareem, [date] author.
Title: Palestine is throwing a party and the whole world is invited :
capital and state building in the West Bank / Kareem Rabie.
Description: Durham : Duke University Press, 2021. | Includes
bibliographical references and index.
Identifiers: LCCN 2020028899 (print)
LCCN 2020028900 (ebook)
ISBN 9781478011958 (hardcover)
ISBN 9781478014096 (paperback)
ISBN 9781478021407 (ebook)
Subjects: LCSH: Economic development projects—West Bank.
| Urbanization—West Bank. | Housing development—West
Bank. | Economics—West Bank. | West Bank—Economic
conditions. | West Bank—Social conditions. | West Bank—Politics
and government.
Classification: LCC HC415.254 .R335 2021 (print) |
LCC HC415.254 (ebook) | DDC 333.33/8095492—dc23
LC record available at https://lccn.loc.gov/2020028899
LC ebook record available at https://lccn.loc.gov/2020028900

CONTENTS

INTRODUCTION

IN 2008, Palestinian Prime Minister Salam Fayyad invited the world to attend a huge party in the West Bank. It was a party of a specific kind, with specific people attending, and according to Fayyad it was a rather big deal (Fayyad 2008):

Dear Investors,

The Palestine Investment Conference [PIC] promises to be a historic event. As the first high profile investment conference ever held in Palestine, PIC-Palestine will jumpstart a process of integrating Palestine into the global economy.

The time has come to invest in Palestine. The international community showed its overwhelming support of the Palestinian economy in Paris last December, and PIC-Palestine intends to continue this process of creating an environment conducive to investment-led growth.

While the conference is private sector run, the Palestinian National Authority offers its full support and is working to make the conference a success. This conference will provide an opportunity to showcase the many promising investment opportunities in Palestine while strengthening public-private partnership and reforming the economy.

We are throwing a party, and the whole world is invited. This conference is a chance to show a different face of Palestine: a Palestine conducive to economic growth and international investment. I welcome you to Palestine for a chance to enjoy our hospitality, and to learn first-hand that you can do business in Palestine.

DR. SALAM FAYYAD
Prime Minister

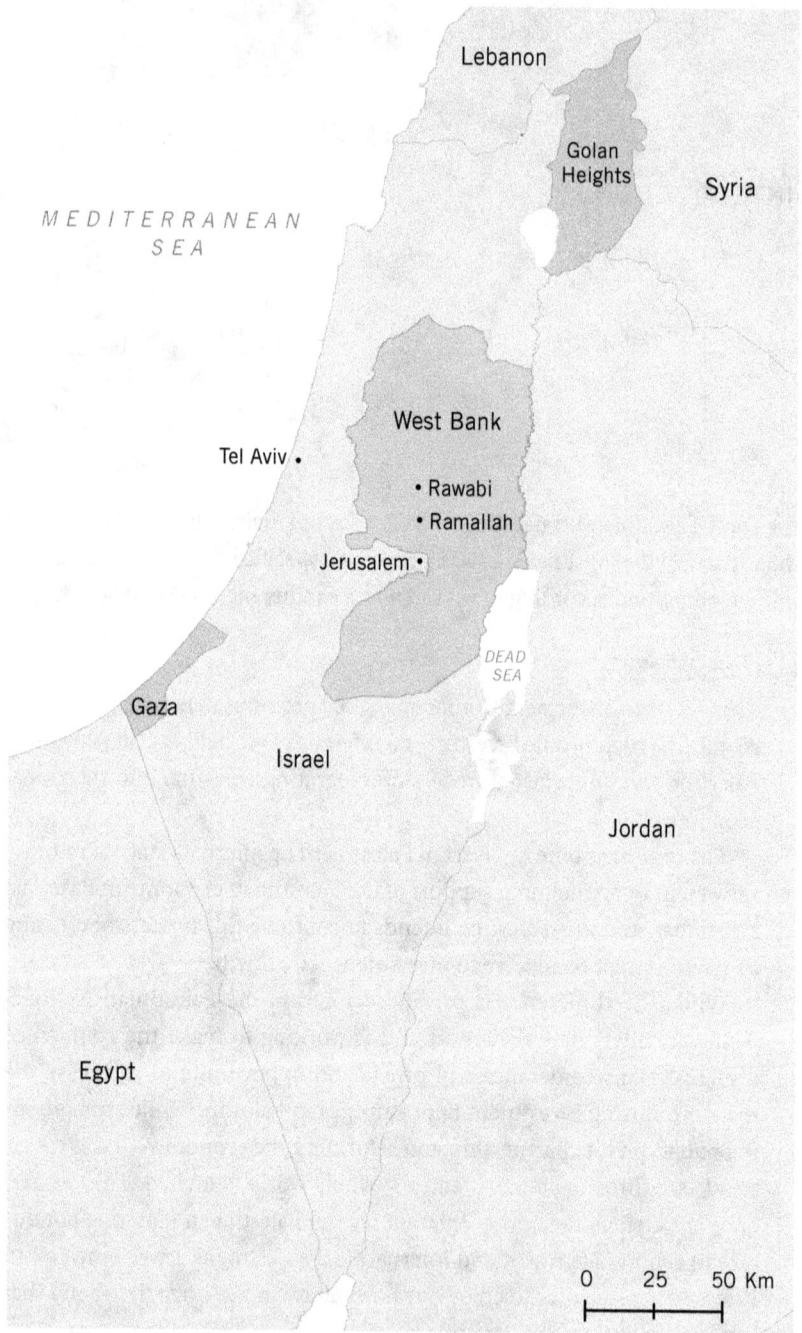

MAP INTRO.1 The West Bank. Map by Meagan A. Snow.

What is in the invitation—Palestine's integration into the global economy, the work to create the foundation for profitable investment, the admixture of public and private, the exuberance and party atmosphere—is as important as what is absent. That is, Israel and its ongoing military, legal, and practical control and integration of the West Bank, East Jerusalem, Gaza, and the Golan Heights. Fayyad's invitation captures the vision and direction established during his tenure, and the ideologies and productive practices I uncover and analyze in this book. Under the rubric of state building, his tenure marked a new phase of market-centric rhetoric and practice in Palestine. With echoes of past forms of responsibility and local control under colonization, the idea was that Palestine could build a private economy and that subsequently, eventually, a functioning and free state would emerge. Formal Palestinian aspiration was slowly translated away from nationalist politics and into practices and political economic languages that circulate worldwide. From the outside, and especially in popular and news media, the situation in Palestine is often described as a series of chaotic, violent, active moments, or as almost apolitically prehistoric. But from a wider perspective on political economic change, the situation seems more coherent and productive. As far as Palestine's relationship to Israel or capacity for self-rule is concerned, ideas and the constitution of power seem stable; significant change anywhere would probably require massive change everywhere.

In response to the failure of the so-called peace process to achieve peace (Massad 2006; Haddad 2016; Hanieh 2013b), its emergence in a period of intensifying globalization (Samara 2000), and given the nature of the contemporary global political economy, the investment conference made sense to its participants. If the peace process was a series of related international attempts to formalize and maintain Palestine vis-à-vis Israeli occupation, the state-building period did the same. But it was framed as though it were possible to circumvent politics through economic mechanisms, a subtle reorientation of political practice. And although Fayyad is gone, and we may be in a different period with a different prime minister today, forms of spatial and political concentration and economic restructuring have not been significantly altered under his successors.

Some of the ways actors in the state and private sector frame their claims about politics in Palestine are new. Instead of describing instability, they focus on potential, with Ramallah as a model. They work explicitly to attach Palestinian politics to capital growth and development by enhancing relations with outside markets, despite the pervasive subordinate relationship with Israel. In other ways this is not new: Palestine has been the target of intervention since well before the establishment of Israel and the global importance of the "conflict" rendered it subject to constant international attention. As Mandy Turner and many others have convincingly argued (Turner 2011, 2012; Turner and Shweiki 2014), development and peace interventions work in concert to produce consistency within Israel's occupation. Yet today's interventions, ideas, and projects for Palestine's economic growth, and descriptions and models of political change, often are based on assumptions that contradict the reality on the ground in Palestine.

Palestine is stratified and geographically fragmented. People in different places are subject to Israeli state and Palestinian violence in much different ways. Israel has long tried to outsource the directly violent parts of the occupation and maximize the distance—political and social, as understood and lived—between Israelis and Palestinians, and between Palestinians themselves. Since 2007 coalitions of Palestinians within Palestine have been openly working to cultivate that distance and enhance stability to produce common sense around practices of investment, privatization, and state building.

The practices that surround ideas and representations go a long way in producing stability and orienting ideas and frameworks around future interventions. In a Middle East characterized by the widespread resistance to autocratic governments—resistance that has often been inspired by the Palestinian struggle against colonization and Israeli occupation—Ramallah might be, in some ways and for some people, one of the more insulated and stable places in the region. In terms of class aspiration and stability, there are not many places in the West Bank other than Ramallah where a refracted image of "normal" everyday life is permissible. "Palestine" refers to less and less territory, and fewer and fewer Palestinians; at the same time, as a target of interventions, it does much more work. Economic interventions orient Palestine toward the global market (Taraki 2008a, 2008b); the Palestine of the West Bank stands in for Historic Palestine, Gaza, and the diaspora and comes to limit wider possibilities. As far as Palestinian cities are concerned, Ramallah and its surrounding areas are the primary sites for development as market building, and they exist in a vacuum enabled by the distribution of Israeli state violence elsewhere. Moreover, Ramallah is an idea and representation that circulates to further plans and interventions—it is a place and an image for aspiration and growth as politics.

If state violence in the West Bank and Gaza is part of the social and political topography there, and class aspiration is a form of safety in this framework, Ramallah presents as one of the few potential sites for partial freedom or return. It is targeted at the national scale, whereas locality is emphasized elsewhere, and it takes on a national character in terms of consolidation inward and population growth, and state- and NGO-scale investments of energy, attention, and capital (Taraki 2008a, 2008b). It is where state-scale planning is most effectively solidifying the political situation in the present.

The same is true for Palestinian society: it is one of fewer and fewer places where a kind of Palestinian life is possible (Karmi 2015). The changes and class character there affect more general Palestinian conceptions and forms of politics and possibility beyond Palestine and Israel. As Ramallah expands at the expense of other parts of Historic Palestine, geographic Palestine is shrinking for most ordinary Palestinians. In a context already defined in large part by barriers to movement, housing debt in particular ties Palestinians to places. Many West Bank Palestinians have treated Ramallah as a "hotel city" during the workweek, and the choice to take on housing debt lessens the means for weekend travel home (Harker 2017). If debt weakens ties between Palestinians and their hometowns, it also deepens ties to Ramallah; consequently, the scale of debt and development strengthens Ramallah at the expense of other cities.

For the Palestinian National Authority (usually referred to as the PA), Israel, and nongovernmental organizations (NGOS), modeling after Ramallah is strategic. For Israelis and the press, it is often the practical outcome of a lack of experience elsewhere. And for Palestinians, especially those in the diaspora for whom the capacity to have a Palestinian place has shrunk drastically, it is structural and political-economic. What it all adds up to is a Palestine increasingly understood through Ramallah's shopping malls, high-end housing, luxury hotels, building boom, its place on something the UN calls the Worldwide Happiness Index, and so on. Buildings, malls, and housing are not accidents; they are built with, and to enhance and produce, stable markets. But these spaces also incorporate people and, like the economy and the state, produce and are embedded within social relations. This has often been described as the neoliberalization of Palestine.[1]

Consequently, the term "occupation" feels increasingly to have exhausted its analytical or descriptive usefulness. When I use the term here, I mean to refer to the forms of practice called "occupation" or grouped under its rubric. My goal is to concentrate and pry from it the forms of governance, practice, and state- and economy-building contained within. Those forms enable and are coproduced by law, investment, and situated forms of capital accumulation that have long since moved beyond the legal structures of international belligerent occupation, while reforming and elaborating the forms of unequal governance and subjugation that fall under its definition. They are practical, material, and ideological.

The occupation is more like a series of localized, piecemeal fixes—routine maintenance, responses, patches—that enable wider settler-colonial imperatives in Israel. It represents one phase, one period of the power structure governing Palestinians' relationships to Palestine, from 1967 to the early 2000s, but it is also an absolute continuation of forms of colonial control, local rule, and dispossession. "Occupation" exists in the present and is logically coherent as a type of investment and economic mechanism for political control. Although the West Bank, Gaza, East Jerusalem, and the Golan Heights are in very real ways occupied by Israel in practice, legally and illegally, "occupation" is not adequate on its own as an analytical framework for covering the political forms prior to 1967, nor is it adequate for the forms of mixed sovereignty that appeared after 2000 and 2008.

Moreover, "occupation" in contemporary academic usage is mainly a West Bank phenomenon. Gaza is a prison and a war zone, its residents collectively punished at regular intervals by a conquering military; the Golan is largely ignored. The temporariness that the occupation once implied has long since been solidified. But it persists in the sense of a future that is deferred and circumscribed by present geographies and possibilities.

Planning for the future in the present consists of material, ideological, and rhetorical projects and practices to shape what comes next. Doing it narrowly within the terms of the present conditions of Israeli control and Palestinian quasi-sovereignty orients those futures that might emerge. Its premise is the future, but it can mostly only function toward solidifying the present. Ideology here is an explanatory framework people have for their material conditions in the present and for orienting themselves to narratives about history and the future. What does it mean to plan for a future in a present that constantly pushes stability further into the distance, but in which states and capitalists are planning to enable specific forms of aspiration within it? In Palestine, planning is in large part a form of speculation that implies a future and a day after the occupation; yet, it does not attempt to bring that day forward. Nevertheless, institutions, places, and relations are being configured within plans in the present.

Hiba Bou Akar historicizes the mutual emergence of planning and development, and asks what can happen when planning narrows and "loses its ethical basis in socioeconomic development—that is, in efforts to address social inequality, poverty, spatial justice, and the redistribution of resources . . . it becomes little more than a tool for ordering space in the interest of those in power, devoid of the normative attributes of equity and social justice that are usually attributed to planning practice" (2018, 147). The Palestinian context is different and in some ways more straightforward than Bou Akar's Lebanon—planning is not about a war yet to come, but imagining a peace yet to come, that no one expects or believes will actually arrive. Planning for a privatized state means ideas of equity are already structured by class and access to aspiration; justice is distributed by the private sector and structured by its particular sense for what counts. Planning and consolidation in Lebanon are in part about protection against future losses. In both Palestine and Lebanon, planning is an ongoing process composed of messy practices and productive work being done that solidifies wider social and political economic relations.

At the scale of state formation, capital investment in the built environment enhances Israeli control as well as shrinks the possibilities to circumvent it. Targeted buildup as urban density means shrinking existing Palestinian space in terms of the possibilities for freedom of movement, association, and aspiration—limited as it is for Palestinians worldwide. The future capital seeks is one with constant growth. Deferral, perhaps the most consistent characteristic of the occupation, has in fact been a primary dynamic of Palestinian subjugation since the Mandate period: the British were to rule until the Palestinians matured enough to do it themselves yet actively destroyed the forms of governance that existed prior to it or would have made such self-rule possible. At the scale of political control of the Palestinian people within Historic Palestine, little has changed since then.

This is a book about those multiple formations of Palestine that occur within the language of temporariness or modern advancement. Occupation frameworks can sometimes obscure analysis of accumulation in favor of focus on the present conditions, and antioccupation analyses have often diverged from political economy. Instead of assuming separation and forms of occupation of the 1967 territories, I want to take the case of private development and housing to understand the productive aspects of global capital, of fixity and circulation, in Palestine.[2]

This is in large part also a book about the social and cultural logics of economic change. My goal is to reconcile local, regional, and worldwide scales of analysis in a political economic ethnography of private housing development in Palestine. In doing so, I hope to give a wider view of Palestine and West Bank politics today, to return capital accumulation to the anthropology of Palestine, and to understand state-form and state-scale economics more generally. I hope to draw a line that connects prior history to the ideas prevalent today to better explain what is happening in the contemporary period; to arrange rather than compose.

Fieldsite

On December 16, 2009, on a van ride between Ramallah and Bethlehem, I heard something quite strange on the radio. In between popular, nationalist songs, the DJ took phone calls, and listeners publicly greeted, congratulated, and wished their friends and families well. One man called about a friend's birthday, another shouted out to his hometown, and a third said he was calling from "the City of Rawabi." At the time of the call, that city's groundbreaking was months away, but the energy, idea, representation, and practical aspects had pierced the public imaginary and begun doing real work in the present. I began my exploration there: in Rawabi, an archetype and a place in the process of becoming. It is a massive new town nine kilometers north of Ramallah that has been under construction for over a decade. Supposedly it will come to house 40,000 "middle-class" Palestinians at a cost, by now, of nearly USD1.5 billion, mostly to the sovereign wealth fund of Qatar as well as to the Palestinian real estate developer Bashar Masri. Masri was educated in the Middle East and North America, and made his fortune as a developer in North Africa and as part of the aid apparatus in the West Bank. He has become a prominent public figure through Rawabi.[3]

Rawabi was announced at the 2008 Palestine Investment Conference, and today it is a place that ties together multiple economic, political, and social phenomena. At the 2010 conference, similar massive development projects had been planned, and Rawabi was the star, alongside Tony Blair, former US senator and peace envoy George Mitchell, and Prime Minister Salam Fayyad. Speakers referenced difficulties and instability, but emphasized investment as a political, nationalist, and humanitarian responsibility. One developer assured the assembled foreign and Palestinian capitalists that "there are returns to be made here." As one of the few noninvestors in the audience, I was surprised to hear the term "return" invoked in this register. Typically, when Palestinians refer to return, they mean the reversal of their exclusion from Palestine; they mean the return home from diaspora and exile. Politically, the idea is that Rawabi will "contribute calm" (Maan News 2015). An interlocutor of Masri's in the conservative *Jerusalem Post* argues, "What is needed is not more walls, but more Rawabis and more Bashar Masris" (Evyatar 2016). With state support and enormous size and scope, Rawabi ties together ideas of social and political stability, and welcomes the rest of the world to participate not through the moribund peace process, but as investors or buyers.

Between 2008 and 2017, I studied the state- and economy-building projects in the West Bank through Rawabi. It is both the vanguard and the cornerstone of a suite of changes to governance, the economy, and the land in Palestine carried out under the rubric of state building. Rawabi is more than an idea: it is a real location, produced through massive political economic interventions and changes, and it both represents and serves as the type of place where Palestinians increasingly hang ideas of their future, politics, and aspiration. New developments are places where stories written in future tense become demonstrably real in buildings that symbolize the future and growth (Searle 2016). Whether or not Rawabi succeeds or a state emerges, new forms of economy, aid, and governance might forever alter how Palestinians live in their homes and their homeland. Rawabi has garnered a lot of attention, but it is just one relevant or interesting aspect of these political economic developments; if not the most important, it is certainly the biggest. And the process of its coming into being makes it easy to see the widespread shift in intervention by actors who understand West Bank political problems to be potentially ameliorated by the deepening of contemporary capital relations. It is the practical application of the ideological work to make accumulation and economic development possible, logical, and sensible.

How does all of this touch the ground in Palestine? Housing and cities are physical manifestations of priorities and possibilities, sites where they are synthesized and combined. Large-scale development and the new city in particular is a place for emerging forms of governance and social life in Palestine. On the ground, the new city entails a few things: investment leading politics, the physical "spatialization of class" (Zhang 2010, 3), investment linking Palestinian individuals to markets in real but subtle ways, and the creation of a site that allows certain forms of politics and aspiration but disables others. The new city is a real place and form where people, ideas, and capital are reconciled; where society and common sense are reproduced. Within a shrinking territory, it helps establish precedents and models for the future of Palestine. In orienting international priorities toward economic aspiration, it renders other experiences outside of what counts or is politically solvable.

Rawabi is located on a previously empty and unprofitable hill in Area A, where Palestinians purportedly have civil and military control; surrounded by Area B under Palestinian civil and Israeli military control; and Area C (more than 60 percent of the West Bank) under Israeli control. As I show in subsequent chapters, Rawabi is a lens through which to see much wider processes. It could not exist without concerted effort by capitalists, NGOs, and politicians to establish the idea of its necessity; a state to enable new forms of economic practice and aid as well as new forms of land tenure; donors and investors to fund Rawabi on a massive scale; and people to live there. The PA state and institutions are not parts of a monolith, but on this issue they work with developers to shape government priorities for growth and capital accumulation. In the following chapters on planning and national priorities, I describe how movement at the top orients practice, even if it does not eradicate debate or disagreement. Not only can the PA work towards its goals for ideological and financial consistency, it incorporates many West Bank Palestinians through its scale as an employer (and through its ability to garnish wages for loan payments and prohibit its employees from certain forms of speech and protest). A significant focus is on bureaucrats and the employees tasked with carrying out government priorities. I do not mean to place undue burden or agency on them, but to try to trace the ways human activity is shaped by and produces wider contexts for ideology and practice, and how the PA and its allies in the private sector work to expand what is possible and who can benefit under current conditions.

Months and years before anyone had moved in, Rawabi was the site and embodiment of new forms of investment, personal aspiration, and political organization. It physically anchors new political economic ideas and priorities in the landscape. Moreover, Rawabi changes laws and sets precedents that enable ongoing interventions. Backed by international aid, the Palestinian Authority and Israel, along with the Palestinian capitalist class, are actively trying to create the kinds of economic and political stability necessary to insure ongoing profit and growth, organized by the idea of an eventual state. The process of state building—and what emerges around and through that process—is as relevant as whatever may or may not ultimately result. The state unfolds over time and emerges in, and makes and remakes, specific places and modes of production through the actions of various actors and coalitions. The form it takes is the outcome of the struggles and projects to form it. This is a perpetually forming state: the "condensation of the changing balance of forces in political and politically-relevant struggle" (Jessop 2014; Poulantzas 1980), rather than a static outcome. The aggregated practices of working to make a state, the ongoing cycle of political intervention, and the strategies organized around the idea of the state shape what is happening in Palestine and among Palestinians. And those practices orient what might happen in the future. Markets are ideological projects as well as legal regimes; but they are produced through and with laws that govern more than economic practice. The seemingly exceptional Palestinian case illuminates general relationships between states, aid, and national economies. The Palestinian state is a hybrid of government, aid imperatives, and private initiative. Some aspects of state building are built on fantasy. But others are more exaggerated than in different kinds of state-scale political formations.

Coalitions of actors create new forms of economic life and market participation; they do not simply emerge from nowhere. They can exist in new places like Rawabi, where developers influence and cultivate consumers and incorporate participants. At the international scale, aid is being reconfigured as funding for the private sector *through* the government. In response to growing privatization and available credit, not to mention decades of exhausting political and social circumstances, consumers are taking on increased debt burdens for the chance to live in the new town. Those loans are backed by international aid organizations, insulating lenders as part of their political imperative to keep Palestine stable. Almost as in aspic, Palestine—the idea of Palestine, the administration of Palestine, Palestinians—is today suspended by and within Israeli political, economic, and geographic imperatives. Many forms of human intervention, international aid and global investment, local projects, and forms of agency work to differentiate Palestine and Israel yet maintain them as part of the same whole—one in which Palestine is a subordinate state, territory, and market within Israel. Private development as a form of state and economy building is one such project.

And that is why Rawabi became a big deal so far in advance of its physical manifestation; for different types of actors, interests, and classes, it has already become an idea and a site on which to cultivate new forms of political organization, economic investment, and class aspiration that had previously lacked clear forms or outlets. And, although there is constant movement, the process has a stabilizing function at the scale of its relationship with Israel. Rawabi fixes ideas from a specific moment in time on the ground, in the law, and in the polity, to orient the structure of possibilities for future initiatives and activity. As a mechanism for class stratification and accumulation, private housing—much of it debt-financed—is itself a site for international intervention. As such development projects become a national priority for the PA and donors, they are altering the experiences of those Palestinians inside and out who are unable to afford to participate or are otherwise outside its scope. Plans premised on class aspiration are potentially inclusive as well as terminally exclusive. Absent the right of return for Palestinians, and return being contingent on affordability, class is a vector for return and a primary way diaspora relations to Palestine are being shaped.[4] This is one unintended consequence for the nation.

Political Economy, Geography, and the Study of Palestine

State building in the West Bank comes out of the Oslo period, but its logics do not begin there. It is, I argue, part of a longer-term project to stabilize Palestine within Israel and to reconcile contradictory imperatives. First is the overarching Israeli imperative to control the Palestinian territories and to do so with as little labor and capital as possible. The earliest European Zionist settler colonists consciously imagined and produced a land without a people, an idea reiterated in practice and historiography that persists despite all evidence to the contrary. Jewish colonists knew they had much to gain from a subordinate and exploitable indigenous population, and they subjected the Palestinians to their power (Lockman 1996). Arab Palestinians and European Jewish Zionist colonists share intertwined histories and lifeworlds. Palestinians and Israelis are separated geographically and physically. They are separated by political formations—the occupation and otherwise—that necessitate specific forms of state and civilian power and authority. Yet there cannot be occupied without occupier, and the massive state structures and institutions that are produced within the occupying state—the generational political, racial, legal, military, and economic mechanisms to police the boundary—are coherent. They are constituted by and constitutive of the settlement, colonization, and occupation of Palestine. Empires are social formations and places (Wilder 2005); that is also true of settlement, state building, and occupation. Israelis and Palestinians are bound in place, and through occupation, by social, political, and economic relations. One of the implications of state building is orientation of work and energy around the assumption that it is possible to build Palestinian markets and institutions separate from Israel. But the context is messily cohesive and better understood through the wider lens of global political economies of settlement, colonialism, and accumulation rather than through an imaginary of separateness.

Central to the Palestinian historical imaginary prevalent in some anthropology and in much political writing is a vision of rural peasantry separate from Israel or the state. Although it might imply something anticapitalist, it does not engage capitalism as a process or set of social relations. And it does not enable broader analysis of the contemporary moment. In chapter 8, I trace that narrative and the ways it is shared and operationalized by both capitalist developers and their critics. It obscures something fundamental that historians such as Beshara Doumani (1995), Roger Owen (1993), and Alexander Schölch (1993) have long since demonstrated—Palestine is and has been incorporated into the world economy. It has a history of capital integration and competition, industrial production, money lending, land tenure and commoditization of land, capture of surplus production, and rural-urban economic relations.

Instead, the histories mobilized have too often been written through the logics of present fragmentation. Part of my goal here is to write against the ways that Oslo has been treated as a moment of rupture, or the occupation as a coherent framework or clearly comprehensible system. Narratives of progress and backwardness, rural and urban, and mechanisms for political and economic integration into the world are neither new nor reflective of the present realities. Many forms of economic practice and aspiration today may seem or be convincingly described as novel, but they have analogs, build upon the past, and putting them into a longer historical framework can illuminate possible directions for the future. Many histories of Palestine take Palestinians to be the objects rather than the subjects of history. There are often good, political, antioccupation reasons to do so, but the typical story accepts definitions of occupation that imply a kind of Palestinian innocence ruptured by the menace of Zionist colonization and modernity. Or it accepts the meaning of occupation in the terms of the contemporary material struggle for state.

In his study of China, Prasenjit Duara argues that while the territorial nation-state is shaped through relations in a worldwide system, representations of political community are shaped by the "transactions between historical narratives and the discourses" of the state itself (1995, 81). In *The Urban Revolution*, Henri Lefebvre (2003) discusses "the urban reality" and "the urban phenomenon" with its specific contours of space and time, but also the concomitant concepts, feelings, and impressions it brings with it. The Palestinian geographer Omar Tesdell (2019) often works against the common argument that "the world is now 50% urban," responding that it means "the world is also 50% rural." True enough, and what Lefebvre was talking about, and what I think the case of private housing development shows, is how they are bound through the same continual processes. The urban phenomenon has more generally shaped forms of economic and spatial consolidation and transition. Changes in Palestine in terms of dense housing are spatial questions; labor and reproduction and productive capacity questions; questions of social change and internal distribution. Urbanism is in part morphological, and the urban phenomenon is part of the explanation for the town-country distinction. Moreover, the urban for Lefebvre means the substitution of customary norms by contractual obligations, so it is also about polity and governance—the relationships of people to place and to categorizations of human activity, potential, and power, as well as place-dependent labor and development. For him, the urban phenomenon is dialectical, and it means change, incorporation, and a much wider unity *through* that change. The urban is a logic that means consequent and relational alteration elsewhere—as a state emerges in Palestine through city-scale urban development and in service of investment in the landscape of Palestine, it also structures a polity and forms of incorporation beyond that investment.

With that in mind, capital accumulation, state building, and private development can be understood as related forms of political consolidation. Once again, they are not new. As part of the Ottoman reform process, land became visible through one of the first attempts to regularize title and create a land market (Owen 1993; Rashid Khalidi 1997). Other parts of Historic Palestine experienced massive dispossession of a rural peasantry through consolidation and market reforms. Early Zionist colonization relied on markets and economics. Palestinians were dispossessed as part of the capitalist accumulation process, which rendered land available for Zionists to purchase as they began to immigrate to Palestine in larger numbers. In all colonial and settler-colonial geographies, land is central as an idea, a mechanism for control and exclusion, and as a commodity. The Zionist historian Yossi Katz (1994) demonstrates how land sales were a vital part of early Zionist colonization of Historic Palestine. There has always been opacity in land markets; private ownership and property have long been parts of how Israeli land control has operated.

Racial separation is fundamental to the Zionist movement, and it too is bound up with processes of market creation and capital accumulation. British economic policy during the Mandate sought to encourage a Zionist industrial sector and contributed to building up more and more separate Jewish and Arab sectors. British support of Jewish immigration occurred in terms of both laissez-faire attitudes and active support through favorable tariffs and monopoly protection—favorable terms for accumulation for a class defined on the basis of its religion and ethnic origin. More specifically, the British allowed Zionists to discriminate against Arab Palestinians in hiring, which spurred the importation of a Jewish laboring class. A growing Jewish working class, which was better paid than Palestinian Arab workers, led to an increase in the cost of living in mixed areas and downward pressure on employed Palestinian laborers (who themselves secured social reproduction with peasant subsistence). The growth of that Jewish working class further excluded Palestinians from participation in new labor markets, and manifest physically in patterns of housing, labor, and movement—the class, race, and spatial bases for a Zionist "state within a state" were created (B. J. Smith 1993).

Beyond labor, capacity for economic growth was inflected by racial and colonial politics, and there was a kind of simultaneous downward pressure on elite Palestinians and on Palestinian capital. Palestine experienced extremely rapid economic change, the emergence of an urban merchant class, and consequent proletarianization of the peasantry. New private property regimes under the British Mandate remade the landscape to enable as well as to limit the scope of Zionist land purchases. This changed ideas of land; it was a site of struggle in terms of ownership and property intertwined with racial and political claims, justice, and rights (Fakher Eldin 2008). Market creation and accumulation are social and political projects, but they have never been about absolute openness. Alongside growth, expulsion—of certain people, crafts, and forms of economic practice—has been central to the formation of global capitalism (Mathew 2016). As certain peoples are excluded, new practices penetrate social and economic life. One way to think about the new forms of building in Palestine is through the ways that Israeli political and territorial control—occupation and otherwise—has aided accumulation. Land in Palestine is empty for very clear reasons related to governance regimes and registration, military intervention, Israeli prohibitions, and so on. Yet, local Palestinians started to oppose the movement and transfers of ownership; Sherene Seikaly (2015) shows how a group almost entirely ignored in histories and historiographies of Palestine—an already established Palestinian bourgeoisie—combined accumulation with a nationalist project of "modern arrival" in the Mandate period. For the Palestinian bourgeoisie then as now, accumulation could be nationalist.

Once a wider perspective on land and state is adopted—one that emphasizes market relations, production, circulation, and class—it becomes clear, as Michael Fischbach (2003) points out, that 1948 was among other things an utterly massive, transformative redistribution of wealth from Palestinians to Jewish colonists and to the state.[5]

It is due to the prevalence of the moment of occupation and separation in historiography of Israel and Palestine—and the consequent sense of exceptionalism—that capitalism can sometimes come to seem like a new phenomenon. Palestine has been one of the most historically important places in the world during the biblical, colonial, and contemporary periods. Simply put, it has never been isolated. Second, if there is a moment when changes to economic structure took material form in the West Bank, it may not have been around Oslo but rather in the early 2000s, during what the artist and geographer Samir Harb described to me as "the siege period." The siege of the West Bank by the Israeli military led to a possibility and an opportunity to remake physical space and to open markets; during that period, the fantasy of a peace process morphed into ideological practices centered around markets as political solutions. And it was when changes to the political economic landscape and the built environment became visible, especially in Ramallah. The analytical point I hope to emphasize here is that linkages and histories produce the context in which further changes can occur and in which individuals' capacities for life and social reproduction take place alongside and through modes of production.

The differences between the images and renderings of wealth and aspiration in the new city and the general reality for most Palestinians under occupation are stark and obvious. But Rawabi is a part of the work being done to make one seem like the other. In the West Bank and with consequences for Palestine and Palestinians, a new city is being made in the image of a political promise and future quite unlike the long-term lived experiences of its prospective residents. Housing is being designed and governed in service of economic and social life formed in relation to an open market and in ways that could only contain a small number of Palestinian subjects of Israel. Modernist and state-scale planning, and architectural programs, are created in service of a specific kind of politics around opening and integrating the Palestinian market and reframing national political agency as market participation; antioccupation political rhetoric and capital accumulation are bound through this project and in this place.

City-State

How then to locate and study the tangled mess of Palestine today? First of all, a kind of state building is happening. And it is happening in the present context, within the contemporary forms of political control, and creating the foundation for a future consonant with them. Second, a context in which there is free movement of capital and information, but not for goods or people, can tell us about neoliberalism and the necessary roles states have in organizing space for capitalist production, distribution and accumulation. Drawing on Lefebvre (2009), what I have in mind here is a state mode of production. As a new state-scale market organization emerges in the West Bank, this adds up to a political, social, and economic situation that appears as a frontier for capitalist investors and a project for opening and integrating the Palestinian market into more general circuits of capital circulation. Socially, it has the potential to reorient national political agency as market participation. It is also monopolistic, given the political and legal institutions forming around state building, and the precedents and barriers it creates for subsequent interventions.

West Bank Palestinians' relationship to Palestine substantially changed after the 1993 Oslo Accords and the PLO leadership returned from exile in Tunis and elsewhere. In 1994, the Palestinian National Authority was created and was expected to function for an interim term of five years, during which time negotiators would iron out the "final status" issues of borders, settlements, Jerusalem, and the Palestinian right to return. More than twenty-five years later, the PA still exists, and final status issues remain unresolved. Oslo also created the idea of a Palestinian interim government operating with meaningful sovereignty at some later date. Second, it carved the West Bank into the A, B, C archipelago of territorial control.

In 2007, in the midst of that holding pattern, the former International Monetary Fund (IMF) official Salam Fayyad became minister of finance, partially at the behest of donor countries. Later that year, at the time of the split between Fatah and Hamas, the Palestinian president Mahmoud Abbas appointed him prime minister. The last time the Palestinian Legislative Council convened was also in 2007. The split and Fayyad's ascendance were the basis for new kinds of pro-privatization initiatives in the West Bank, and governing could happen relatively unencumbered by law, in effect setting precedent as it went along. Fayyad focused on calling in capital and encouraging investment and reform at the national scale. He established an economic agenda based on the need for profit and growth and worked toward a national economy that would encourage stability, investment, and ultimately the state. In a celebratory column on Palestinian moderation and economic growth, Thomas Friedman (2009) coined the term "Fayyadism" to describe it.[6] But it is a mistake to give Fayyad all the credit or the blame. The year 2007 marks an important shift in the political economic orientation of Palestine: it was the year that many large-scale private economic development and stabilization projects were formulated.[7]

If history is a question of narrative and representation, and it shapes the land, ideas of the land, and what might be possible on that land, then representation and representational space is vital. Representation is an important aspect of this analysis: What needs to happen to make interventions into physical space seem possible and coherent? What work needs to be done?

Who benefits now and in the future? The Palestinian case allows me to shed light on the ways economics is understood as a means for political stabilization and improvement. Such a context, where a territorial state is unlikely to emerge, demonstrates crucial features of the neoliberal state and the ways states can organize markets even without production or well-defined territorial relationships. Ideas, institutions, and practices of state can be productive even without territorial sovereignty. Moreover, the geographies of political and economic control, occupation and otherwise, enable new forms of intervention and accumulation. In my analysis, I aim to go up to the general scale and political organization, and down to the landscape, and tell stories that are at once discrete and connected. Taken together, they help clarify the bigger picture in Palestine today. Although the concept of scale has ebbed and flowed in human geography, I want to keep and maintain a basic part of it. Scale is spatially productive, and it implies, utilizes, and is constituted by political and geographic interrelations. Neil Smith describes the urban scale, the scale of centralization; the global scale, the scale of the world market; and the nation-state (1984, 189). The erosion of the nation-state through the world market has multiplied roles and capacities for governance and economic organization at the urban scale, and cities have been made and remade as objects and containers of economic and social activity. Investment in housing, I believe, is a place where general dynamics of spatial production and Palestine's strange market and politics are apparent. Moreover, it is a local node for regional and worldwide economic processes and for making and remaking ideas about economic, cultural, and political universality.

In this period of globalization and absent a national economy or clear nation-state territory, city-scale governance is increasingly important, and the emerging state may not have a straightforward relationship to its territory. The nested state political organization in Palestine emerges upon, by, and for the benefit of the market—not simultaneously, as in Karl Polanyi's (2012) formulation, but because one necessitates the other. Capitalism implies, seeks out, and produces markets, and it necessarily incorporates different territories in different ways. The universalizing tendencies of capitalism do not equalize or render uniform.

Capitalism and neoliberalization are worldwide, dynamic processes of unequal incorporation. As Andy Clarno (2017) has described it, neoliberalism is a context-specific process of political economic and social change. It is, after all, a form of capitalism. In this text I emphasize features like accumulation, differentiation, aspiration, and so on, rather than using the broader category as shorthand; it seems more fruitful to parse than to lump. The scholarly literature on neoliberalism is huge, and a handful of features are most relevant to my study. First, privatization is part of the continuous formation of the state, governance, and state–civil society relations, and it is often a response to administrative and political problems (Hibou 2004). Second, neoliberal forms of capitalism extract labor value but do not replenish social reproductive capacity either through wages, types of infrastructure development, or state forms of aid such as health care (Peck 2010). Third, the reproduction of labor power has cultural and social dimensions (N. Smith 1984). Finally, the nation-state, while it never was totally self-sustaining or bounded, is now almost entirely a node in a global political economy (Harvey 2007). The inherent capitalist imperatives for accumulation presuppose certain kinds of states and relations between them; neoliberalism means the responsive reformation and repurposing of the state in line with those imperatives.[8]

The state in this account is an ongoing question. What that means is that as the idea of a state is forming, it does what states always do—draws boundaries between people and the state, between the public and private spheres. It reiterates, strengthens, and realizes the idea of a state itself. If the state is political power in territorial form (Jessop 2016), I want to separate state power from sovereignty, for reasons that are obvious in the case of the subordinate authority presently managing state building in Palestine. To dig down a bit further, I want to emphasize jurisdiction as a mode of the exercise of legal power over people and population in place (Pasternak 2017). Here, the ways state power and jurisdiction exist in the absence of sovereignty do not weaken the idea of a state; in the contemporary global political economy the state is now more than ever a mode of managing and organizing power and possibility. And if a primary reason for having a state in the first place is to operate in relation to the network of nation-states, then contemporary forms of communication, capital flow, uneven development, and labor mobility mean that a state can operate through market organization and concomitant political power over local market participants. It does not require strict boundaries. One of the primary mechanisms of the state is to produce the idea of itself as it obscures its operation and fundamental aspects; it is a historically-constituted social fact (Mitchell 1999; Abrams 1988; Trouillot 2003; Watson 1990; Allen 1990).

Moreover, the state is the scale of political organization that operates within what Bob Jessop calls the "world of states" (2016, 194). In this period, it does not at all disappear or lessen its hold over a polity; instead, it pivots. As for the state in the West Bank, I show one part: how capital comes in and becomes fixed as a way to circumvent the political stagnancy of this particular territory and translate it into nodes, infrastructures, and political relations that enable and ensure the local necessities and global relations for capitalist accumulation. The world of states is coproduced by, within, and through states themselves and is part of the continuous management of the relations between state, territory, and market. Like Karl Marx's commodity, it is an object that not only conceals relations, but translates them into common form to enable communication, circulation, and motion (Marx 1990).

This is what state building means in Palestine: the creation of a scale of economic practice that replaces liberation and moral claims with modernization so as to stabilize local jurisdiction over a territory within Israel. The economy has not replaced the state, but the state project is one to create a national economy that can be made in lieu of a state.[9] But state and market are parts of the same whole, the same ensemble of characteristics, and one could never supplant the other. Today, and in ways that make sense in the contemporary global political economy, the West Bank state can be weighted almost entirely toward producing a market. I use language of accumulation, aggregation, and solidification to try to understand how these things come together in this place, and what it can tell us about general phenomena. Accumulation is an individual question, but it can also be much larger and organize political forms and geographies. This state is an accumulation strategy (Jessop 2014); in Harvey's terminology following the French Regulation School, it is a regime of accumulation that is at once economic and political, but just as importantly, a social, cultural, and human relation (Harvey 1990; Aglietta 2016).

My point here: I emphasize the imperatives of accumulation that drive the state-building process and marketization through urban development. It is piecemeal, it is not monolithic, it is in part spatial, and the ways that combinations of its attributes appear are not inevitable. It is a "worldwide" process rather than a unified global phenomenon (Lefebvre 2003; N. Smith 2002). It is a process of becoming. Critical work on Palestine has tended to emphasize capitalists over capitalism, and development over class. I hope to explain the modes of exercise of power rather than its location (Roitman 2013).

Contemporary ethnography has tended to emphasize messiness and contingency at the expense of wider phenomena, and recent economic anthropology has often paid more attention to moral or ideological economies or questions of historical development than to social and structural relations under capitalism. There has long been a greater ease assuming difference in context; consequently, differences are framed in ways that demonstrate a lack of structure. As a question of method, there is, I believe, a way to understand structural links and social life without being overdetermined, but it requires assumptions about human activity and social reproduction. The strange exceptionality of Palestine, both real and as presented, helps clarify the complex interaction between local context and dynamic processes of capital accumulation and market creation.

If state building is an explicit goal intertwined with economic liberalization and market creation, how does the state come to exist, and in what form? The state emerging in Palestine—here shorthand for both the process of change organized in its name as well as the set of political institutions for managing the polity—is part of what accounts for the longevity of the complex political and ideological forces lumped into the "occupation" terminology. On multiple occasions during my years of fieldwork, I was told that "there is no state," that it is a "fantasy," or worse, it is "bullshit." While each is correct in its way, those descriptions are partial. The state, even if it is fantastical, is formed through market logics and solidifies not only as a set of laws and institutions that manage things like infrastructure and development, but as a scale of political and economic relations with Israel and other states. It establishes and formalizes priorities at the scale of the state. Within that state, the idea frames—but does not determine—social relations among a people and a polity.

Political rationality takes the form of the state process in the West Bank, subjects are incorporated, and new laws are written to govern practices and relationships. In nonsovereign Palestine, law is malleable, often more descriptive than proscriptive, but the laws that coalesce as part of the state have material effects. Housing is one place where these multiple dimensions of political, economic, and social life can be understood; it is simultaneously an effect of and precursor for much wider relations. Drawing on Antonio Gramsci's framework, Louis Althusser (2006) describes those aspects that are part of the state but operate primarily through ideology rather than repression. Crucially, these "ideological state apparatuses"—the media, schools, family, political parties, and so on—are part of how the state becomes obvious to its subjects and reproduces existing social and political economic relations. For Althusser, social and cultural organization is fundamental to how state power, distinguished from a repressive state apparatus, operates. Analytically, a clean separation between public and private is impossible here and anywhere else. Housing is fundamental for establishing the political and cultural contexts for social life and reproduction, in providing shelter for people, and to shaping conditions for jurisdiction. Targeted private developments like Rawabi are produced as the image of political economy at the scale of markets and the network of national economies, manifested into the landscape, and productive of future capacities there.[10]

Charles Tilly (1990) famously described the state in Europe as a form of organized crime, and what he meant was that state formation involved protection, violence, and extraction in service of capital accumulation. States also formalize legal relations in part to establish geographical and economic consistency and predictability. One of the primary ways this happens between Israel and Palestine is through laws that formalize geographical separation *within* Israel. One of the important outcomes of housing in the West Bank today is its practical elaboration of jurisdiction. Jurisdiction, as Shiri Pasternak explains, is about how authority is established and managed in ways separate from sovereignty. She points toward a question Harvey asks about how "the territorial logics of power, which tend to be awkwardly fixed in space, respond to the open spatial dynamics of endless capital accumulation?" She argues that "forces of accumulation and state formation that seek to integrate Indigenous lands into the capitalist economy have in turn been shaped by Indigenous assertions of jurisdiction of their lands" (2017, 26). If state power consists of the capacity to organize and order relations of production (Gilmore 2007), what happens when the most authorized indigenous articulations become about formalizing and stabilizing politics through markets and state building? When the question for Palestinian governance becomes about how to invest and profit in this unstable environment? How do these changes inflect social life and change?

In the West Bank, the fluid relationships that neoliberal capital and states have to territories and national markets are not fundamentally at odds with the present conditions of occupation, military rule, and colonial control. Moreover, state- and economy-building projects work to create stability at the scale of the national economy and the relationship with Israel (upward), but they may distribute instability socially (downward). As a question of capitalism and neoliberalism, the territorial state was successful . . . until it stopped being so. Capitalism is both crisis prone and resilient; the ways that it regulates itself and overcomes contradictions are sites for analysis of its persistence and ongoing formation (Boyer 1990; Boyer and Drache 2005). Power is exercised as a series of endless patches on a tire. But the wheel keeps moving. Unintended consequences continuously appear as both new problems and new opportunities. In *Lineages of the Absolutist State*, Perry Anderson (2013) suggests that histories of above are no less important than histories from below. I hope that this ethnography of the above emphasizes the continual production of the state and the local contexts in which a general political phenomenon is formed and reformed.

Housing and the Topography of Class

The PA state is suspended within an Israel that works to maintain its limited practical responsibility to the Occupied Territories, while maximizing its territorial control, jurisdiction, and sovereignty. For the PA in the West Bank, there is a body of state law forming around state practice, practical authority, and moderate independence—jurisdiction and increased stability. For developers like Masri, occupied Palestine presents either a "ticking time bomb, or an opportunity" for accumulation (Cuen 2017). Housing is a form of fixed capital, and those spaces that dominate and shape everyday life are made through and in the image of capital under occupation.[11] Value is appropriated and created in space and spatial arrangements. If urban environments require and necessitate fixed capital, and if they incorporate people—people who live real lives beyond the abstraction with which they are targeted as consumers or through national plans—then the scale of human habitation is bound to imperatives, ideology, and movements of capital. Worldwide and international political economy and events at multiple scales can bear directly on individuals' lives.

In complicated and murky ways, international aid has also been reoriented as investment, providing loan guarantees that insulate Palestinian banks from potential default. This, in turn, makes foreign investment in housing development feasible—risk is minimized in the name of political and economic development. Attempts to create stability in a colonized territory through foreign investment, class consolidation, and capital accumulation lead to little change in the broader context of political and territorial control, but increasingly orient individual practice toward class aspiration and servicing debt. As ideas about open markets inflect government practice and form the basis for new government institutions, those ideas materialize in plans and the stuff of housing developments. Mundane, everyday qualities of life are produced through wider political economic and social relations. Housing is as much a commodity and vehicle for accumulation and circulation as a place for people to live (Madden and Marcuse 2016). Given a PA focus on international investment over local capital, and the distorting and separating effects it has on the Palestinian economy (Samara 2000), what happens to the dynamics of control, nation, and state when Palestinian and foreign capital come together? Forms and ideas about politics—empowerment and resistance—change along with and through the wider context (Kuttab 2010).

Adam Hanieh (2002, 2008, 2013a), Toufic Haddad (2016), and others have charted the complex connections that Arab capitalists and certain wealthy families have to different regional political regimes and the ways they work toward ongoing accumulation. For Hanieh, it is through spatially productive and regionally and internationally oriented market building; and for Haddad, this is through neoliberal state- and peace-building efforts. Tariq Dana describes the role that Palestinian capitalists have had in shaping the national political movement, through funding and political mediation, but who have, since Oslo, become beneficiaries of the occupation. He describes how PA monopoly protection and support of accumulation through banking reform "enables capitalists to pressure the PA" (Dana 2014).

This is true, and taking the PA as a moving target—with actors and interests continuously shaped through a different scale of market imperatives—shows both pressure and cooperation. My goal here is less to define class and interest than to look at how ideas and priorities are generalized, established, and made meaningful through interventions and plans. Class is an ideology, an identity, and a set of practices that shift along with politics and modes of production (Bhattacharya and Vogel 2017). Palestine itself changes as ideas about the future are incorporated into the landscape and as new spatial arrangements take off, start to exist, or otherwise gain legitimacy.

Investment into private housing for a burgeoning middle class implies questions of social change and class orientation. There is little consensus on what exactly the "middle class" consists of in Palestine. In an interview, the sociologist Jamil Hilal told me that 38 percent of Palestine is "middle class" as defined by a unity of cultural values. I have also heard the argument that, in the absence of productive sectors and without a working class, *all* Palestinians are middle class. There is also the opposite argument that, given the economic difficulties and occupied economy, it is not worthwhile to describe *any* Palestinians as middle class. Where does that leave us?

Hilal outlines the ways the Palestinian middle class emerged under the Mandate, was stagnant for decades under Israeli de-development, and is re-emerging in the present, with difficulty and barriers imposed by the current iterations of Israeli settler-colonial imperatives (2006, 2014). Although it is vague, the "middle class" invoked via development means essentially two things: first, it refers to the kinds of educated people who live mostly in Ramallah and who work in the PA or development sectors (or are potential employees of the high-tech sector long-desired by the same classes and actors brought together in the Rawabi project). Second, and perhaps more importantly for my account, it refers to a potential or aspirational middle class, the people targeted by Rawabi and people with the desire to orient themselves, their families, and their lives in relation to the political, economic, and consumerist promises that Rawabi makes. The idea of Rawabi as a private form of governance, and the fact of its existence, provides a site for the spatialization of a middle class defined through it.

Moreover, middle class is the population that is targeted as a class, produced by and through interventions that enable it. Within a local node of global political economy, class is being made in an environment in which labor, wage, and property ownership are not determinative in ways they might be under different state-scale political economies. Because of political instability and lack of production, in an environment where public sector employment, remittances, and development aid are foundational, place and changing social relations are crucial for understanding class. Even where there are already-formed states to speak of, these problems are exacerbated by neoliberal governance schemes in which states no longer prioritize social reproduction. Here as elsewhere, political economy requires a concept of class that emphasizes relations and the cultural and social aspects of circulation and fixity.

In her "Vagabond Capitalism and the Necessity for Social Reproduction," Cindi Katz (2001) points out that, under forms of global production, as production and social reproduction are decoupled, social reproduction nevertheless must occur, and must happen in those places people find themselves:

> Social reproduction is fleshy, messy, and indeterminate stuff of everyday life. It is also a set of structured practices that unfold in dialectical relation with production, with which it is mutually constitutive and in tension. Social reproduction encompasses daily and long-term reproduction, both of the means of production and the labor power to make them work. At its most basic, it hinges upon the biological reproduction of the labor force, both generationally and on a daily basis, through the acquisition and distribution of the means of existence, including food, shelter, clothing, and healthcare. (Katz 2001, 711)

Katz, in turn, offers the research strategies of topography and topographical knowledge, and the political potential of counter-topographies. In a Palestine where housing is a primary aspect of state-scale political economy and mode of production, and when housing profitability depends on filling it with people who can afford it, new housing becomes a site of a much wider form of class reproduction—mode of production appears as a place, container, and site of social relations. Fragmentation of the Palestinian territories greatly affect labor migration and labor markets (Farsakh 2005), but it also presents an opportunity for investment in physical space and aspiration. Thus, Hilal's "unity of cultural values" is illuminating precisely because class is not a fixed entity, but shifts in relation to wider social and political economic changes in Palestine, and through interventions like housing developments that presuppose, need, or cultivate certain forms of class cultural values. For real estate developers, the middle class means single family homebuyers, but also a form of urbanization and vernacular (J. Hilal and El-Sakka 2015).

Recent literature on political economy coming from Palestine tends to fall into two main sets. The first is the critical work I have drawn on here and throughout, on the current condition in Palestine that works to aggregate a class analysis through the deformations and peculiarities of the occupation. The other is policy-oriented analysis undertaken in concert with NGOS and guided by considerations of development, lack of development, and political barriers to development in Palestine. There, class is not often central, but when it does come in, its composition is assumed or stable, ancillary to national development. Part of the reason for the focus on development rather than class might be the legacy of a national movement that purposefully subsumed questions of differentiation and stratification to national problems. Disunities would be dealt with after the occupation ends. When class is discussed through Oslo and returnee capital, it is itself framed as a critique of Oslo and as a deformation of the national movement, a skewed form of development that produced internal differentiation and stratification. It is a discussion that occurs from the top-down and focuses on the petit bourgeoisie and capitalist classes—the most visible and expanding classes post-Oslo—and their political economic relations to Israel.

A more complex rendering emerges when political economic relations to Israel are treated also as part of Palestinian class composition. Ali Kadri (2014), Toufic Haddad (2016), and Ghazi Surani (2009) suggest that the petit bourgeoisie emerged as a kind of comprador response to the political situation, while working classes shifted toward selling their labor to Israel. Surani makes several astute arguments: that the occupation has economic and lifestyle affects; that it is a socioeconomic relation; and that Oslo was not a moment of rupture in the occupation but one that enabled a shifting and malleable conception of class, especially among a nonproductive middle class. Gilbert Achcar's (2018) outline of Marx in this context pushes toward the argument that the forms of productive relations are themselves a barrier to development. And Raja Khalidi (2015) more hopefully argues that a nationalist bourgeoisie has extra-economic interests that can more actively aid development.

Class analysis and a focus on internal differentiation demonstrate that economics are not simply problems of national development, but are also so-cial relations among Palestinians. They are intertwined and constitutive, and political economy appears as a contextual social—cultural, value—relation. This is starting to become more visible with a resurgence of Marxist political economy in the Middle East (e.g., *Bidayat Magazine* 2018) that treats class structure as context-dependent and the outcome of politics, violence, and geographic relations. Such an approach can join and elaborate earlier discus-sions of class and labor in Palestine (Mansour 2012; Farsakh 2005) that focus not on development but on the intersection of war and colonization with cap-ital. In his early work on agricultural labor and the de- and re-peasantization process in Palestine, Salim Tamari (1983) provides several crucial insights. First, the fluid land regime works as a form of protectionism for the Jewish market and to subordinate local Palestinian capital. Palestinian proletarian-ization thus tends to be at the scale of the national division of labor with regard to Israel. These trends are still evident, and tenure and landholding—property—are vectors for Israeli territorial imperatives.

Politics of landownership and markets inflect Palestinian class structure; today, the global apparatus of conflict has enabled a capitalist class in Pales-tine with an outward orientation and capacity to create new markets there. Internally, there is still a continual process of class building and constitution and reconstitution interceded by colonization. The topography of class is the topography of ownership and accumulation within the dynamics of Israeli settler-colonial, political, and territorial differentiation. For West Bank Pales-tinians, that differentiation is also the topography of both permissible growth and future aspiration, as well as consequent barriers to either growth or aspi-ration. In my account, class is not static; it is the context-dependent and con-tinuous mutual production of labor, ideas, desires, and economic capacities vis-à-vis new markets in a Palestine subordinate to Israel. The middle class as a debtor class is framed through market growth and development in housing, planned and invested into existence. But growth is also a framework for both national development and personal aspiration and desire.

Politics, Stability, and Accumulation

Developers work to engage the global economy ostensibly in support of the Palestinian nation through their housing development project. Masri often presents himself as a "visionary," a brave nonconformist against Israeli bar-riers, against the PA for failing to live up to its obligations and sometimes against Palestinians for their incapacity to understand what he is doing. He has railed specifically against "left wing living rooms" for making his project difficult (Monni 2017), as well as against the Israelis for failing to establish a truly open market. Masri and the Rawabi marketing department have promoted the hashtag نتحدى_العالم# (#WeDefytheWorld). He is quite open about wanting to make money as one part of his politics: "We want to make money," he says. "But more importantly, we want to make a better surrounding and life for our people. We want to inspire young people and give them opportunity" (Howard 2017).

Rawabi is a form of fixed capital and an idea in formation. It is an idea that supports capital ties between Israelis and Palestinians. The developers have close relations with Israel and liberal Jewish supporters. Masri, who became quite famous as the development's public face, is deeply engaged with managing perceptions of Rawabi and himself. He speaks regularly with a range of supporters and stakeholders abroad and in Israel. Locally he has had public disputes with boycott and antinormalization youth activists, and in interviews he has blamed Palestinians for the lack of progress (Hamdan 2018) or the PA for failing to meet its obligations under their memorandum of understanding (MOU). Andrew Ross (2019) outlines rumors that Masri has long had obscure business dealings with Israel. Masri is adamant that he does not negotiate with Israel as a private businessman, but only through his position as a PA appointee. If contemporary political economic logics emphasize the transfer of economic forms into governance, where is the difference? Rawabi overlaps with the government in many ways, not least when negotiations for developers mean concessions elsewhere in the West Bank.

As economic development stands in for the state, why bother with the peace process at all? The answer is twofold. The peace process organizes relationships between Palestine and Israel, maintains the occupation, and suspends and sustains the market. Here as elsewhere, capital needs a state to organize free markets in relation to one another. Rather than equalizing Palestinian and Israeli markets, the occupation manages their inequality. Masri, the PA, and Israelis are working through Rawabi to project an image of a Palestine in which they would like to intervene, and subsequently intervening and working to produce that Palestine. The geography of Palestine and the peace process have enabled these actors to politicize "modern arrival" in service of accumulation within the language of an eventual state.

For real estate developers and their allies in government, what they are doing is new and important; it is a radical break. The opposition, Palestinian and otherwise, often also describes privatization as somehow a new imposition on the land and polity. My sympathies are with those who do not view indebtedness and privatization as adequate to national politics. But in similar ways, both sides are nearsighted. Accumulation and appropriation are not new. One common version of the imposition critique is to describe Rawabi as a settlement, a type of building unsuitable to Palestine. Opponents look at its style and position on a hilltop and compare it to Israeli typology. They are correct in one respect: the Israelis pioneered homebuilding alongside state building as a strategy of land defense, something Rawabi also claims to be doing. Yet such a critique absolves Palestinian capitalists for their role in shaping the wider Palestinian political economy, and it minimizes the aspirations and desires many Palestinians have for freedom and stability through ownership. It displaces an analysis to rhetoric and aesthetics. The occupation seems as pervasive as ever and stock in Palestine is trending upward; capital is being called in; and laws are written so that more and more credit is offered (Wainer 2018). Credit incorporates ordinary Palestinians into projects like Rawabi. It is heavily backed and suspended within Israel, but who covers individual loans if projects fail to materialize in the intended way? And will the economy collapse? In a video that circulated very widely on Facebook in the summer of 2017, Palestinians visiting Rawabi asked: "Is this freedom? Could you afford it?" What constitutes success or failure from this position, when occupation is not a barrier to business, if you happen to be in the right business? Capital is not an external form imposed on Palestine, but a more general set of imperatives into which Palestine is unevenly incorporated. I try to describe the messy and complicated ways these imperatives appear on the ground in Palestine and how they might shape it in the future.[12]

Encouraging class aspiration in smaller swaths of Palestine makes it possible to map a topography of class and safety in contrast to other parts of Palestine. In his study of private land registration in the West Bank, anthropologist Paul Kohlbry (2019) argues that individual market relations contradict collective Palestinian territorial ambition. But not exclusively: as representations circulate, Rawabi and projects like it give form to those representations and collective logics. Architects Sandi Hilal and Alessandro Petti have pointed out that in Palestine, like other places under repressive regimes, home life becomes a sort of commons (2018). Home life is being transformed as a scale for smaller forms of collectivity, and at the scale of the state, homes are ancillary to the other benefits that housing provides.[13] Housing is a general category and a question of fixed capital and commodification, but also fundamentally of representation and social reproduction. Needless to say, this raises questions about the limits of politics in a private city under occupation where planners emphasized discussions of the planned community in Columbia,

Maryland, and modernist architect Le Corbusier just as much as the upscale clothing retailer Zara, technologically advanced 4-dimensional movie theaters, and the Israeli settlement Modi'in.

Confusion arises in the Palestinian case when such politics contradict and overwrite nationalist politics. But nationalist politics cannot be assumed to be coherent, static, local questions. Characteristically as well as rhetorically, global capitalism—through its emphasis on liberalism, openness, and universality—is presented here as a kind of freedom, something Neil Smith (2003) described as the universalism embedded in the empire of capitalism. In a global context where value can be more easily appropriated through circulation and the production of space than through commodity production; in a local context in which occupation presents barriers to both, it might be both logical and transformative to see Palestinian politics increasingly attached to worldwide economic questions than to local political ones. How do these logics take hold politically among Palestinians, in the landscape, and achieve coherence? How is it that flourishing development exists within the same framework as violent repression?

Promissory Note

Palestine is not currently a territorially sovereign state and is unlikely to end up as one. One task for neoliberalism is to eradicate institutions of state and enhance the idea of the state as a relation between itself and others. In a worldwide context of uneven geographical division of labor, a neoliberal state—a state-scale of political and market governance—in a Palestine that necessarily lacks coherent territory or much national production makes a kind of sense. In its separation from Israel, the West Bank is already a scale of organization and, given subordinate market relationships within Israel, a national-scale market. If neoliberal state building means aggressively emphasizing markets and global economic links over political or territorial control, not only is nothing else suited to the Palestinian context, a nonterritorial state is a coherent outcome of neoliberal practice. International actors, Palestinian capitalists, foreign governments, the PA, and Israel are working in concert to imagine, make, and remake into existence the kind of Palestine in which they would like to intervene. This approach raises two questions that Neil Smith (1984) has asked of other contexts: What does capitalism do to geography, and what can geography do for capitalism?

Those questions drive the story I am trying to tell. It is a complicated one about convoluted, intertwined economic, political, representational, and social logics that operate at multiple geographical scales. General phenomena and things that happen far from Palestine directly impact life there. Despite the ways the occupation has often been understood as an outlier or world-historical exception—the last colonial context—this is as true of Palestine as anywhere else. Capital depends on certain configurations of state form and produces context-dependent versions of them. The state has always been intertwined with capital markets, and public-private partnerships might be contemporary language for the same kinds of political economic relations at the heart of colonialism, settler colonialism, and enclosure (Mironova and Stein 2018). With this in mind, a globally linked, occupied market state is being produced out of stateless Palestine in ways that make the relationships of market and governance to geography, territory, and polity most visible. Within a settler-colonial state, what better form of local governance could the settler regime want than one that does not affect the sovereign state, allows territorial and practical control, creates new opportunities for accumulation in Israel, and does not fully or equally incorporate native populations? With Israeli imperatives and the scale of markets in mind, the condition of governance in Palestine looks less like an anomaly in the present; it shares attributes with other contexts of stripped-down autonomy, such as Detroit under emergency management or the sovereignty of nearly state-scale governance in peacekeeping missions. It is a state based not on a territorial outcome, but the continual process toward something that Nasser Abourahme (2019) has described (in terms indebted to Mezzadra and Neilson 2013) as a postausterity shift from the sovereign moment of decision-making to the duration of management.

Palestinians, and the Palestinian middle class, are the people defined through intervention and the intertwined capacities for social reproduction—the material and social practices through which people reproduce themselves on a daily and general basis and through which the social relations and material bases of capitalism are renewed (C. Katz 2001). Those things happen in and through places. Consequently, class and production have to be taken together and conceived broadly alongside physical space. In an environment where so much is about the land, the built environment on that land is also a topography of class, a way to map capacity for aspiration and what it means for the future of land elsewhere in Historic Palestine. In the sense of building and allowing classes to emerge safely in narrowly specific parts of the West Bank, new ties to place emerge—through debt but also through desire and ideology—at the expense of others. Class is spatialized through new forms of building, and opportunities for return and for a relatively free Palestinian life are narrowed; Ramallah and its suburbs flourish as other Palestinian places are disinvested, cut off, or ignored. This is a messy argument about a messy situation, but it is how place, political economy, and class aspiration are bound in Occupied Palestine today.

Over the following ten chapters, I approach the problems of state and development in Palestine from different angles, aggregating accounts into an analysis of semicoherent structural forces. First, I set the scene and introduce Rawabi. I give a sense of its scale, its placement on the landscape, and some of the experience of its emergence in the hills beyond Ramallah and Birzeit.

In the next two chapters, I present data drawn from dozens of interviews in English and in Arabic carried out with Rawabi and other private developers and financiers. I outline some of the ways that, in the context of structural and legal instabilities, they are working toward an open market for development. As international aid increasingly supports privatization, the PA increasingly serves as a funding agency for private developers, enabling those developers to extract public funding for private projects. Moreover, working specifically through housing, developers seek to create both demand and supply. They hope to represent and create new sensibilities among first-time buyers and to reconfigure people's relationships to their homes and to the land, as well as to draw potential buyers into developments through debt financing. Large-scale development is fundamental for reforming markets in Palestine—operating at a large scale, and by consolidating huge tracts of land, developers and the PA work to alter laws governing land tenure and to create a capital basis for a financial sector.

In chapter 4, I draw on Anthony Coon's (1992) work and describe the ways that planning operates as two overlapping spheres of control, one Jewish, the other Arab. After Oslo, the PA became the overseer of this framework, consolidating it under its authority and formally subsuming the whole apparatus within the occupation structure. Confusion and opacity are part of the legal system and the context for privatization. The law is something actors invoke and reference, but "the law" is vague and often contradictory. There is authority and power held by the PA under the law, but to reform laws or to call something "legal" or "illegal" is as much about strategy, practice, and prerogative as it is about jurisprudence. Planning is part of the reform process, enabling both development in the present and drawing previous bodies of law into the structure of possibility for future plans and relationships to the environment.

Chapters 5 and 6 focus on the PA ministries of Public Works and Housing (MOPWH); Planning and International Cooperation (MOPIC); and Local

Government (MOLG) and their different roles in supporting and implementing Rawabi. I build on the second chapter's analysis of how the private sector presupposes an open market, to look at the ways the Palestinian Authority both actively supports and has been reconfigured by private development projects. An important aspect of how housing emerges in the West Bank is through constant document production and the idea of a housing shortage and the subsequent national priority to develop affordable housing. The shortage in Palestine is not a dearth of housing, but of affordability and priority; housing shortages and shortages more generally emerge from social relations and material inequalities, not absolute physical facts. The specific type of middle class targeted by real estate developers is one willing to maintain a standard of living through debt, and that middle class is assumed—both assumed to exist and assumed as an identity—and made in terms of worldwide norms of middle-class attainment and aspiration. In previous moments or in different places and regimes of accumulation, this is a class that may have earned well. Today, the growing middle class is the class that can take on and consistently pay down debt; its members are the targets of development, intervention, and financialization.

In chapter 7, I look more closely at the people who interact with and are transformed through their interactions with Rawabi. Diverging visions of Palestine and Palestinianness can be based in new sites and the opportunities that emerge around them. I describe the contours of contemporary critique of privatization in Palestine and argue that visions of Palestine as a smallholding, agrarian society neglect long histories of industrialization, modernization, pauperization, and stratification under colonial and occupation rule. Zionist settlement of Palestine before and after occupation drove forms of economic and spatial change: it destroyed urban Palestinian life in places like Jerusalem and Haifa and spurred internal migration. Chapter 8 narrows the focus to the shared landscape for developers and critics of development. Ideas about stewardship and who has the capacity to adequately use the land are as old as capitalism (Wood 2002; Bhandar 2018). Pervasive and ahistorical engagement with the idea and image of peasantry often neglects class, work, and history, and illuminates a common ideological framework for discussion of development and the direction of modernization.

I begin the ninth chapter with settler opposition to Rawabi and one relatively new Israeli organization, Regavim, The National Land Protection Trust. The overlapping legal and administrative structures for Jewish Israelis and Arabs that I described in the third chapter become clear in practice here. In the context of the occupation of the West Bank, the Israeli state advances control by mechanisms that are both legal/administrative and de facto/prerogative. Given the legal confusion, one way that Israel formalizes occupation is through the extension of civil control and jurisdiction over Jewish settlers who move into areas under military rule. The interplay between people and territory is crucial to the way Israel circumscribes Palestinian capacities and encroaches on land with Palestinians on it. Chapters 9 and 10 are based in part on research I conducted with Nicola Perugini, and chapter 10 introduces Regavim's legal claims made through "mirror petitions." The languages of civil and human rights are not contradictory with Regavim's goal of maximizing Jewish land and minimizing Palestinian presence. Settlers and their opponents are using the same specific sets of human rights, yet Regavim does it to dismantle the rights of one population on the basis of race and nationality. Regavim argues that Israeli state enforcement discriminates against Jewish settlers in favor of Palestinians. It demands equal protections manifest as greater enforcement against Palestinians. Its aim is to make ostensibly universal human rights and humanity a question of Israeli practice, prerogative, and civil law and, consequently, to make Palestinian *areas* more subject to the legal jurisdiction that often follows civilian-led repression. This does not suggest that Regavim is misusing human rights; instead, I believe it widens the picture of what human rights and a liberal state can encompass. Law here is malleable, more often descriptive than proscriptive. Legally and in terms of the incorporation of a population, the state of Israel can easily contain a subject Palestinian territory and state with moderate self-rule but little to no territorial sovereignty. Like the shared ideological backdrop of the previous chapter, an expanded view makes clear some ways the state form in Israel and Palestine shapes the contours of contestation. Rights are contextual: settlement legal activism makes clear that both sides of the conflict exist on the same landscape not just mediated by occupation, but through territorial administration and race-dependent law within a liberal democratic settler state.

Taken together, these stories describe a set of phenomena that are at once physical, conceptual, ideological, and productive and that circulate and aggregate in multiple registers and places. Strands unfold and weave together throughout the following chapters. This text is less a proof than a set of descriptions that draw on and bring together discussions of Palestinian politics, human activity, history, and experience that are often assumed to be necessarily local.

Rawabi is a city based on partial accounts of history, documentary expertise, capital, and political priority rather than social life within it. It is a weird kind of hope, memory, and dream of future possibility superimposed onto the present. Development and planning are in part about world making and imagination; I parse what is fantastic and what is real and explore how they are intertwined. Part of the way in is through the technical work that needs to be done to reconcile competing understandings of the past and disputes over visions for the future.

It often feels overwhelming to try to capture a multitude of actors and imperatives and scales together, let alone to try to think through those connections that do not always neatly overlie the narratives we might share as Palestinians, social scientists, political actors, or otherwise. A primary takeaway from this account is, I hope, that there are local articulations of general phenomena, even in Palestine. I look at a Palestine that is unevenly incorporated within a settler state and where all of its racial and territorial imperatives, accumulation, security and stability, rhetoric around security and stability, state building, and class and spatial segregation all intersect. And where they aggregate is the material basis, the materiality, of place and social life today and for the future. I hope what follows serves as a provisional attempt to link wider logics to some of the details.

Chapter One

The Site

■

WHEN I BEGAN VISITING, Rawabi was a huge, dusty construction site spread over several hills about nine kilometers north of Ramallah, and formally approved by the Higher Planning Council on June 23, 2009. For the first several years of construction, the drive from Ramallah consisted of bottleneck after bottleneck: you would go through a checkpoint; over a narrow bridge; winding and bumping through villages; weaving through closures, hills, and towns, catching glimpses of the landscape beyond. Developers had placed signs for miles down the road, indicating where Rawabi was, some ways further in the direction you were traveling. On my first trips in 2009, I had to take the windy, steep road to Birzeit and, a few minutes past the university, take a left toward 'Attara. After a few minutes the road widens and comes to the 'Attara checkpoint. This checkpoint blocks the entrance to the restricted Route 465, which connects Ramallah to Nablus and points north in one direction, and to a narrow bridge in the other that begins a narrow road toward the villages of 'Attara and 'Abwayn. Although the checkpoint was ostensibly decommissioned in 2009, it still exists and appears to be staffed constantly, giving not only the appearance of an Israeli presence, but also of Israel's ability to close the roads at any time.[1] Historically, the 'Attara checkpoint has been a primary mechanism through which Israel has prevented Palestinian students from attending university in Birzeit.

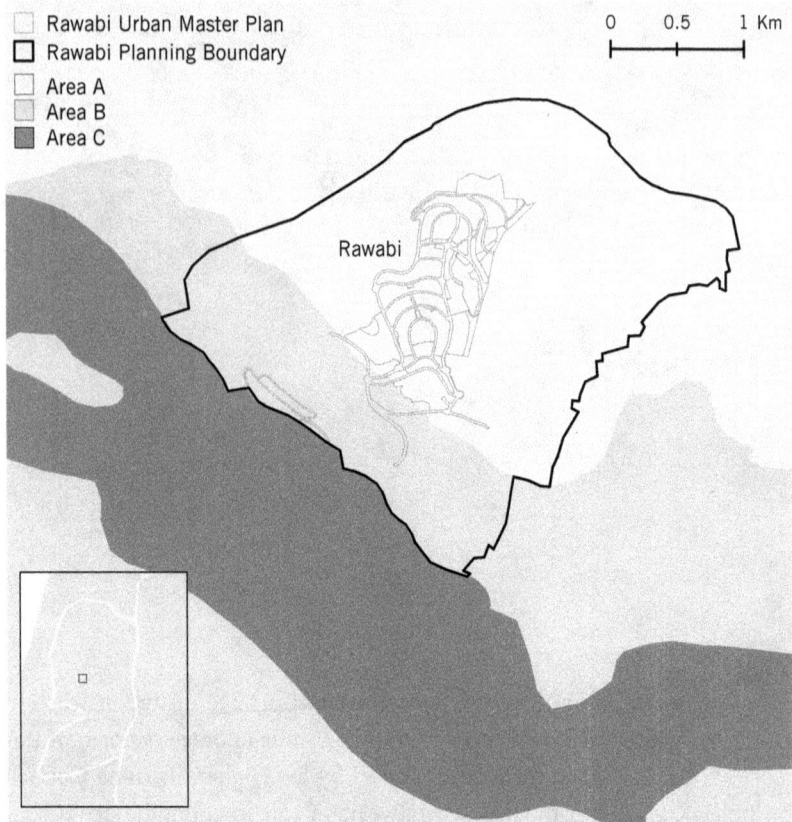

MAP 1.1 Rawabi and its plan boundaries. Map by Meagan A. Snow, based on data from the Palestinian Ministry of Local Government.

Since 2000 at least, Ramallah has seen large-scale architectural transformation, and an increase in scale and density. Apartment blocks have replaced small single-family homes. Within a broader context in which Palestinians are losing territory and economic life has transitioned away from working the land, Rawabi solves a problem for development: how to build and profit in the landscape of Israeli control and Palestinian fragmentation? This trend is not just about local vernacular and quotidian change, but how local forms are related to worldwide phenomena (Harker 2014a).

At the turnoff to Rawabi, the West Bank would open above the town's central square, immediately giving a sense of the massive scale of construction. As part of the Oslo Accords, the West Bank was carved into Area A (Palestinian civil and police control), Area B (Palestinian civil and Israeli military control), and Area c (total Israeli control). Area c makes up more than 60 percent of the West Bank, although the degree of actual Palestinian autonomy in other areas is relative. The development—which is primarily built up in Area A and abuts Areas B and C, in the middle of "rural" Palestine—contrasts substantially with its surroundings, the environment both built and unbuilt. "From the ancient hills of Palestine," a new, modern city is said to be emerging.

Rawabi ("the first new city built since Herod!" one developer told me) is portrayed as part of the landscape, both forward-looking and indebted to the past, a good steward of natural Palestine and Palestinians. It is designed to give the impression it has been there forever, but also to look like a distinctly new form, habitable place, and typology. After the Israeli Civil Administration conditionally approved a new access road, visitors now circumvent the checkpoint, driving directly from Ramallah, through Birzeit, to Rawabi. The new route turns the ride through Palestine into one long Palestinian bottleneck, and enters the site from below, the landscape suddenly widening at the new town.

Although far-reaching, the arguments that follow begin here, in this landscape, from this viewpoint, and as this place emerges and is made real. Rawabi is the manifestation, visible indication, and precedent for a whole suite of changes to the legal, economic, and built environments in the West Bank. It exists, not necessarily as evidence of successes, but evidence of viability. Infrastructures are social, and part of how political changes are reiterated and grounded is through their social life and the social lives they incorporate. Rawabi produces economic relationships and geographies as amalgamations of precedent. But this is also a private, for-profit development project conducted under the rubric of national politics. Beginning in 2008 or so, and as a physical place around 2010, Rawabi is unfolding over time, and the time of the project development, like everything in Palestine, is continually deferred, but nevertheless productive.

In subsequent chapters, I aim to move slowly beyond the site to describe some of the political, social, and cultural changes that such regimes of accumulation entail. But first, what is actually there? And why does it look like such a massive change? What parts of these changes are immediately visible, and which physical, rhetorical, and political forms obscure the rest? Initially, there is the land: land sales at scale required a new market, and markets almost always require a state to regulate them. State regulation presupposes certain priorities in the PA statelet and among its international donors, and more generally about attempts to stabilize the West Bank through economic

FIGURE 1.1 The approach to Rawabi in January 2010. Photo by the author.

logics. Such questions raise others about the idea of the state and about global political economy and neoliberalism generally.

According to developers, the name Rawabi, "hills" in Arabic, was submitted to a contest to name the development. The site sits on 6,300 dunams (1,557 acres) on the hills between the villages of 'Ajjul, 'Attara, and 'Abwayn, and about one kilometer from the settlement Ateret. Villagers share anxieties generally about the project and specifically about the prospect of being subsumed into a Rawabi municipality at a disadvantage.

Much of the land in the West Bank is not formally registered, and varying regimes from the Jordanian and Ottoman periods cover those lands that are registered. Moreover, land can be collectively held, and there may be many plausible claims to individual plots. The footprint of Rawabi will encompass approximately eight hundred dunams (which the developers sometimes call "Rawabi I"), and the company has planning jurisdiction over the 6,300 du-

MAP 1.2 Rawabi, the surrounding villages, and settlement. Map by Meagan A. Snow based on Esri World Imagery and data from the Palestinian Ministry of Local Government.

nam outline of "isolated" land, "natural blocks" already marked by hills, rocks, and use patterns. According to the company, developers bought much of the land under the site, but not all of it.[2] After the company managed to purchase 51 percent of a parcel it wanted to tie together, the rest was "reparcelized" by the PA through *istimlak*, an eminent domain process based on existing Jordanian law. This process enabled them to take control of the site, and depressed land prices in the wider area (phenomena I discuss in chapters 7 and 8).

According to a plaintiff with an ongoing suit against the company, the Rawabi developers bought something like six thousand dunams all throughout the site, which they then sold to their Qatari partners; they have the ability to effect wide reparcelization or eminent domain because of the diffusion of those parcels throughout the site. And although there was some early dispute about whether Rawabi will comprise an official municipality, it always seemed likely, and the company claimed there were ongoing negotiations between it and the leadership in 'Ajjul, 'Attara, and 'Abwayn. By 2013, the Rawabi municipality had been created and was being run mostly by representatives of the private sector, headed by an NGO leader, and including mostly business people, mortgage financiers, and some private sector engineers (Zawya 2013; AME Info 2013). This municipal structure will allow the company to control zoning in the area and to collect taxes.

The site has views of the West Bank on three sides and the settlement of Ateret on the fourth. The development advertised as the "first planned city" in Palestine hopes that it will eventually house forty thousand people. It is being built at an initial cost estimate of about USD500 million from Palestinian and Qatari investors, a number that is continually revised upward and may now be somewhere near USD1.5 billion. The idea of "middle-class" or "affordable" housing is central to the way that the project is being conceived and sold, and the hope is that it will establish not only a new urban environment, but enable opportunities for a new style of life for Palestinian inhabitants. The company describes a Palestinian desire for "stability" and "security" from the present political situation but also from a constantly changing Palestinian urban form, given not only settlement building but also Palestinian building in other cities (for example, they say, if you build a house, there is no guarantee that a neighbor will not build one later blocking your views). Rawabi developers strive to project stability and certainty, and growth: they claim they will create jobs and jump-start numerous sectors of the economy, such as the production of building materials and a new real estate market.

In this new market, the idea of this being a city that will serve young families and first-time buyers is central: developers hope for new habits among young Palestinians, where buyers will move to new homes rather than expanding on, say, a family building, and they are creating new mortgage financing to enable these purchases. And there is enthusiasm; one person I spoke with, a potential buyer and former employee, has discussed it explicitly in terms of modernity, a desire for services such as TV on demand and as "a little Dubai in Palestine," but it is also tied closely to an image of Palestine that resonates with certain classes in the diaspora, and against the logics of the occupation; it is "natural," "green," and so on.

The Image of Rawabi

The representations that the company produces are important in its project to model a new Palestine and, like the state-building project, to provide the image and attempt to orient a reality and set of practices around it. The ways that image organizes practice are just as fundamental as what is happening in the hills north of Ramallah. From nearly the beginning in 2008 or 2009, through advertising, word of mouth, not to mention through critiques and academic papers, Rawabi had pierced the public imaginary long before there was any Rawabi to point to. The first representations of the site were 3D renderings of a clean town with functioning transportation and opportunities for shopping, banks, doctors, and so on. The video and the representations ask, implicitly, what might it be like to have a Palestine without the occupation, where Palestinians could flourish and succeed in an open market free from the obstacles of the occupation?[3] And indeed, this place apart is powerfully appealing to many people—it ties class aspiration to a view of a life without military occupation. The development will have hotels, private schools, a country club, movie theaters, and other businesses that fill leisure time. It already has a large amphitheater that has generated press for the firm through high-profile concerts (and attendant controversies). It also offers luxuries and services unavailable elsewhere for West Bank Palestinians, such as a track for racing all-terrain vehicles, bungee jumping, and so on.

Studying something in process presents certain methodological difficulties. But given the greater importance of process and practice than success or failure, interviews and the ability to capture a segment of that process can help to show how actors are working toward something, even if that thing might be shifting or perpetually unreachable. Rawabi has a prominent place in Palestinian public discourse. But there is a danger, as the sociologist Salim Tamari once warned me, of even critical academic projects like mine generating continual attention and being "the greatest advertisement for Rawabi." Rawabi is not as important as the huge amount of press coverage would indicate. It is an indication of one direction in which Palestine is moving; it is a large intervention by Palestinian capitalists and their allies in various governments and NGOs; it is something they hope will succeed and influence future interventions for building economies and private political institutions, even if success in their terms may not result in a fully completed Rawabi, let alone an independent state.

It is important as a test case for a swath of reforms that have the potential to fundamentally alter Palestine politically and economically for Palestinians,

FIGURE 1.2 The central shopping district under construction in 2010. Photo by the author.

FIGURE 1.3 An early developer's rendering of Rawabi. Source: Rawabi

and it says a lot about Palestine at scales beyond the local. Rawabi is a material project that the PA and the private sector are hanging various institutions and reforms on—new markets, a debt and finance sector, urban governance, and the reformulation of direct humanitarian aid into investment. It can mobilize and orient change, and it can tell us a bit about what coalitions of governments, capitalists, and aid institutions have in mind for Palestine: what they are doing to shift it, and what happens around those projects in intended and unintended ways. A former cabinet minister told me, "The cooptation of the middle class has been total and complete" as a result of Oslo, making transaction costs too high for them to do business, and making capital—capital that "can come and go easily"—totally dependent on the occupation. What does it mean to build an open market under occupation?

I first contacted the Rawabi office by phone, explaining my project and interest and asking if there was someone I could meet. I was put in touch with George Rafidi, then the director of sales and business development. At that time, the main Rawabi offices comprised two villas on a street that houses the Palestine Development and Investment Company (PADICO) and other large private firms. The main office was a nicely redone, bustling place. I remember marble floors, glass conference rooms, young people at computer banks, and the impression of work—real work—going on, in contrast to the shabbiness and languor typical of Palestinian bureaucracy. In this first meeting with the young, likeable, passionate Rafidi, he explained what makes Rawabi different: that it will be contrasted specifically with other Palestinian places. There will be a town center with retail, banks, services, and a cultural center with "name brands" and "Jordanian businesses" that will form a "destination" for other parts of the West Bank. This is a vision both scaled to the town center and ambitious in relation to the rest of the West Bank. At that time, early winter 2009, developers reported that over six thousand people had registered their interest online. Rafidi told me that, while Palestinians currently get holiday permits from Israel to go shopping, he hopes that Rawabi will reorient commerce, so people can shop "without restriction and without [travel] permits." This is a vision for Palestine that essentially does an end-run around the occupation by building the occupied West Bank. At that time, Rafidi was projecting that there would be eight thousand to ten thousand jobs created during construction (it is hard to know how this was calculated, since construction crews were small at that time). Andrew Ross (2019) quotes Bashar Masri as saying that ten thousand job openings had been filled by 2017. It is unclear if that number refers to long-term direct employment or "job creation," but either way it would put him just behind the PA in scale.

FIGURE 1.4 Stalled private construction near the site. Photo by the author.

On an official visit to the site with Rafidi in spring 2010, after work had started, I understood how big it is and how far it reaches. We entered the site past a few houses that had had expansion stalled because they were within the footprint of Rawabi and, all of a sudden, subject to its bylaws. I had just missed a CNN crew and was told that more than sixty journalists had visited the site since they broke ground only a month prior. There was much more infrastructure: a new, attractive fence, and offices and meeting rooms to serve foreign visitors. At this time the company was actively courting the foreign press, foreign dignitaries, and Israeli politicians, and promoting an image of a new Palestine.

A slick new sales center had been built, with small offices for banks offering mortgages and displays of the options and finishes available to buyers. A huge stone quarrying and cutting operation was in place. It was slow, but it was real, a self-contained, actual city in the making, moving and positioned to generate interest and get people into it.

The town center of Rawabi sits on thirty-three dunams, around which

FIGURE 1.5 Rawabi in January 2010. Photo by the author.

the neighborhoods 1, 3, and 5 (to the west) and 2, 4, and 6 (to the east) were to be built—eighty-seven buildings in all. Subsequent phases go down the hill to the north and up the hill to the south. The first phase was projected to take 2.5 years to complete; in fact, it took much longer. The company imagines the possibility for more Rawabis on the 6,300 dunam site—"Rawabi II" and "Rawabi III" and, although they do not anticipate being the developers, it is likely that they will be the service providers.[4] The relationship between Rawabi and the surrounding areas is not entirely clear, but they were still actively buying land, and still benefitting from structural changes in the land market that their project has enabled.

By summer 2013, many buildings had been built and the site had become recognizable as housing. By spring 2015, it seemed like parts of it were ready to be inhabited. In 2016 a small number of families lived there, although only two of the twenty-three neighborhoods had been built (Kirk 2016), and the company's webcam showed mostly blackness at night. The company was actively trying to bring in services for the small number of residents: I saw a dry cleaner and a bodega but few people on the streets. It was, despite their efforts, a "ghost town." By 2016, Masri was saying it would still take another

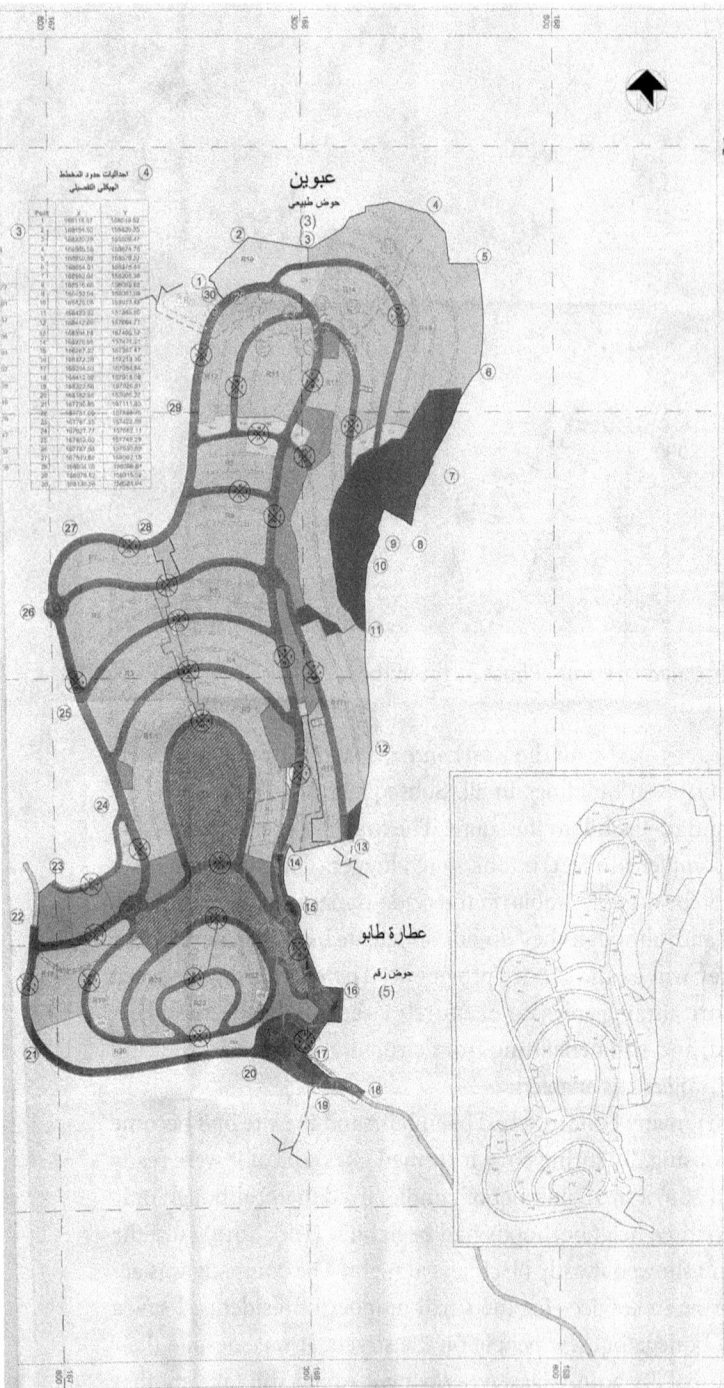
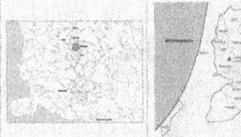

FIGURE 1.6 Approved planning map. Source: Higher Planning Council.

FIGURE 1.7 The sales center. Bank offices are to the right. Photo by the author.

FIGURE 1.8 Stonecutting. Photo by the author.

FIGURE 1.9 Construction in 2013. Photo by the author.

FIGURE 1.10 Construction in 2017. Photo by Léopold Lambert for *The Funambulist*.

FIGURE 1.11 Israeli road sign pointing toward Rawabi. Photo by the author.

six to eight years to fill. Six to eight years has the potential to scare off the people who were interested in 2009 and the people who looked into loans in 2011 and 2012. Yet the entire project and Rawabi process continues to move, to make changes, and produce precedent.

More generally, and in terms of its relationship to the rest of the West Bank, it was surprising to see the site marked in the landscape, integrated into Palestine, and into space far outside of Rawabi itself. In 2009, developers made Rawabi visible by putting their own signs everywhere along the route from Ramallah, showing people the way, where it was located, indicating that—somewhere down the road—Rawabi was there. By 2013, they had taken on a new meaning and had become a lot more formal: the Israeli Ministry of Transport and Road Safety had erected signs for the site (see figure 1.11).

Signs and markers have long been sites of conflict. The Palestinian-Israeli activist group Zochrot and others have demonstrated how these function for the erasure of Palestinian towns and villages in Israel, and they are implicated

FIGURE 1.12 Jerusalem road sign. Source: flickr user ingmar, shared under a Creative Commons license (CC BY-NC-ND 2.0), 2009.

and embedded in the politics of naming and erasure in Israel and Palestine. They set the scene and orient movement and the ways the landscape is experienced and conceived. As recently as 2009 and 2011, the road signs and various bills to formalize them made international news. Arabic and Palestinian place names have been replaced with Hebrew, including the replacement of Jerusalem's Arabic name, "al-Quds," with an Arabic-language transliteration of the Hebrew "Yerushlaim" (see figure 1.12).

Rawabi is an economic, legal, ideological, and political precedent that is also visible, material fact. In the process of becoming visible, developers worked to inscribe it into the landscape and to keep the idea of it in public circulation. As a series of buildings, it takes a form that implies and enables the continuing mystification of many processes external to its site, and the things happening in the site itself provide a narrow object to support, or fight, or dream about, or fear. Its place in the landscape makes it seem as though it was always a part of it and parallels logics that have run throughout Historic Palestine since the occupation, if not before. Symbolically and physically, changes in the landscape such as Jewish National Fund forestation, designing architecture and public space to project autochthonous origins (Abu El-

FIGURE 1.13 Construction in 2017. Photo by Léopold Lambert for *The Funambulist.*

Haj 2001; Weizman 2007), and signage are produced with political and social goals in mind. Physical space orients people's relationship to the land and to the built environment. Al-Quds had been erased and replaced by Yerushlaim, and a construction site had been marked on the landscape officially and linguistically uncontested—a new city and a real place, Rawabi. The landscape was clearing, and the scene had been set for Rawabi and all of the ideas and aspirations contained within it.[5]

Chapter Two

Developers
and Designers

RAWABI OPERATES AS A PLACE, an idea, an image, an organizing principle for economic and political practice at different scales and in different ways. At the stage of conception, Rawabi and the projects around it are part of a continuously forming economic and political framework in the West Bank, organized and justified in terms of a wider state-building agenda. Eventually, ideas are made material and touch the ground; developers are producing physical places to anchor and fix investment, new forms of economic practice, social life, and accumulation in previously unprofitable areas and markets. Not only do they create a physical form for projects, they also establish physical and ideological bases and precedents for future projects and interventions there. More specifically, they have figured out how to extract ground rent from fallow, isolated, and otherwise unusable land, and how to move financial and political capital toward their own projects.

Rawabi is implicated in wider political changes and institutional arrangement and rearrangement in Palestine. Private investors and the private sector are leading the work of state building, and the image of the development circulates and incorporates different groups of people in different ways. Palestinians are consumers but not critics, liberal Israelis and Jewish Americans can be investors and supporters, the PA acts as a political force able to reshape international interventions and capital toward development, and NGOs and international aid agencies are ideologically and financially intertwined.

This chapter focuses on interviews with Rawabi developers and other private actors working on economic development projects in Palestine. I introduce some main characters (and one by his absence). Who is making Rawabi? What do they hope to accomplish, and how are they doing it?

First Contact

Amir Dajani is a tall, bald-headed, gregarious man, who, like George Rafidi, exudes competence and professionalism with a kind of easy familiarity. He was the project manager of Rawabi; a director of Rawabi's parent company, Massar; and the second in command through whom many day-to-day decisions are made. Prior to his work at Massar, Dajani was with USAID, and, like many others in the West Bank, he has moved between development and the private sector. During my first meeting with him, and after an introduction to the project, we started talking about politics. I asked about the relationship between Rawabi and national political goals and to the Palestinian state-building project, and how Rawabi mobilizes a kind of a politics emphasizing a desire for stability and normalcy. Dajani was explicit about Rawabi's placement in the occupation landscape—it will create a territorial link between Ramallah and Nablus. Furthermore, it operates sympathetically to PA state building and is a crucial node in the public-private development of Palestine outlined by the Fayyad government and in the 2008 Palestinian Reform and Development Plan (PRDP). Even so, he told me that to make the project happen, they had to "work with the PA for twelve to eighteen months in order to educate" them about water, traffic, the desirability of removing water tanks from roofs, and so on. The general attitude is that a great deal of the state building will be—and should be—determined and led by the private sector, with the PA as "regulating authority." These attitudes are reflected in an MOU under which the PA will provide all offsite and public infrastructure for the project, largely funded by international aid organizations. And, as I suggest in chapter 6, through the MOU and with Rawabi's municipal designation, developers have worked to blur the distinction between public and private in Rawabi, to drive down their own costs and political and economic risk. They do so by extracting external funding through one part of the sprawling PA and creating precedent for further public funding for private development. They model the admixture of priority, scale, form, and polity through practice. Large-scale development is making land and governance increasingly private, and public support of private initiative is making the two increasingly indistinguishable; public-private partnerships are turning one into the other. The PRDP, as Adam Hanieh put it, is so central to discussions of contemporary capitalism in Palestine precisely because of how it came to define politics and political practice, not just as an implementation of a development plan (2013a).

As Dajani and I began to discuss NGOs and the PA driving costs down for the company, he got a call from former British prime minister and then leader of the Quartet Tony Blair's office. I asked if I should leave, and he shook his head and held his finger to his mouth. From my side of the brief conversation, it seemed as though the Quartet were working closely with the firm and on behalf of development in the West Bank. Dajani discussed the road issue and the possibilities for istimlak, and the need for more public funding. He told me that what is required (from the Quartet and in general) is an effort to reduce the overall cost of the project. USAID, he said, would be coming up with the first USD5 million payment to the PA for infrastructure, but they still needed more money to keep the costs of apartments low enough that the Palestinian middle class could afford them (at this time they were saying additional funding would lower apartment costs to approximately USD65,000–USD70,000, from USD90,000–USD100,000). He also said that the firm needed the Quartet to help the PA gain control of land for an access road. He was critical of segments of the PA for their lack of help and for failing to advance the interests of the Fayyad government and other leaders "who have some sanity." He explained that "we are in the business of moderation, building harmony, coexistence, supporting the visionary two-state solution that is hoping to be the way forward under the circumstances," stating that he is "not in the business of politics, [he is] in the business of job creation." He ended his phone call by offering, "Please feel free to ask me any questions that may be helpful to advance your arguments with the other side" (a reference to Israel).

Dajani told me that Rawabi is working "theoretically in the same vein" as Fayyad's state-building project and would substantially add to the new state's economy in the next five to seven years (e.g., they will jump-start nail manufacturing, support door importers, cement, steel, stonecutters, and so on). At the same time, they will contribute to the reality on the ground, helping with the housing shortage and relieving congestion. For Dajani, practically speaking, there was no separation between public and private forms of development. Given the occupation and weak PA—while diffuse and in some ways inchoate, also real in terms of its capacity to implement priority, shape funding, and interpellate Palestinians—Palestinians were more or less unable to develop forward-looking economic activities. They could not build export-related services given current restrictions on access and mobility, and they were forced to work locally, even if they had wider issues in mind. "This is not a sovereign state at the end of the day," although it is part of why Palestinian capitalists and their allies in the PA—as well as in international aid organizations, in Israel, and regionally—can create political precedent and political organization around economic projects. He fully expects Rawabi to create precedent and orient further interventions: development in the area will increase, and USD1.5 billion will be invested in formerly unprofitable land in a formerly unprofitable part of the West Bank. And Massar will center itself in all the economic activity sited there—as service providers, with venture capital to accumulate Palestinian intellectual property, and of course with housing. From the outset, the wider political stakes are intertwined with the economic rationales for development; in this environment, state-scale politics and markets are linked. In some sense, the developers see barriers as technical or engineering questions related to the enormity of their task, whether economic, social, cultural, or political.

Scaling up Economic and Political Development

Massar is not the first to attempt large-scale housing as a form of economic intervention in Palestine; several groups claim that credit, and there are similar projects emerging, although none on the scale of Rawabi. How did Rawabi itself come about? The Palestine Investment Fund and its Al-Reehan housing development position themselves in these conversations as a more sober, less risky kind of an initiative, and often claim to be the first. One of the main characters is the Portland Trust, an economic development firm—an "action tank"—founded in 2003 in England by former military and intelligence personnel and economists who wanted to work in the field of economic peace.[1] Samir Huleileh, then head of the USD250 million Palestine Development and Investment Company (PADICO), is the chairman of the board. Through Rawabi, Al-Reehan, and other interventions in the housing market, the state-market relationship is being reformed even if (and especially because) "at the end of the day," Huleileh observed, we are "not a sovereign state."

Nisreen Shahin, then the local director of the Portland Trust, who later moved to a Masri firm, has traveled through numerous economic development organizations—PADICO, the Palestine Real Estate Investment Company (PRICO), and others—and had been at the Portland Trust for about a year when I spoke with her. She told me "the idea for doing affordable housing" started with the Portland Trust and with the question, "What is it that prevents developers from doing affordable housing?" They settled on the value-added tax (VAT), the land shortage, and an overly renter-friendly Tenants Law, and tried to figure how to make apartments affordable as a consequence of a pro-privatization reform process. They conducted stakeholder meetings with funders and "relevant actors in the private sector." Ideas that are generated internationally have long circulated in the West Bank, and attempts to express donor ideology are, in some ways, comparatively easy: the entire apparatus of government is wholly dependent on them. And as early as 1993, a World Bank report, "Housing: Enabling Markets to Work" (1993), articulated the need to turn housing into a national priority and economic growth sector. These ideas are reiterated in the Richard Martin report (2009) I discuss in chapter 6 and are materialized in private interventions into the West Bank. The admixture of economic, peace, stabilization, and market logics does not emerge solely within government, but it enables a reorientation, opening, and basis for legal changes in favor of private-backed intervention into the cultural and housing spheres.

I was told that the idea of Rawabi was hatched at a 2008 meeting. Little about it is publicly known, and despite asking, I never got clear answers. At the very least, the Portland Trust brought together Bashar Masri, architect Raffie Samach of the multinational engineering and architecture firm AECOM (known for massive infrastructural projects and Olympic villages), the Palestine Investment Fund, people from the construction sector such as Palestine Real Estate Investment Co. (PRICO) and Baydar in Nablus, banks, the Ministry of Public Works and Housing (MOPWH), and the contractors' union. It is unclear how they were chosen or what happened, but in those meetings, Shahin says they "initiated the concept" of working on affordable housing, a "long-term, high-growth" sector. A Harvard Business School case study puts the meeting in 2007 in Tel Aviv, with the founders of the Portland Trust, Israeli government minister Rafi Eitan, and Samach followed by meetings in which Masri was involved. Given that Masri had already begun real estate purchases and speculation and had development experience in the Middle East, the Portland Trust/AECOM and Massar came together (Segel et al. 2014).

They discussed barriers such as the high cost of transport and building in the West Bank; the scarcity of available land, given the planning laws, Areas A, B, C, and so on; and "the VAT issue," which "the PA doesn't want to get rid of because it is a good source of revenue" but the private sector views as an obstacle to development. While it is clear that the private developers want state intervention to benefit them, there is a limit to what they can change given Israeli practical control of Palestine. The VAT is not something that the PA could get rid of without abrogating the Paris Protocols, and no developers are talking about doing so. They criticize the PA when it fails to completely support them; but a West Bank without it, without its aid, and without security coordination with Israel would be terrible for investment. At best, the occupation is assumed, and at worst, its forms shape private development.

Shahin told me that "more than 35% of the population make only USD800 to USD1200/month," too little to afford a down payment, and a figure that makes it "difficult to decide what an appropriate monthly payment would be." To target that 35 percent, the Portland Trust found a gap between supply and demand and organized studies on the viability of mortgage financing with professors from Najah and Birzeit Universities.[2] Those reports helped establish ideas about scarcity and the imperative to lower barriers to market participation through financing. Reports became important to the ways that planning is organized and privatization is materialized, and in terms of legitimacy and capacity in Palestine. Reports are continually produced and referenced and circulate to aggregate authority to the ideas and practices they elaborate. For the Portland Trust, the MOPWH is "not ready" to do this, so the private sector must step in, armed with its accumulated research and expertise, and push the PA. At the time I first spoke with Shahin, the cabinet had just approved changes to the health insurance and pension laws, enabling the creation of pension funds, a crucial foundation for the financial markets that the Portland Trust hoped to create and a clear opening for further private intervention. In 2016, a PA Law by Decree dismantled the social security system in favor of private pensions, a clear example of the kind of state privatization that means drawing and redrawing boundaries between public and private to establish new forms of governance and authority (Hibou 2004).

Housing for Whom?

Raffie Samach became involved with Rawabi sometime in 2007, during the Portland Trust meetings on how to achieve a "peaceful resolution" to the conflict after the 2007 Annapolis Peace Conference and attempts to restart the peace process. The question was, If the peace process is dormant, if "the political track is stuck," what other options could there be for the private sector? Samach was brought in by the Portland Trust because he knew its head, venture capitalist Ronald Cohen, and because of his experience working with AECOM on "large-scale projects in emergent markets" such as China in the

1980s, Vietnam, and Indonesia, and "using large-scale construction to jump-start economies and to provide affordable housing for impoverished populations." Samach had a political and humanist motivation: he is a believer in Reform Judaism's dictate "to make the world right." Samach is a good representative for the kinds of investment developers have in making the project a desirable idea outside Palestine in terms of a kind of universalist liberal utopianism. For Samach, planned, large developments put people to work, especially underutilized skilled labor, and produce economies of scale. The group that included Dajani and Masri, the heads of the Portland Trust, and Samir Huleileh "put together a vision" for planned towns, and when the Rawabi project got off the ground, Samach and AECOM were hired to design it.

Part of that vision, he told me, was to establish a "new" urban environment for Palestine, "a new urbanism." However, given the context of Palestine, there were massive structural impediments—not only challenging topography, but the scarcity of sites in Area A, which maps onto places that are already built up and thus prevent Palestinian expansion. Through conversations, meetings, and focus groups with a target audience that they identified, the developers asked the following questions: What do Palestinians aspire to? To US-style suburbs? Do they want to return to villages? Samach came to believe that Palestinians would need a "community-driven" plan. Given that "there is no urbanism in Palestine," his team would need to provide a vision for things that do not really exist in Palestinian cities—horizontal spaces, neighborhoods—and the kinds of buildings that could incorporate "universal aspirations" toward decent housing. Given site constraints, plans, and buildings would have to also move "inwards and upwards."[3]

According to Samach, "multiple families living in a structure is not the prevalent form" in Palestine, and it is a "sociological/cultural challenge to create these new forms." And, through focus groups, developers learned what was acceptable and how much was too much. The focus groups influenced the design in minor ways—certain kinds of units were desirable or undesirable, it was important for the design "not to look like a settlement" but instead "as part of the environment," rather than placed on top of it. It became clear that stone cladding, which the company had hoped to avoid because of the expense, was necessary.[4] The settlement issue is crucial here—not only is it a dominant critique of Rawabi, but it is enhanced by the company's explicit interest in settlement planning and its relationship with Moshe Safdie, the internationally renowned Israeli architect and the designer most famously of Habitat '67 in Montreal and Yad Vashem: The World Holocaust Remembrance Center, as well as the settlement bloc Modi'in. Developers were interested in Modi'in as a model for the type of building possible in Palestine, and the scale and neighborhood form they wanted. Safdie told me he approached Massar after he had read about Rawabi and the comparisons they were making to Modi'in. He served in a casual advisory capacity, as a supporter and friend of the project, and spoke with developers and planners not only about his work in Modi'in, but the forms of town planning for growth that he had pioneered for Israel.

Naturally, developers were proud of his interest and involvement, but after the relationship opened Massar to Palestinian critiques of Rawabi as a settlement, the firm stopped discussing Modi'in and has minimized references to Safdie on its website. But the relationship had nevertheless been close, and it influenced their thinking about the need to build a "holistic city" rather than a "bedroom community."[5] Developers and planners wanted a city where a child could walk to school, where residents could circulate in a town center, where there would be an industrial sector. Bashar Masri told Samach to look at the Tel Aviv Port, an area with "a sense of place, a town center, multiple options for retail and entertainment, places for social interaction," things that enable "universal aspirations." This is quite unlike what exists in Ramallah, where there is "no organization, no parking, no easy walking," etc. Tel Aviv Port is a Baltimore Inner Harbor, new Times Square sort of a place (Petersburg 2011), not the kind of area that typically exudes an inherent "sense of place," but one that does work as a sort of manifestation of a representation.

Although Modi'in and Tel Aviv were part of the argument, and planners and developers saw settlements as both an influence and a model to avoid, politics rarely came into the equation for Samach. He said that, although there is some political responsibility given the context, "it probably didn't impact the design much." Later he told me that politics did not impact design "at all." More important were the "passion" that the "significance" of the project motivated. For Samach, what Palestine needs is community and cohesion, and Rawabi, like Palestinian cities with longer histories, will be able to create those qualities. But his vision extended far beyond the local; Samach took inspiration from a project he had worked on in Vietnam.[6] In a context where people had "long been colonized," he made a plan that was "wonderfully appropriate." He created a similar synthesis of styles, and indeed, has more freedom to design, since long histories of colonial vernacular have overwritten "traditional Palestinian architecture [since the time of the] hut." For Samach, housing has to be different in this period—"urbanism is a global phenomenon . . . practically universal." Old ideas are finished, so the imperative is now for planners to create urban environments that are forward-looking and oriented toward creating a future out of the present.

Samach's role was to "bring a level of expertise and transfer his knowledge to the local populations" that would carry it out. After all, in 2010, there were global links and people were responding to certain "axiomatic, universal" things like care for children, the need for good schooling, and the importance of small scale; his job was simply to take those universals, overlay certain historical cultural forms like the *hamula* kinship structure within the constraints of the site, and create something new and unique for Palestine.[7] Samach told me about his experience in Shanghai in the late 1980s, "Kids would crouch and defecate outside. You don't see this anymore," and a big part of the reason is home ownership, a sense of belonging and commitment that will reflect itself in the public realm and, in the case of Palestine, in the realm of national politics. The need is for "owner-occupiers" rather than speculators, to make people care about their environment and to protect it. And that is also why the Qatari and Massar co-owned Bayti Real Estate Investment Company is "quite serious about" all the bylaws that will exist. Rawabi is being organized around universals and the idea of an open market, mixed with ideas about appropriateness, possibility, and class aspiration, and attempts to embed those qualities in the environment, in the law, and among its future inhabitants.

Planning

Ideas about the economics and vernacular forms of housing scale upward, primarily through the idea and the act of planning. Shireen Nazer, a planner with Rawabi, told me that town planning is key not only to Rawabi's success but also to addressing the shortage of housing in Palestine. It is a "compact urban form" that may have some qualities that were "inspired by the colonies"—the settlements—but is part of a "national project to build on our lands" and to help ameliorate the unemployment and housing problems. As planners working in an unstable environment, difficulties are more trying because they need to speculate about and plan for both conditions of peace and the current status quo.[8] Any kind of planning that implies a future requires contingencies because "you can't guarantee a long-term in Palestine." What exactly are they doing short and long term? How are they establishing a sense of the long term, if their work is oriented to what happens in, and in relation to, the present? How does a compact urban plan scale upward, and how does it orient nonmaterial interventions?

For Rawabi developers and planners, planning provides a chance to impose order, to engineer a future in their new city, and to model one for Palestine. They hope to establish new opportunities for consumers to desire and

FIGURE 2.1 Rawabi advertisement across the street from perhaps the most upscale coffee shop in Ramallah: "Big jobs and lots of opportunities." Photo by Raja Khalidi.

FIGURE 2.2 Adjacent Rawabi advertisement: "The best view from the top of the hill." Photo by Raja Khalidi.

need goods and, unlike in "random" Palestinian development, they believe that Rawabi will allow for a Palestinian environment that enables a sense for the future and forward-looking politics. The quality of life will be higher; there will, Nazer says, be more water, there will be shopping within walking distance, there will be coherent rules.

Increasingly, and through the creation of a physical place to anchor investment, changes in building typology, services, and local governance structure, and relationships between public and private are remade. The company would classify areas within its site—roads, streetlamps—as public so as to utilize funding from the PA under the MOU. According to internal company documents, in the early budgeting phase, developers were planning to request around USD87 million from the PA for infrastructure costs. In form, administration, and culture, developers envision a city unlike what exists in Palestine presently, but it is not clear just how public a private city can be. It is hard to imagine the town center would remain open if it becomes a site for teens to linger or if it gets covered in graffiti, let alone if it becomes the site of demonstrations. And the relationship with the general public, even the public encompassed by the huge Rawabi municipality, is not yet clear. I learned about a dispute between the developers and the Ministry of Planning and International Cooperation (MOPIC): schools were to be built along with the phases of construction, but PA planners did not want to pay to build them long before construction would be completed. "We have needs in areas that are populated," they told me. At the same time, developers need schools to attract buyers. During one visit, a laborer told me that the schools will be better than the alternatives and that "the villagers will bring their kids to these schools." Nearby, a company higher-up grimaced. The city was likely to end up with private schools, and internal documents outlined proposals for a country club, a place for horseback riding, and other services likely to be prohibitive for the residents of ʿAjjul, ʿAttara, and ʿAbwayn. (These later manifested as an extreme sports concern with bungee jumping, four-wheeling, and a zip line—RAWABI EXTREME.)

The Open Market

Clearly, parts of the political negotiations with Israel were oriented toward driving down costs to developers, and the PA is actively supporting this particular development. Thus, some strong critiques come from other corners of the private sector on the basis of that support (rather unlike left critiques of Rawabi that tend to focus on its relationship to Israel, similarity to Israeli forms of building, and some of its statements on occupation). Khaled al-Sabawi heads UCI, another large development firm, and he makes clear that the reorientation of public and private has something to do with specific actors mobilizing political and financial capital to minimize their individual risk. Sabawi suggests that Rawabi's developers have been able to position themselves as recipients of government and international aid in contravention of the open market. There is a tension, he suggests, between open market rhetoric and practice. He has written about "unfair competition," where other developers "literally copy" their ideas but receive funding and aid from the PA and others. He seems particularly incensed by Rawabi, which "received a road paid for by USAID and received financial support from the Qatar Government while we pay for infrastructure on our own expense and the other projects are funded by the government and the donor countries" (UCI 2013).

As developers contest the meanings of politics and economics, and freedom and competition in the open market, the scaffold of Israeli control and aid economics reappears. It is possible to use the situation to drive down development risk and produce markets in land, housing, and financing. But even for Rawabi and despite handshake agreements with the Israelis for vital infrastructure, there is instability and contingency. Even after their road, wastewater treatment plant, and water allotment were approved, Israel built in instability—it requires constant renewal for the road and political concessions were necessary for water approval. When I first started interviewing around Rawabi, they had worked with the Palestinian Water Authority and the Joint Water Committee to ensure a hookup from Mekharot, the Israeli private company that manages water in the West Bank. The connection was confirmed, but the quantity had not been settled—in a letter to Israeli authorities, developers asked for an amount much higher than the West Bank average, itself only two-thirds of the World Health Organization's (WHO's) minimal recommendations. The road had still not been approved, and Dajani had been waiting eighteen months to hear from the Israeli Civil Administration. He was "not optimistic right now." But when I returned to Rawabi in summer 2013, some of the instability had settled, if in unsatisfactory ways: Mekharot would not be increasing the water allotment to the West Bank on the grounds that, according to one employee, Rawabi was simply "reallocating people," and the road had been granted short-term, renewable permission. The issue reemerged in summer 2014, and in 2015 the water hookup was approved, supposedly in return for the PA backing down on threats to join international organizations.

Clearly all of these initiatives require direct contact with both the PA and the Israeli Civil Administration and for the PA to negotiate on Rawabi's behalf. Developers work to create the image of an open market, but it is highly constrained. The continuing and continual process of building and accumulating capital, of creating markets under the ongoing regime, is as important as their stated goals to build housing. I asked one firm higher-up, is it worthwhile to expect goodwill from the Israelis? "Israelis are interested as a business opportunity. There is political and economic will for this project to succeed." You're optimistic? They laughed and jokingly responded, "Well, I'm getting paid."

Chapter Three

Image, Process,
and Precedent

■

SOMETIME IN 2008, Bashar Masri approached RTI International
about self-funding a study and plan, with the possibility of turning it into contract work. RTI is a massive, billion-dollar, nonprofit
development firm, and Masri had a previous relationship with it from his
work with USAID in Palestine and elsewhere in the Middle East. The plan,
like many others, established the sense of expertise, experience, and seriousness around Rawabi. In practice it was utilized selectively, but the way it
circulated was as important to the process of place-making as its content. I
spoke with a few current and former RTI employees who worked on the project and, although they would not release the report to me, they told me about
their experience (I ultimately got the report another way). To them, Masri
is "an extraordinary entrepreneur . . . very wealthy, very successful," and the
idea of working on a project that is "at once profit making and also embedded in the failure of the state and the inability of the world to do something"
was appealing. And it was appealing enough that RTI fronted its own money
for research under the assumption the work would eventually be linked to
the wider aid economy as part of a USAID project it could help implement.
A senior researcher was very taken by Masri, "struck by what a remarkable
entrepreneur he is . . . the guy is all business . . . all about the bottom line." He
had "never seen a private sector guy so completely pro-profit." But one simul-

taneously driven by national politics: Masri's attitude was "hey, if the prime minister can't do it, I'll be the private sector PM." "He thinks large . . . he is so dynamic." He is also "very impatient." For RTI, this was a "fascinating opportunity" to do a different kind of development; it had "never encountered a situation where the private sector imperative is also a public policy imperative." That intermixing does not happen in isolation but, rather, through the idea of private development as state building, private developments themselves, and the aggregation of expertise and documentary evidence—like the RTI report—that circulate to establish, confirm, and strengthen the approach.

Another RTI specialist in Palestine explained that the firm is experienced in large-scale economic planning, so while creating a strategy for Palestine required a discussion of its unique situation, Palestine's is "not all that much different from [strategies] in Kentucky, Florida, etc." A primary issue for Rawabi is that there are "two classes of workers, but that the uneducated, low-skilled workforce could provide a basis for growth." So "you need an industrial sector . . . stone and marble are not enough." But part of the problem—and a source of disagreement with the developers—is that "economies are regional" and must reach beyond the town. Developers wanted to control industry locally. So, in coordination with Massar, and given the clear impediments of occupation geographies, they created a plan that was technology-oriented and based mostly on outsourcing IT to Israel and beyond, and utilized the structure of foreign aid. Ultimately, there was a bit of a break with Massar. Although there was mutual agreement that "the future is in outsourcing," RTI tried to "hammer out a strategy" and to figure out how to move forward concretely, but "the folks at Rawabi weren't ready for it." Or, as a former Massar employee said, "They won't use it."

Like AECOM, RTI sought to overlay universal ideological and liberal economic principles as mechanisms to solve problems specific to this political context. Plans are often made to be invoked and to orient the next set of plans. Planning is a form of anticipation, but also a way to orient activity toward a future. In an environment where there is no clear developmental trajectory, plans oriented toward the future solidify in and shape the present.

Plans also reflect precedent and decision-making for the institutions and individuals empowered to make decisions. The distance between planning and reality is where work takes place. A few months into my interviews with Rawabi, I got a surprising call from a frustrated employee. A Massar employee asked me to send an email reminding him of a few documents he had promised: a schematic for legal approvals and their economic plan. One employee heard from another who heard from someone else: "See what he wants." Finally, one of them called the number in my email signature rather than replying, believing work emails to be monitored. The employee told me that they would be unable to give me the documents because "sometimes these guys," the firm higher-ups, "talk too much" and "there is no comprehensive roadmap for approvals." They said they were unlikely to share the RTI economic plan I had heard much about because they did not plan to adopt it.

At first, I was reluctant to believe my luck; up to that point I had been given mostly superficial information, and the developers had politely declined to offer any kind of participatory access. At the same time, I felt certain I did not rate highly enough with them to be a legitimate concern, and I knew that the firm was interested in having people write about it. I asked for a meeting and began one of my most important informant relationships. I gained access to more information, people, data, and documentation that clarified and complicated my understanding of how the developers were imaging, imagining, and producing their project both rhetorically and materially, as well as to knowledge and documentation of discussions around discarded plans.

I interviewed several current and former Rawabi employees on multiple occasions, and they told a story of a work environment without clearly defined tasks, where work was done piecemeal, and where comprehensive frameworks were kept away from employees. They were assigned to do research the company constantly cites, although they may or may not have been qualified. They described Masri as the sole decision-maker. Even the origin story is his alone: supposedly he was on a drive with a friend who owned some land in the area. The friend was excited, showed Masri the site and said that he loved the hills, the beauty, and planned to be buried there. Masri "saw a city there" and "decided to buy the whole thing," including his friend's plot. "This is a man with a vision." Like reports that are invoked but not necessarily followed, this singular vision does not completely line up with the Portland Trust meetings in 2008, or the broader context (how did he come up with a city, one employee asked another. "Did he get the idea from Modi'in?" "Probably, yes. He is in love with it"), the firm's dependence on PA and international aid, or the kinds of compromises such a huge project requires. Masri is constantly described as smart, ambitious, innovative, and pragmatic. One former RTI researcher described him as a man who has "availed himself of opportunities" and is a success "despite his management style," an often harsh exactitude. While these particular employees were ambivalent about his personal approach (another former employee I spoke with had tears in her eyes about the admiration and excitement she felt for him, for Rawabi, and for the future), they admire his vision and charisma and his macho ability to *create* opportunity for himself. He brought the Qataris in, and he has oriented the government to serve him, they said. The employees had many critiques of Masri's plan, but one asked the other, "Would you prefer a minister that steals, or Masri, who is making money legally?"

Two former employees I spoke with were not confident that the homes would be affordable for ordinary Palestinians. And to some degree they wonder if that is even the point; whether or not it improves quality of life for those who can afford it, they believe one of Masri's primary motivations is his own status: "He is so happy whenever the Israelis or Americans mention him." Over and over I heard the language of "he" rather than "they" or "it." Rawabi is Masri's plan, he is making it happen, and he will be the primary beneficiary of this ostensibly national project. But of course, Masri is not doing this alone, he is a visible representative of a coalition of class actors, capitalists, NGOs, and PA officials roughly intertwined in a similar ideological project. Moreover, many Palestinians want to live there, to buy what developers are selling. Masri and that coalition have successfully shifted the putative state's political agenda, mobilized resources, and worked productively with Israelis. At minimum, the project has required close ties with the occupying authority to bring in investment, to be granted building permissions, to gain special business travel permits for its West Bank employees, and so on.[1] Rawabi seems to run fairly smoothly, despite the complications and difficulties of doing pretty much anything in the West Bank. Partially this is due to Masri's connections, power, and local celebrity, but it is not his alone; his persona shapes the specifics and makes the work visible, but focusing too much on individuals makes it difficult to see the productive and lasting effects of wider capitalist political interventions in Palestine.

Image Circulation

If the image of Masri and Rawabi—or Masri as Rawabi—obscures some of the complications of building in the West Bank, how does the idea of politics at the national scale become material through investment in the land? Part of how it operates is to bring different groups of people together in the project. In October 2010 I visited the site with George Rafidi. Later that day Tony Blair visited, and the day before Gilad Erdan, then Israel's minister of environmental protection, was there. Erdan is a hard-line rightist known for shouting in 2006 at Azmi Bishara, an Arab Palestinian member of the Knesset, "Why don't you just go back to Syria?"[2] Prior to his visit to Rawabi, he had also tried to cut Gaza's power and accused Mahmoud Abbas of being a member of Hamas. He supported bills against Arab "disloyalty to the state" in 2008. He is aligned with the most far-right and ultra-nationalist elements in an already rightist and nationalist legislature. Yet Massar welcomed him to the site and invited him to discuss regional wastewater treatment and environmental plans with the firm and the United States Trade and Development Agency (USTDA). Moments after concluding his visit, Erdan turned to his retinue and the media and announced that Rawabi must be stopped, that it would necessarily be bad for the environment and that in light of the so-called settlement freeze, it reflected an unfair and unbalanced government attitude toward building in the West Bank (Waldoks 2010).

One employee told me that he "was against the visit, but don't quote me—I don't want to lose my job." The rationale, he said, was "they are an occupying army, how can you tell them not to come?" Ultimately, the company thought it would be a "good gesture to invite him in" and were "quite surprised" by what he said, "especially with all the money" put toward "master plans and environmental designs." But this should not have come as a shock, and it demonstrates some potential political limitations of using universal, shared concepts like class aspiration or the environment as a venue through which to model and promote development and normal relations. In this context, it is the surprise that is more surprising than the minister's speech. The rhetoric of peace and universality cannot easily project across the conflict and above overlapping geographies of dispossession and forms of race-based territorial governance. Universals are not shared or available to Palestinians; they are encompassed and unevenly distributed within Israel. The potential benefits of Erdan's visit were unclear to me and to the employees I spoke with about it. But what they got was clear: "The minister used environmental crap to try to stop the project. What about the settlement waste they're dumping on Palestinian villages?"

Clearly the liberal Jewish Israeli public is an important audience for Masri and his firms. At the time of Erdan's visit, I was also working mostly on the material for chapters 9 and 10 on settler human rights. One of my interlocutors, a well-known leftist Israeli activist, was interested in seeing the site. They asked me to make an introduction, but the public outreach people at Rawabi never answered. When I asked a higher-up why, they said, "We are private sector, not an NGO. There is a developmental aspect to be sure . . . but we are too busy to take the time to organize meetings." "We are not a political organization." They were at that time, however, *constantly* organizing meetings; a visit like Erdan's presumably seemed somehow beneficial.

Developers have tended to be defensive with Arabs and in the Arabic-language media, for example, angrily reacting to critique and "losing composure" when asked if Rawabi will house Israelis, a claim they had made in the past (Ramallah News 2017) and continue to talk around with the language of openness (Ross 2019). Masri in particular seems to conflate general Arab opinion with those leftist activists who have accused him of being a comprador or a profiteer. In my many official interviews, it was almost impossible to get to the details beyond PR. But as a matter of method, even superficial accounts accrue weight through repetition. They start to look like principles around which politics and intervention are based and organized, and they point toward the things that developers find important, worth prioritizing or demonstrating. The firm has engaged the Palestinian public mostly through events like large concerts by international Arab stars, and they have also sought out the triumphalist British pop rock band Coldplay, who visited the city (Haaretz 2017; Brinn 2017).

So, Palestinians are engaged mostly through spectacles of normality, safety, and achievement, and through desire to have the same opportunities as those outside Palestine. Palestinians are treated as an abstract population, assumed to be willing to be cultivated. And although developers could never stifle public debate, they work hard to craft the information available and how and where it circulates. The firm seeks to mystify the ways that it is carrying out its business and to present a tailored version to its international audience. The firm returns that version to Palestine after it has circulated and accrued authority from outside. Capital and influence are not evenly distributed; in this instance Palestinians are consumers, Israeli and international audiences are supporters, and NGOs and elites are funders. Put another way, my experience made me wonder whom the project is for. At least at this stage, developers are concerned to mobilize resources—financial as well as in terms of liberal ideology and culture. Rawabi is a massive, "national" project that is not only real but symbolic, and it circulates far beyond the West Bank; indeed, at numerous times throughout the history of the project, there was more coverage in English-language outlets than in Arabic.

As one of the first, if not the first, social scientists to attempt long-term study of Rawabi, I have regularly been sought out by students, journalists, documentarians, and other researchers dozens of times. As I was working on this manuscript I was contacted by graduate students, college students, filmmakers, and a playwright, mostly non-Arabs. Many were granted easy and quick introductions to Masri. For the entire time I was in Palestine, the company was regularly hosting researchers, Jewish American community organizations, and foreign press, and it seemed like anyone from outside was welcomed. Those visits are reflected in a long record of stenographic newspaper articles, blog posts, and student papers. On the other hand, it took me wading through nearly a year of promises and follow-ups before being definitively put off. As a Palestinian-American, a scholar, and an Arabic speaker, a lot of doors were open to me during research. This was not one of them, and I worried my identity and deeper interest led them to ultimately question my intentions. Given the realities of the context, the company appeared to see alliances with Israeli and international liberal publics as, at least, equally important to Palestinian public opinion, with the possible exception of potential consumers, lumped and treated as an undifferentiated unit.

Clearly, the firm is scripting its relationship to the various groups that it hopes to convince and incorporate. It was in October 2010, just days after Erdan's visit and near the end of my longest fieldwork stay, that I was finally put in direct contact with Masri's young personal assistant (who very quickly rose to near the top of the firm). I called and was told to call back in a day. I called the next day and was told to call back in another day. I was then ignored, followed up, and finally received a reply:

Hi Kareem,

I got your message Kareem, and I told you that I will get back to you as soon as I have an answer; as Bashar was out of town in the past few days and I was extremely busy. At any rate, Bashar's schedule is very tight, and I am afraid that it's not possible to meet him; furthermore, we don't think that there is any further information that Bashar can add to what Amir & George have already briefed you.

I had seen Masri in the Bayti Real Estate offices during that time so, confused, I asked one of my informants what was going on. They told me I would not be given access because developers had decided I would not reproduce what they had told me. They hoped my account would lack legitimacy without quotes from Masri.[3]

A little later, I found I may have been wrapped up in the firm's image management to a degree I had not expected. After I had given a paper at a Birzeit University conference, that same informant called. They had been contacted by one of the higher-ups and before going in to meet them wanted to know, "Could it have something to do with your paper?" I reminded them

I am ethically bound to protect informants' identities, that my paper barely mentioned Rawabi, and that I certainly had made no public denunciations or anything like that. Which developers would have known to be true since one who I had interviewed previously attended my talk (and only my talk). After the conference, I pointed the informant out to a very prominent Palestinian academic, who half-joked that she "probably came to spy." Anyway, the informant's meeting was totally normal and work-related, but in this case the pervasive paranoia reflected something real. On my final research trip in 2017, I met with a different former employee who confirmed much of what I had managed to piece together. Without prompting, they told me I had a reputation among the senior people—they know who I am, have passed around my articles, and view me as someone "critical." Having published little of anything about Rawabi this book, it is hard to guess why that might be so.

The economist Raja Khalidi had a telling experience in 2014. A public intellectual, a heterodox development economist with nationalist commitments, Khalidi found it difficult to get an article published in the local Arabic language media. He critiqued private development in favor of a more national approach and argued that Rawabi was in financial trouble. He somewhat mischievously suggested that, if indeed it is a national project, it ought to be used to house Palestinian refugees from Syria. The idea was that developers could at once help work toward resolution of a humanitarian crisis, put Israel in the position of opposing such aid, and fill and enliven Rawabi. The critique was one, I think, based in a bigger set of questions about the role of the private sector in politics: far from wanting it gone, he wanted it oriented toward the things it might be well placed to help.

Part of the reason newspapers did not want the article was that earlier in 2014, the center-left Bisan Center for Research and Development released a two-page report on Rawabi and the "normalization" it represents and advances. The report was skeptical the housing will be affordable and made an issue of the firm's relationship to Israelis such as Moshe Safdie and the attorney and fixer Dov Weissglass. Bisan claimed that not only is Rawabi based on a settlement model but that it benefits Israeli firms. The report demanded that Palestinian capitalists and the PA clarify their positions regarding normalization, and that the PA should not actively aid private firms at the expense of antioccupation politics (Bisan Center for Research and Development 2014). Almost immediately after it was released, Massar sued Bisan for USD1 million, and the report disappeared (Kutub 2014).

I do not mean to suggest that developers have managed to shut down debate; the fact that Rawabi is such a public issue proves otherwise. But developers are working hard, at times successfully, to limit debate to the kinds of images they want to project. They present a Palestinian unity to the outside world, an image that returns to Palestine through foreign media. Rawabi is best for them as a topic of conversation, not something controversial or debatable. Typical discussions in the Arabic press might refer to "Facebook activists" (Palestine Today 2018) or to regular problems, sometimes in a gossipy way, such as the Rawabi school's headmaster stepping down (Ultra Palestine 2018a), critiques of venture capital and normalization (Ultra Palestine 2017), various severe anxieties and arguments about complicity (Ibrahim 2017), or sightings of Israeli delegations and soldiers in Rawabi (Ultra Palestine 2018b, 2018c). But reports are more often laudatory or focus narrowly on project details rather than the politics around it or its constituency.[4]

At the earlier stages when the site was closed to the public, developers could manage researchers' access more easily. They continue to work to control the images that circulate in the West Bank and among Palestinians more generally. They are certainly not averse to press or even academic study outside of Palestine. By 2017, the firm had started cold-calling elite universities, proposing that they "work together" with Rawabi on the grounds that they "are facing some interesting challenges . . . which could be the subject of some academic research/case studies."[5] The goal here too is to accrue authority to the project and to bring back that authority to present to states, NGOs, and eventually to consumers.

The point is simply that developers seek out specific audiences, utilize the press, and manage their image. Given the political situation, there has been a lot more attention given to convincing outsiders than those Palestinians who are passively incorporated. All of these representations aggregate to give weight to arguments for financial aid: articles from 2013, around the time of John Kerry's renewed peace process and "Marshall Plan" for Palestine, emphasized both the peacefulness of the project and the fact that developers did not receive sufficient or promised aid from the PA or international organizations. Countless articles in the English press indicate the importance of the audience abroad, who can potentially pressure states and NGOs for further aid and economic reform (Al Jazeera 2013; PBS 2013; Rosove 2013; Sherwood 2013; Voice of America 2013). The question of emphasis on the outside is not very complicated in this case; powerful publics do not tend to exist within Palestine.

A more direct example is in an event I attended in December 2016 in Chicago, a fundraiser for the liberal Zionist organization J Street. The featured speaker there, alongside members of Congress and local political dignitaries, was Bashar Masri. Masri spoke in front of a large crowd that had serious anti-Trump energy, a group of funders genuinely committed to a peaceful resolution to the conflict. The first several speakers talked about resistance to Trump and electoral activism against him. They spoke of their commitment to a two-state solution, to working "within our community in a pro-Israel way." Although many Palestinians would be skeptical of Masri's relationship to a Zionist lobbying group, his presence is one outcome of the logics of the two-state process: if American Jewish activists believe, correctly, that the peace process is at an impasse at the level of government and want to find Palestinians working in an explicitly two-state mode, they have discovered they need to go to business.

When it was Masri's turn, he started with a promotional video, followed by a conversation with the founder and head of J Street, Jeremy Ben-Ami. The video was more aspirational and future-oriented than descriptive of the current status of the site. It showed crowded areas, shops, and a vibrant downtown that had yet to be created. The video said that there are several hundred families living there. But the point was the image of success, peace, and prosperity. During the conversation, Masri talked about his initial excitement for Oslo and how he was at Andrews Air Force Base in 1993 to welcome Yasser Arafat on the trip where he would famously extend his hand to Yitzhak Rabin.[6] He continued to discuss how he returned to Palestine in 1995 and wanted to start a business. At first, he wanted to do something in manufacturing ("I'm an engineer") but realized that assembling anything would be impossible if it had to be disassembled at a checkpoint. So he decided on real estate. If, as I have suggested, these economic initiatives aim to turn the West Bank into a market and ensure ongoing accumulation, they use the only thing they really have available: the place where they stand.

He proudly stated that he is pushing USD70 million to USD80 million into the Israeli economy and that "our historic enemy—Israel—could become our best friend." Over a few minutes of banter between friends, Ben-Ami discussed the first outside employer to commit to Rawabi, an Israeli tech firm that has a relationship with the US-Israeli chip designer Mellanox Technologies. On a J Street-organized trip to Rawabi, a Mellanox board member saw what was going on and became inspired to work together. Ben-Ami urged the crowd to "reach out to our networks" and get involved personally and through investment. For Masri, Israel and Palestine are intertwined, and he has spoken out against Boycott, Divestment, and Sanctions (BDS) being applied to Israel beyond its settlements (Jacobs 2018). Palestinian activists have called this "normalization" (Abunimah 2012), and they are not wrong in that, at least to this audience, Masri is openly and successfully working within the presently normal condition of occupation in the West Bank.[7]

The political questions that are alternately mobilized or discarded by Massar become the framework for motivating economic intervention and even for explaining the strange forms that the "open" market takes under occupation. Here is Masri, from a Dutch documentary:

> As you grow [up] you understand things better, and you learn things as you grow. Resisting the occupation always takes many forms. And some of them move parallel, some drop, some increase, and so on over time. I believe since, again, we signed a peace agreement, all our resistance of the occupation should be peaceful means. Even when the occupation quells us, and shoots at us, and tear gasses, etc., I believe at this stage—although I participated in rock-throwing—I should, we should not respond in that way, we should respond in passive ways. We need to become more sophisticated by using smart ways of battling the occupation. Building a city is, in a way, fighting the occupation. It is the more progressive way, it is the professional way, it is the human way, it is the modern way. (Al Jazeera 2013)

Still, I did not quite understand why the firm was so guarded toward locals and could not square what seemed like a disproportionate outside focus. One former employee had a hunch: they described Masri's firms as being so intertwined, and with so many opportunities to extract so many different pieces of foreign aid, that the whole could really only function if the specifics were opaque. Once I met an employee interlocutor in an old Ramallah coffee shop—a dingy, smoky, mostly male kind of place he chose because it was not frequented by foreign residents and the kinds of young, upwardly mobile people working for Massar. I described being given the runaround, and he said, "Of course they won't set up a meeting for Masri to see you." Why not? "Because they are assholes." Oh, come on, that can't be it. "There is propaganda" about state building and politics, but if you dig deeper, it is "pure capitalism." It is "perfectly legal corruption," he said.

Development aid is present and important, even in the supposedly independent private sector. Massar is a local partner for Chemonics International, one of the larger USAID subcontractors operating in the West Bank. For every project it works on, it allegedly takes an 80 percent overhead—"even for development agencies, this is high."[8] When I asked why Massar gets these contracts, he replied, "I would guess because of Masri's good contacts with the

US and the Israelis." Similarly, he says that Rawabi is profligate with "Qatari money," buying multiple Mercedes SUVs, raising wages for favored employees, paying other firm's employees out of the Rawabi accounts, and so on.[9] He describes a company that was just as much about process as results—"all Rawabi does is spend money . . . only the finance department is doing anything." And as part of the process, current and former employees report a dearth of accountability, haphazard promotions, constant turnover and widespread dissatisfaction, complaints about "management style," and the belief that even senior people have to ask permission for everything (indeed, a disgruntled former staffer joked one must "go to him if you want to fart"). Another employee told me that, from the perspective of the press and "PR-wise, Rawabi is number one," but the details? "Not great." Despite all that, nearly every former employee I spoke with felt invested in Rawabi's success, used "we" to refer to it, and described himself or herself as "loyal."

These companies are constantly producing new companies that become beneficiaries of indirect and direct foreign aid. In summer 2010 Massar had just started Siraj Fund Management Company, a venture capital fund for small to medium enterprises (SMEs). Siraj received funding from the Overseas Private Investment Corporation (OPIC), the US government's private development agency, and immediately bought shares in PalGaz, a utility that installs large central gas tanks for buildings rather than the portable tanks common in Palestine, and the company that Massar planned to use in Rawabi. Allegedly, although it is a separate firm, Siraj employees are being paid out of the Rawabi payroll. When I asked how this was possible, a former employee suggested, "the Qataris are not investing for profit," and do not really notice what "the Palestinians are doing with their money." Do the Qataris send auditors? "The auditors are all Ernst and Young," a company with close ties to the chief financial officer. Neither does the procurement process happen openly. Rawabi does not solicit bids and tenders; the employee in charge of procurement solicits "price offers from his friends." At that time, Rawabi had bought a large amount of equipment, including Caterpillars, and supposedly had circumvented the Palestinian market and the authorized West Bank dealer, instead purchasing from Israel. The dealer authorized in the West Bank sued them, so they simply continued with their purchase under the name of an individual employee with an Israeli ID. "Wherever you look there's something wrong with what they're doing." "The term 'building capacity' to me means we are wasting money."[10]

In 2014 and 2015 there were widespread rumors of a sort of critical mass of malfeasance. Supposedly the Qataris had cut funding based on an audit showing "millions" misallocated and of massive landholding obscured—land dealers told me that developers had sold their own land to their partnership with the Qataris at significant markup. The popular version around Ramallah was they were tipped off by people around the wife of a knowledgeable employee as retribution during a difficult divorce proceeding.

I was unable to find evidence for this gossip and these claims, and they should not be taken as fact or legally actionable. Many of the rumored allegations are very serious, and I take no position on the extent to which they are entirely accurate or even true. But I believe public discourse around Rawabi is nevertheless meaningful and productive. Rumors are valuable because they index the kinds of anxieties and fears about practices that both flourish in and continue to shape the Palestinian context. These descriptions of how private developers operate are also images that circulate, intersect, and sometimes diverge from the reality, and they are part of the public experience of development in Palestine. The details are necessarily obscure—any private firm would do the same—but the conversations around Rawabi reflect worry about privatization, development, and frontier capitalism at the expense of the national political project. Again, as one former employee put it, "the term 'building capacity' to me means we are wasting money."

The lack of coherent law or jurisdiction in the West Bank enables developers to operate by setting precedent around their practices. Developers are not creating free markets as much as easing their own entry and orienting the framework for who can enter after them. Aid subcontractors are doing work funded by donors without a profit motive. The public sector generates documents for donors that become political frameworks as these private projects materialize. Foreign capital creates and insures markets that function for local capital accumulation, and fixed capital in the built environment enables it all. Complexity among Palestinians is glossed over, and the people, as a people, end up somehow ancillary or redefined in the process of being invoked. Investment in Palestine is organized around an ideology of "politics," the idea of investment as nationalism, what Raja Khalidi and Sobhi Samour call "neoliberalism as liberation" (2011, 6).

Developers and planners shape their interventions in terms of ideas about universal aspiration, and in doing so they produce local forms. Complexity is minimized in favor of a polity treated as undifferentiated, waiting to be developed. I return to a point I made earlier about the 2010 Palestine Investment Conference in Bethlehem, where a speaker put it this way: "It is difficult, to be sure, but there are returns to be made. It is our national duty, but be sure, there are returns to be made." While almost all Palestinians could benefit from increased financial returns, this is a different kind of return than the one Palestinians in refugee camps, in the West Bank, in Gaza, and in the diaspora imagine. In the Rawabi return, Palestinian elites can serve simultaneously as outward-looking and collaborative, as well as nationalist bourgeoisie. By extracting profit from an unstable political situation and working actively with the PA, NGOs, the US government, the Quartet, and the Israeli Civil Administration, they are producing a West Bank that serves market liberalization as political liberalism and potential liberation. There emerges an ethic of individualism and class aspiration that does not negate previous forms of collective nationalism but alters its form and objectives.

Chapter Four

Public
Urban Planning

GOVERNMENT AND URBAN PLANNING exist in Palestine in spite
of uncertainty about the future, within a constant politics of deferral, and they help to produce forms of politics and social relations that will have lasting consequences. Planners and practitioners are quite
aware of the difficulties of making a roadmap there, yet they do it nevertheless.
Absent a path toward political liberation, ideas of development and modern
arrival—both necessarily about economics and capital accumulation—have
overlaid and begun to reorient political aspiration. And for some Palestinians, especially those capitalists who benefit from a stable, ordered, investment landscape, that is enough. Today, large-scale planning has a class logic,
and it enables subsequent stages of accumulation in the West Bank. It builds
upon and subsumes other articulations of the national planning project. It
does so by formulating and authorizing national priorities around privatization in narrowly accessible places for Palestinians to move.

Today, private-led planning is possible for reasons specific to the Palestinian context as well as more generally through investment and aid pressure
congruent with a worldwide movement away from national-scale or public
service provision. Not only is it part of the alchemy of turning Palestine into a
stable, productive market as a form of state-scale management, but plans are
materialized in built environments and in institutions of state governance. In

many ways, planning is a form of anticipation, it presupposes a future. Yet in Palestine there is no real political or practical capacity to build toward one. If, as Bou Akar (2018) writes, anticipation of violence is an urbanizing process and form of urban governance, this is what happens when it becomes possible to act as though one could anticipate peace. In Palestine the context and scaffolding of the conflict is organized around perpetual anticipation. Planning and deferral are forms of urban governance and state-scale management in Palestine, written into vernacular form.

Law in the West Bank is an important part of the context for interventions into the Palestinian built environment—their limits and possibilities, shapes and extents. The act of planning frames, orients, and justifies interventions in a landscape produced over time and in part by Israeli legal, practical, and military restrictions on Palestinian life. The absence of clear law—if not necessarily clear jurisdiction—enables the placement of Rawabi on open land. Various forms of law are mechanisms for the exercise of power and for the elaboration and creation of the physical site and, at a more general scale, an open market. This chapter focuses on the context in which Rawabi is built, and how, as a project of urban and master planning, it encourages and produces urban governance and practical and legal precedent as it intersects with current PA strategic "national planning" in the West Bank. Planning implies and creates visions and possibilities for the future, and it weaves practice together with other kinds of laws that enter into this story at different scales, such as land tenure, state form, and human rights.

Palestinians in the West Bank are continuously separated and segregated from Israelis through a system of military orders, legislative action, judicial decisions, and contracts that specify which body of law applies to which people. Taken together, they constitute what Israeli legal scholar Amnon Rubenstein calls the "enclave law" (Nakba Files 2016). There is a dual legal system of local governance, and the separation of the land from people was a strategic response to legalize violations of the Fourth Geneva Convention (Hajjar 2005). Israeli civil jurisdiction slowly creeps into the occupied West Bank, mapping onto Jewish Israelis rather than land (in ways that are different from how it works in Jerusalem and the Golan, which are actively annexed). Taken together, that agglomeration of law and practice enables Jewish Israelis to move freely between the 1948 and 1967 territories (Nakba Files 2016). The geographical imperatives of the Israeli settler state require a push and pull between the need for territory and the undesirability of fully incorporating its inhabitants. On the one hand it means the application of law onto people rather than territory, on the other to a legal system that coalesces around those imperatives, maintaining and formalizing them. Planning and state formation—those Palestinian institutions emerging separate from Israel yet in the same place—bring Israeli restrictions into the body of Palestinian jurisdiction and practice. Rawabi forms in the primordial soup of the PA statelike law, massive as both a project and a national-scale priority. Palestinian Authority law is modeled upon and lightly overlays previous legal regimes. As Palestinian self-rule slowly and partially emerges, investment priorities combine with previous forms of colonial and occupation law and practice, drawing capital imperatives into a preexisting system of control over people and territory. This is how planning, a roadmap for the future in the present, contributes to legal reform, the foundation of state law, and maintenance of a web of legal and practical regulations that organize populations within the occupied West Bank.[1]

Palestinian Planning in the Oslo Period

Planning has served changing political imperatives, first to formalize activity on the landscape, and second as a language for enforcement and to circumscribe Palestinian existence and possibility. Today it is used to open previously unprofitable land to capital investment, but that approach was not preordained. Prior to the Fayyad regime, there were attempts to use it to establish an alternate political and spatial practice that served Palestinians and worked actively toward a future state.

In the Oslo-era hopefulness of the mid- and late-1990s, a Palestinian-led planning movement emerged in one part of the PA, demonstrating one side of an internal fight, practically speaking, that apparently lost. The 1998 National Plan was the first serious attempt in more than a decade to institute a planning regime for the West Bank (and, at the time, Gaza). Palestinian planners set out to use their new authority under the PA to create a comprehensible system as well as a road map for formalizing Palestinians' interactions with the built environment for the future. Planners knew their authority in the moment could be fleeting, so they attempted to fix certain things such as regional planning and resource use. They came up with a detailed plan that was ultimately stymied structurally and legally and had little power or possibility for implementation.

The plan frames its goals in terms of the need to create a responsive framework for addressing the structural, physical, economic, and environmental problems that decades of occupation have imposed on Palestine. As Palestinians gained greater sovereignty over larger parts of the West Bank and Gaza, they had to build capacity at the same time as they defined land use and pro-vided an overall vision for linking and growing regional Palestinian settlement.

There has never, in modern times, been planned development of the built-up environment in the West Bank . . . . The West Bank has been en-croached and divided by external rulers without structuring in relation to economic forces or an administrative-political order. There has been no development strategy for population distribution, nor allocation of land for future expansion . . . . The system of built-up areas developed more or less randomly and wherever possible, scattered by man-made interference, with the topography lacking the essential inter-linking infrastructure in terms of network facilities that characterize a mature and well-developed settlement system. (Ministry of Planning and International Cooperation 1998, 6)

The technocrats then in the Ministry of Planning and International Coop-eration (MOPIC) argued for a robust, diligent system that would help oversee Palestine's transition to a centralized state in the following years by curb-ing bad planning and haphazard development. Their planning was based on needs rather than forecasting or speculation, and presupposed a much more specific day after occupation than the private sector and presentist ap-proaches to planning do today.[2] Samih al-Abed's preface states:

As we are at the end of the 1990s, Palestinian society is embarking on a new era. For the first time in modern history, Palestinians will be able to shape and direct the development of their future, limited to the areas un-der their jurisdiction. The signing of the Declaration of principles by the PLO and the Israeli Government in September 1993 and the election of the Palestinian Legislative Council in January 1996 have created a new framework for Palestinian control over the planning process and the de-velopment of the built-up environment . . . . During Israeli occupation, Palestinians were not allowed to participate in any form of planning, as development was entirely controlled by the Israeli Civil Administration. Israeli withdrawal from areas under Palestinian jurisdiction and from Palestinian civil affairs after the signing of the Interim Agreement on the West Bank and the Gaza Strip on September 28, 1995, left no basic data and planning capacity for future development. Consequently, the [PA] through the Ministry of Planning and International Co-operation (MOPIC) has had to take charge and create a physical planning system from nothing. (Min-istry of Planning and International Cooperation 1998, i)

Their baseline was as follows: "It is assumed that by the year 2005, the Palestinians will have full authority over the entire West Bank and Gaza Strip. Borders will be opened between Palestine and other countries and the bulk of Palestinian refugees will start returning to Palestine" (Ministry of Planning and International Cooperation 1998, 13). And "it is presupposed that by then (East) Jerusalem will be under Palestinian sovereignty . . . it is assumed that . . . settlements will become under Palestinian authority after the year 2005" (Ministry of Planning and International Cooperation 1998, 13). Those assumptions about both the future and the inherent capacities of Oslo were not borne out. The plan was neither approved nor adopted. That it was not adopted is not unique: little is formally adopted in Palestine. Yet, unlike other documents, this Palestinian-led proposal was not invoked, it did not circulate continuously, and other ideas and documents took its place. The 1998 plan talks about universal and other needs: "Economic growth and development under guidance of sustainability should be allocated and distributed to achieve balanced regional development, a well-functioning utilization of resources over time, and a fair distribution of income and welfare among individuals for the benefit of all" (Ministry of Planning and International Cooperation 1998, 10).

Today, the Palestinian leadership and capitalist class benefit from the lack of formality. MOPIC no longer has the directive to conduct national planning of this type. Instead, it produces optimistic reports of institution building for international donors such as the Palestinian Reform and Development Plan and "Building the State of Palestine: A Success Story." Moreover, the 2003 Constitution enshrines free market capitalism as the sole economic system for Palestine. Planning is as rhetorical and ideological as it is material. It exists within and becomes a component of the occupation, and aid economies and planning and law are designed to produce landscapes for privatization and accumulation. (This is not to mention that Rawabi is in a location the Oslo-era technocrats would have rejected: the 1998 plan proposed building up existing centers to aid service distribution as well as expanding boundaries around cities to aid development and reduce density.)

It is true that many of the assumptions in those plans—especially the idea that Ramallah, al-Bireh, and Jerusalem could be considered a single urban unit—no longer hold. However, prior plans assumed Palestinian political autonomy. They aimed to eradicate some of the worst legal and material effects of the occupation, and they did not presuppose and work around colonial boundaries. Present-day urban planning must conform within the occupation area system. But it also benefits from the consequences of previous plans that kept land around villages clear of development, and now affordable—one unintended consequence of the area system is that it has created a rent gap. Rawabi's explicit claim is to create new privately owned infrastructure for services and utilities under its control. Politics, laws, and national priorities were reoriented, and the desire for formalization turned into the need for openness. Whatever problems previous plans sought to address were opened to market forces and profit-making intervention.

If for no other reason, this planning was important because it was a *government* project. Unlike the countless speculative plans that appear and evaporate, it demonstrates the state's priorities and relationship to the future. Planning only later became about formalizing capacities in the present. The future is conceived in the late 2000s state-building agenda as something that will emerge, not quite actively, once the present is stable.

Rawabi and the Practice of Planning

The way a PA national planner explained it to me, there are three legal areas of planning: the local level, the domain of local authorities; the regional level, which used to refer to either the West Bank or Gaza and is now unclear; and the national level, the jurisdiction of the Ministry of Planning (MOPIC) and now effectively restricted to the West Bank. In fact, the Ministry of Local Government (MOLG) has been doing the local planning and creating precedent for municipalities because, as someone in MOPIC said, "There is nothing to prohibit them from doing it, [even though] logically they should not be doing local planning."

Local plans must first be approved by municipal/rural planning councils; and second, by the regional planning committees responsible for approving local planning, as well as projects outside of localities and in the in-between areas; and third, by the Palestinian Higher Planning Council (HPC), the final decision-maker for disputes between other councils and, most importantly here, the body that approves plans with "national dimensions." Rawabi, a local unit with national dimensions located in between jurisdictions, has no clear precedent for approvals. Because of the added confusion between national and regional levels in a fragmented West Bank, and because post-Oslo plans were never approved, MOPIC's national planning has become more about establishing state-scale ideological orientation in documents like the Palestinian Reform and Development Plan (PRDP); the ministry has no clear procedure for something like Rawabi. The HPC is increasingly synonymous with the MOLG, the ministry with growing authority over West Bank planning. As a rule, one PA planner told me, "that Ministry is in support of private development" and, as such, developers are "defining the priorities."

Planning has thus become not only about the nitty-gritty of making buildings and infrastructure but about fanciful thinking, and proposing and aggregating authority to the ideological framework in which Palestinian relationships to the land are shaped. Legal bodies work in service of the various "national projects"; bureaucrats, many of them from the early PA period, implement the various directives. National projects are where symbols and ideology meet the law, and demonstrate the limits and possibilities for reforming the law.

Economic sectors also become national priorities, and government plans formalize a road map for orienting governance toward the private sector. Planners who believe in the utility of planning have no clear idea how it could work in this context, and the private sector, I was told, "is in front." The Ministry of Local Government moderates the relationship between the government and developers. For Rawabi, because of the Oslo area system and Israeli urban plans, and because there were few coherent plans to approve, the site could be built where they were able to buy and reparcelize land. Given that there are no coherent planning or legal frameworks, "development is occurring in a disorganized way." Urban planning just sort of happened, as the domain of people who are rich enough or otherwise empowered to do it.

Dr. Azzam Hjouj, then head of the Ramallah office of the Ministry of Local Government, described the new ways large-scale planning is starting to happen in the West Bank. Prior to projects like Rawabi and Al-Reehan, companies would buy the land, and then plan for the land they had. Most large-scale housing was done by unions for their membership, or by the PA for its employees, and in general housing was financed by workers over time and planned in consultation with the relevant authorities. This form of development was built from the needs of existing classes, rather than imagining who they could become through planning and speculation in the land market. But now, he says, financing has been inverted, the land acquired and planned, and buildings put up quickly on credit. In Rawabi, investors facilitated financing, brought plans to the planning boards expecting approval, and the law is changing around existing buildings and investments.

One such example is the "Rawabi bylaw," which granted planning authority on an area of land far greater than what developers actually own, and where, according to another bureaucrat familiar with the HPC, "people cannot utilize their land if it is not within the principles of Bashar Masri." Planners I spoke to believe that part of the rationale for this law is to consolidate further land: the bylaw has provisions for maintaining green space for public use while dense areas are on land the developers own. Those landowners, they fear, will be forced into market or otherwise unable to use their land, despite its not having been reparcelized or expropriated in the ordinary sense. The master-planned town expands its plan, authority, and jurisdiction far beyond its boundaries.

Many people in the MOLG and in Rawabi reiterated the idea that planning will shape how people interact with their homes and land. The lack of coherent planning law or practice in Palestine enables development, and planners believe that Rawabi will be a model for future practice. Planners argue that clear planning regimes—a legal relationship to the land—are necessary. Both supporters and detractors believe Rawabi is a "pilot project," although they mean different things by that.

Legal Inheritance

Shifting ideas and laws around the land are vital parts of state formation in the West Bank. The overlapping and baffling systems that weave together to regulate Palestinian land control form not only the structure of possibility for building in the present (Zeid and Thawaba 2018), but the models for future Palestinian law. More than simply about priority, planning is part of how Israeli systems of control are brought into the present systems of governance by private initiative. Slipperiness exists within that context of Israeli occupation and control and is an important part of how laws and institutions are made. Although it was written prior to the formation of the PA, I draw heavily on Anthony Coon's work (1992), to date the most comprehensive on the intertwined planning regimes in the Occupied Territories, and one of a small number of texts that does not focus primarily on settlement practice. Coon elaborates those laws that would form the basis for PA authority. Urban and national planning in the West Bank after Oslo operate on shifting legal structures between Areas A, B, and C; Ottoman, Jordanian, Palestinian, and Israeli Civil and Military law and practice; the 1980s Israeli special outline plans that circumscribe Palestinian building (Shehadeh 1982); and contemporary Israeli planning discourse on the necessity for Palestinians to learn new forms of urbanism and build "inwards and upwards," given the scarcity of land available to them.

For Coon, planning is a tool of occupation. If the PA took over physical space and a legal system somehow composed of Ottoman law, Jordanian and Israeli amendments, and so on, the end result is that de facto practices of occupation make up a significant part of a de jure Palestinian system subordinate to Israel's—Israeli law is often based on enabling or justifying military prerogative or on "facts on the ground." The PA inherited a specific system it had to figure out how to use. Rawabi operationalizes the confusion inherent in that system in concert with and in order to materialize ideological and economic imperatives for the West Bank. The planning structures that the PA draws upon to fill the landscape are often the same that Israel has used to keep it empty.

After Oslo, the PA had to confront a complicated and conflicting system of laws, but what does the law mean in an environment where laws are rarely followed and almost unknown? How do they shape practices as either prohibitions or positive inducements? The 1998 Palestinian national plan outlines at least some of the dated colonial-era, and colonial-infused foundations for PA planning authority, foundations that are still somehow binding—out-of-date but legally valid (Coon 1992, 64).

The principal plans, still in force for the West Bank area, were approved on the eve of the British Mandate period. They are:

- RJ5, covering the southern part: Regional Outline Planning Scheme Jerusalem District, approved 1942
- S15 for the northern part: Series of plans for the District of Samaria, comprising Samaria District Regional Outline Planning Scheme, approved 1942, with modifications of 1945, and the Samaria Development Plan

During the Israeli occupation there have been some alterations to these regional plans regarding maps and regulations, [as well as] Israeli road plans and military orders that constitute the occupier's conditions for regional development in the West Bank. (Ministry of Planning and International Cooperation 1998, 1)

The previously existing structure—a mishmash cobbled together over more than a century of colonial administration—was maintained but placed beneath new institutions of moderate, supposed oversight. The PA administers the old structure but is subordinate legally and practically to the Israeli Civil Administration. With respect to Israel, the whole PA operates something like the Palestinian Land Authority does internally—not as a ministry but as an authority with, as some there described it, "diminished power," tasked to invent some kind of working practice from Jordanian 1956 and 1966 codes to register land and computerize records, and doing so today explicitly to expand the land market.

Ottoman, Jordanian, and Israeli amendments overlap and work to separate different types of interventions for Jewish Israelis and Palestinians in the West Bank. And that agglomeration results in the opening in which the PA legalizes land development, based on the ways Jewish settlements are legalized in the West Bank. Structures are built and then incorporated continuously into existing plans as amendments. Coon emphasizes: "Although the legal basis of these plans is anomalous it should not be forgotten that their preparation and implementation are the dominant concern of the Central Planning Department, and that the priority accorded by the administration to establishing colonies for people of their own faith is the reason for the inadequate coverage and stunted opportunities provided by the plans for Palestinian development" (1992, 65). Planning law justifies building, or else law is disregarded as necessary for ideological, or racial, or economic, or whatever other imperatives exist among those empowered to use it. And where there are gaps in the law, the military intervenes (Thawaba 2019). Israeli planning for Palestine is one mechanism used to prevent economies of scale for Palestinians.

Take for example the "blue line" plans that were drawn around villages and submitted to, and approved by, the Israeli Central Planning Department (CPD) in the late 1980s and early 1990s under Ottoman town planning procedures. Coon describes the strange and opaque process of making and approving these "boundary plans." Drawn by a member of the CPD, they were made public during a two-month comment period nearly six months after they had been submitted for approval. The notices themselves were "characteristically vague as to the status of these plans, with no reference to legislation; the plans are categorized as 'outline local particular partial:' a species of plan unknown to legislation" (1992, 89–90). A year after that comment period, eleven more CPD plans had been opened for comment, six of them *already approved*. Beyond those eleven, nearly *four hundred* Palestinian villages had been subjected to unwritten planning requirements to constrain future growth. There was little centralization of the various Israeli antigrowth initiatives.

"The CPD plans," Coon writes, follow earlier plans "both in format (being crudely drawn, mostly on air photos) and in their policy implications." "They also lack any explanation for their proposals; new laws are made with the same practical effects. Their most important feature is again the 'plan boundary' within which all future development [is] to be confined" (89–90). Planning is almost exclusively about putting barriers around Palestinians.

Coon describes an important example of a dispute: once the existence of the plan for the village Kfayr became known, the village complained to the CPD that the boundaries were too narrow. The CPD replied, "in that case 'high-rise development' could be the answer for this remote rural village which consists at present of about 120 houses."[3] Coon continues:

> This indeed may be the purpose of these plans, since the notice of deposit mentions that an objective of the plans is to "increase the number of floor levels," and the three zones of development into which these plans (and virtually all plans since the Mandate) are divided define a bizarre form of land use control in which the three zones represent progressively more stringent controls on the *range* of activities allowed, rather than on the maximum *density* allowed as in the previous practice in the West Bank. (1992, 90, emphasis in original)

Planning regimes are opaque, or are not public, and were designed to limit Palestinian expansion. The law may not fully exist, but it is invoked, touches the ground, and frames possibilities. Jurisdiction precedes law, and it is the mode through which sovereignty is practiced (Pasternak 2017; Ford 2010). Much of the law here is fluid, and jurisdiction is the power to change it to maintain and operationalize control over territory defined at different times as land and as the people on that land. The blue line plans, which we will encounter again in chapter 10, maintain their status if not their name. Planning is the exercise of jurisdiction in ways that enter law and formalize relationships between planned spaces and the state, producing boundaries either by drawing or contesting them. It has long been about separating people and putting different ideas, facts, and political visions into circulation and into the landscape. Questions of race, territory, and jurisdiction are fundamental to the ways that Israel has maintained the West Bank in a state of suspension.

Israel has worked in the places in between plans to broaden legal, formal authority over its Jewish subjects in the Occupied Territories (Nakba Files 2016). In 1957, Israeli civil law was extended to civil servants there; uncontroversial at the time, the law has applied for decades along with the system of overlapping military orders and so on, to incorporate Jewish Israelis wherever they are without offering the same civil rights or protections to Palestinians. Under International Humanitarian Law precedent and the law of occupation elaborated as part of the Geneva Conventions, existing Jordanian law covering the West Bank prior to occupation should be the predominate body of law. Yet, various Israeli amendments and practices have limited Palestinian space and extended rights and civil protections to Israelis. The existing Palestinian municipal system is overlaid with Coon's "Jewish system" of local settler councils. The context of generalized legal confusion and PA outsourcing public functions to private developers enables the creation of something without precedent—Rawabi, the first Palestinian municipality created since Oslo (but not the first local government unit). Nested as they are within prior regimes, the current practices do not look much like the historical "state within a state" (B. J. Smith 1993), or the foundation for a political and economic system that could become the basis for one. Instead, the current situation looks more like a system of concentric partial jurisdictions produced around the imperative for economic and political stability—regularity, the rule of law, and political pacification—within the broader context of Israeli control. It looks less like the successful foundation of the Zionist state than the embedded sovereignties Audra Simpson (2014) describes under the settler-colonial regime in Canada; sovereignties that cannot possibly be equal, under a process of solidifying jurisdiction that could not possibly be complete. Practices around planning make jurisdictions, institutions, and government priorities; planning is part of how reform occurs, and priorities are manifested. The next chapter explores some of the technical work needed to operationalize new political, economic, and spatial priorities in the putative state.

Chapter Five

Housing Shortage
and National Priority

LIKE PLANNING, the policies that go into the foundation of the Palestinian state process are built upon and structured by prior remnants, a kind of compressed strata of decades of magical thinking and intervention solutionism. The aggressive focus on privatization that characterizes such thinking in the contemporary period engages the government and inflects laws and projects that have long circulated, giving them a new focus and orientation, but maintaining their central characteristics. This chapter explores how such government and economic planning quantifies and produces an abstract polity through the simultaneous construction of the idea of a housing shortage and the increasing government "national priority" to cede itself to the private sector. That process has the potential to materialize and incorporate Palestinian participants through new mechanisms for local governance, housing, and debt.

The Palestine Development and Investment Company, PADICO Holdings, is one of the largest holding companies in Palestine. PADICO was one of the leading think tanks supporting private housing development, and it worked on surveys of the housing market undertaken along with Rawabi, the Palestinian Central Bureau of Statistics, the World Bank, and the Ministry of Public Works and Housing.[1] According to a principal researcher in the PADICO business development group, there were "no clear criteria" for how to define the segments of the population that ought to be targeted as new consumers in new housing. They settled on income brackets and focused on low- and middle-income Palestinians, the 34 percent of the population who make 2,400 to 3,400 Israeli shekels (ILS)/month (about USD600–USD1,000). Some 51 percent are poor and the remainder is wealthy enough not to need financing. Although these numbers are "not very formal," they are calculated based on the costs for essential goods, health care, schools, and so on. "All the basics" at minimum.

One researcher told me that during the second intifada, the real estate sector collapsed, and demand accumulated. From 2000 to 2007 there was a shortage of about 40,000 units, and an annual demand of about 52,000 units. Based on the permits that were given at the time, fewer than 4,000 were built annually. There was both a gap between supply and demand, and a mismatch between construction and what most Palestinians could afford. PADICO and its allies decided there was a need for affordable housing and financing that was missing from the market. According to them, there are manifold problems in housing and financing within the government and in Palestinian culture that would all need to be addressed simultaneously. In their framework and assumptions, market defines both supply and demand, overwriting those extra-economic dimensions they are unable to address. That combination of problems—cultural, political, economic—was opened to a market solution aimed at Palestinians in certain income brackets. A national-scale housing shortage could be produced as a market problem with a market solution and a government priority.

Making Demand

What is the actual demand for home ownership? Having already decided on real estate as the economic sector with the most potential in Palestine, the Palestine Investment Fund), the Portland Trust, and their peer organizations produced reports and documents that simultaneously create and presuppose a need for housing. In 2012, according to the Palestinian Bureau of Statistics, three-quarters of Palestinians in the West Bank were living in homes that they or their families owned. That number increased in the 2017 census to nearly 87 percent despite the lack of movement in large developments (State of Palestine, Palestinian Central Bureau of Statistics 2018). And it is still higher than in the United States (67 percent). Many families in Palestine live in large, extended family homes. The rest are split between renters and the "other" category—camps, work for housing—and probably not part of

Supply, A Past Shortage & Projected Future Lag Behind *Demand*

> According to current market dynamics, supply will rise but will stay short of demand resulting from newly formed households resulting from marriage.

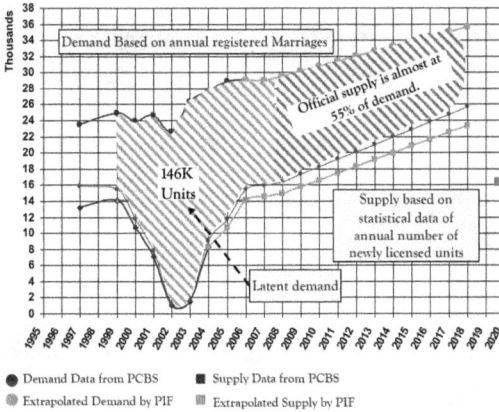

Market Trend

The graph shows a fixed gap between supply and demand. Much of this difference is being absorbed by:

– Increased Household densities.

– Splitting of homes among households.

– Living in unregistered buildings.

– Supply doesn't include units added to refugee camps because of their inadequate conditions.

Latent Demand

For the sake of this study, latent demand is assumed to be that resulting from supply falling below its natural growth trend especially as a result of political unrest. Total calculated latent demand is 45K Units.

Source: PIF Analysis based on raw data from various sources.

Note: Chart accounts for natural growth only, Information extrapolated assuming a declining growth rate.

10

FIGURE 5.1 Forecast of latent housing demand. Source: Palestine Investment Fund.

any potential middle-class buying pool. Yet the PIF says there was a latent demand of about 146,000 units in 2008. These figures exclude refugee camps, undercounting the number of units, and overcounting the potential market by describing the camps as unstable (see figure 5.1).

The current supply meets only the needs of the rich. According to figure 5.2, fewer than 5 percent of Palestinians can afford what is on offer. The PIF says it will get worse: demand will grow to nearly half a million units in the next decade! (See figure 5.3.) Yet that number is roughly the current number of households in the West Bank.

How do we reconcile the difference between developers' projected demand and the government's? One former member of the Higher Planning Council questioned the idea of a housing shortage entirely. "It is important," he said, for the private sector "to eradicate real analysis." "I can find a house in 24 hours if needed." The 2017 Palestinian census shows 35,176 housing units in the cities of Ramallah and al-Bireh, 30 percent of which are unoccupied

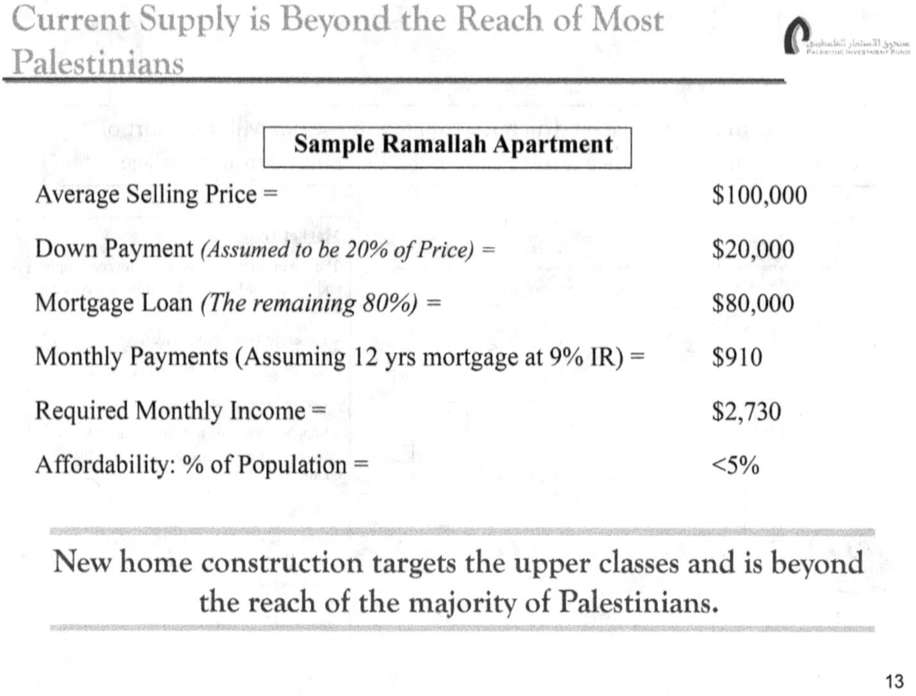
Current Supply is Beyond the Reach of Most Palestinians
Sample Ramallah Apartment
Average Selling Price = $100,000
Down Payment (Assumed to be 20% of Price) = $20,000
Mortgage Loan (The remaining 80%) = $80,000
Monthly Payments (Assuming 12 yrs mortgage at 9% IR) = $910
Required Monthly Income = $2,730
Affordability: % of Population = <5%
New home construction targets the upper classes and is beyond the reach of the majority of Palestinians.
13

FIGURE 5.2 Mismatched supply and demand. Source: Palestine Investment Fund.

and possibly for rent or for sale (5,053) or otherwise "closed" (5,589) and currently uninhabited (State of Palestine, Palestinian Central Bureau of Statistics 2018). According to him, there may be a deficit and a need, but it is nowhere near the numbers cited, and there are vacancies. Does it mean that people will move to Ramallah rather than commute? Is it a rural-urban problem? It is at best "approximate." And he notes that building patterns around Ramallah exist because of, and in response to, the current normal conditions of military occupation, Israeli control over the majority of the West Bank, and closure.

In 2017 there was a total of just fewer than 800,000 housing units in the West Bank (State of Palestine, Palestinian Central Bureau of Statistics 2018); developers and investors suggested that by then, demand would rise an additional 60 percent. Yet at least at the local scale in Ramallah and al-Bireh, 30 percent of units are vacant. One way to reconcile the difference in these trends and emphasize the high-end projections was simply to remove the

227K New Houses During the next 5 Years

Forecast for the demand of households in the coming 10 years:

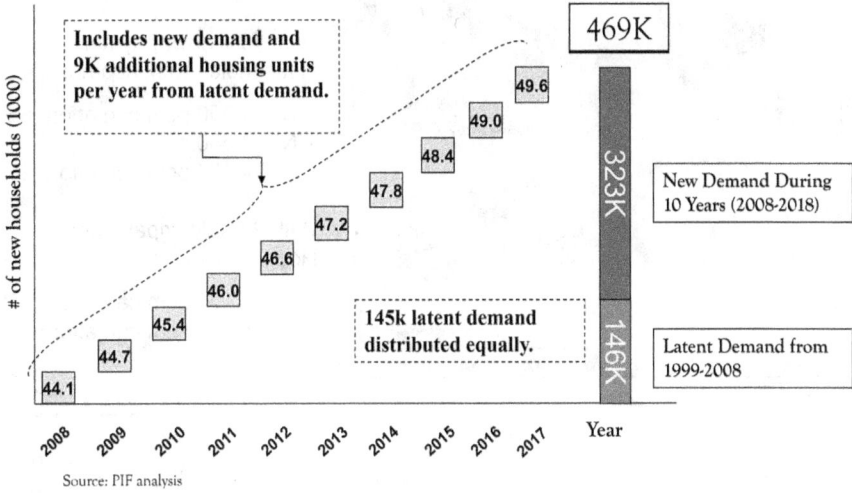

FIGURE 5.3 A growing problem. Source: Palestine Investment Fund.

numbers. The Ministry of Public Works and Housing's draft contribution to the 2011 national plan said that 82 percent of Palestinians lived in family homes. That figure disappeared before it made it into the national plan, helping inflate the number of nonowners. Without a replacement and given government support for ongoing development projects, the national plans validate developers' numbers. Once legitimated, international and nongovernmental organizations incorporate the data. (UN-Habitat views their work as so intertwined and complementary, they are able to simply re-present PIF PowerPoints without removing the logo.)

If that is one way that numbers and priorities enter government, how do these numbers touch the ground? How do Palestinians in the West Bank become potential buyers if they have homes and cannot afford currently supplied apartments? First of all, as figure 5.4 illustrates, the Portland Trust puts the sweet spot of affordability at about USD60,000 per apartment, based on loans with a 6.5 percent interest rate.

Affordability at 6.5% interest

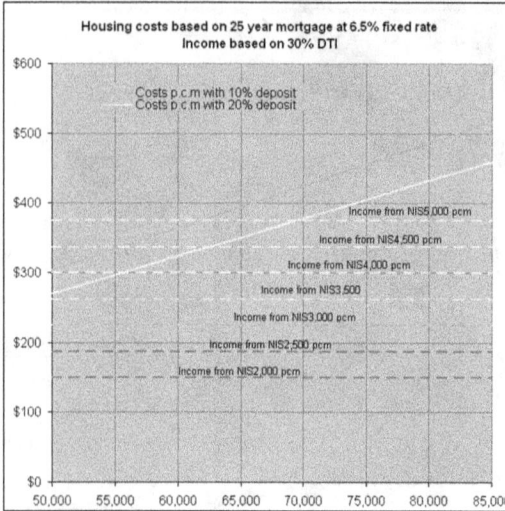

Housing costs based on 25 year mortgage at 6.5% fixed rate
Income based on 30% DTI

More affordable.

Scenario: 30% DTI ratio, 6.5% interest

With 10% downpayment.
Households with income:

= NIS 4,000 pcm can afford $50k
= NIS 4,500 pcm can afford $55k
= NIS 4,800 pcm can afford $60k

With 20% downpayment,
Households with income:

= NIS 3,500 pcm can afford $50k
= NIS 4,300 pcm can afford $60k.

21

The Portland Trust

FIGURE 5.4 Affordability and interest rates. Source: the Portland Trust.

As in figure 5.5, the PIF proposes housing costs to consumers that fall within that band. The Portland Trust and the PIF know what people can afford. But they also know the current market cannot meet either their own demands for profit or what they believe and hope to be buyers' demands for housing. They found an elegant solution. They proposed apartments that are a bit out of reach (see figure 5.6).

Coalitions of developers, pro-privatization and international NGOs, and quasi-governmental authorities created a need for debt and a loan mechanism in the margin. In the West Bank there are currently high rates of home ownership but low rates of home financing. The PIF and the Portland Trust are doing the technical work to change that.

Throughout all of these documents it is clear the priority is not to make housing available to low-income people with state subsidies or to otherwise drive down the cost to consumers in any absolute sense. In the case of new large housing developments, the goal is to make housing potentially affordable through mortgages, displacing costs from the private sector.[2] The process is key, and housing is often secondary to the ideological and practical

PIF's Affordable Housing Program Will Increase Affordability By 30% Through Additional Supplies Of Lower Cost Housing

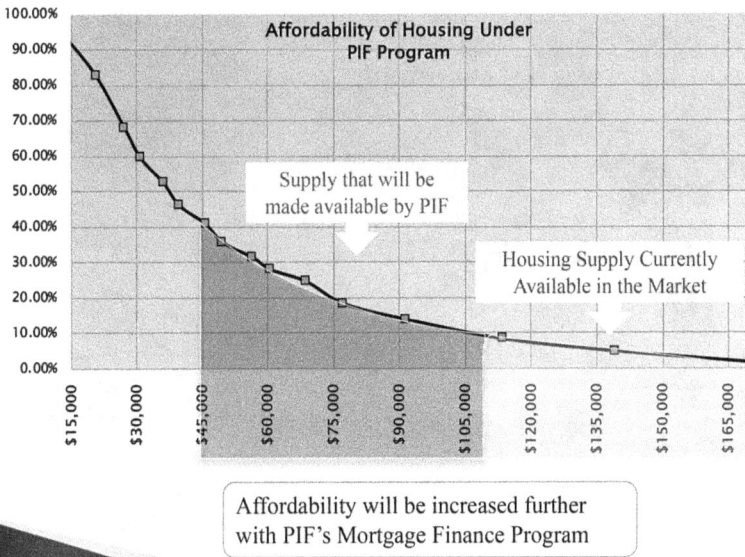

application of political goals. At least by 2014, the practice of lending to drive a market had become clearly unsuitable as a primary mechanism for market creation; there may have been a drive for home ownership among a potential buying pool, but continually increasing costs of housing stretched what is possible. The Harvard Business School study on Rawabi and West Bank housing based an average mortgage on a USD110,000 apartment with a USD16,500 down payment and wages as collateral. This entailed monthly payments of USD1,028 on a ten-year loan, USD638 for twenty, after which point the housing will be transferred into the residents' names (Segel et al. 2014). This average is more expensive than the figures that the Palestine Investment Fund had given as the "current supply" that was affordable to only 5 percent of Palestinians.

Indeed, in 2016 the World Bank appraised these forms of mortgage lending in "emerging countries." Its report argues for the political and practical need for housing that can benefit political and economic stability and general

Affordability of Housing Will be Doubled With the Establishment of AMAL- A New Long Term Mortgage Finance Facility

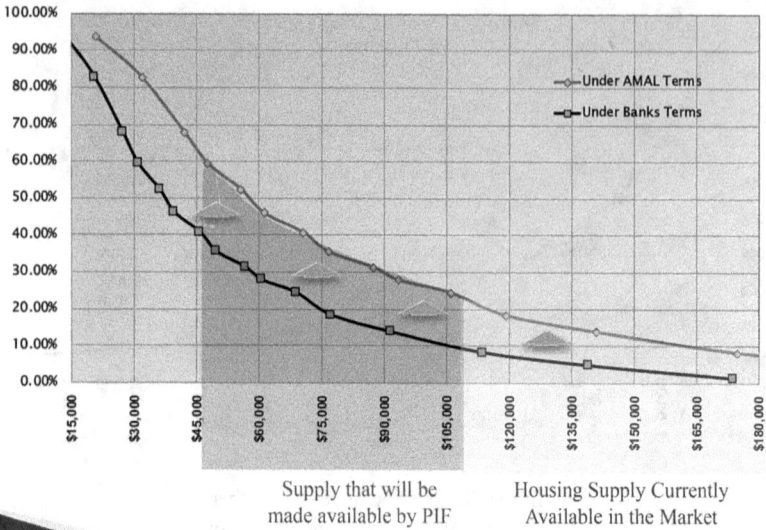

FIGURE 5.6 UN-Habitat/Palestine Investment Fund on the prospects for making more expensive apartments accessible through financing. Source: UN-Habitat.

welfare. But despite the tremendous (and potential) growth of home financing, "housing is frequently unaffordable to all but the top earners" (Independent Evaluation Group, World Bank 2016).

When there is no mortgage financing in the market, it may not be appropriate to target low-income housing. In the West Bank and Gaza, the World Bank project initiated a small mortgage market where none existed before and refinanced approximately 300 residential mortgage loans totaling US$28 million. While the availability of long-term financing made housing more affordable in general, the project nevertheless failed to reach out to other lower and middle-income segments of the population. The refinanced mortgages were far fewer than the 2,000 mortgages estimated at appraisal. This translates into an average mortgage loan that was three to four times higher than the one targeted for lower- to middle-income households. (Independent Evaluation Group, World Bank 2016, 20)

The World Bank's goals, they say, for developing a market in such a complex environment with unsettled land tenure issues were "exceedingly optimistic" (Independent Evaluation Group, World Bank 2016, 23). The loans that were dispersed went to housing "three to four times higher than the targeted housing price for lower to middle income housing" (30). If the loans and financing that emerged as a part of the real estate development process do not meet most Palestinians' needs, or are not sufficiently responsive to the specifics of the political environment to be able to do so, what explains the persistence of national priorities around development?

At least part of the goals and reasoning must be beyond housing, toward state capture and reform in the present and goals for the future. Investors require political and economic stability and regularity. Market logics and economic plans are increasingly made available to Palestinians for whom hopefulness about the future remains difficult to grasp. Not only do housing and debt enable one another, they are formed with the same goals in mind. For developers and willing Palestinian participants—as well as for NGOs, the United States, the PA, and Israel—regularity, enforceability, and political pacification are enabled and coproduced by new forms of capital accumulation and new markets. Land ownership, political localization, and capital accumulation are intertwined. The first step in making a new housing market is establishing the idea of need and figuring out how to get people into new buildings. Demand is a social category, cultivated, encouraged, and subsequently quantified and projected into the future. The second is to disentangle foreign aid from humanitarian development logics and use reoriented political priorities to back privatization with development aid. Third is to operationalize political instability to reform the law to create the physical foundation for the movement and growth of capital.

Meeting Demand through Mortgage Loans

The Affordable Mortgage and Loan Program (AMAL) is a USD500 million project bringing together international development agencies, several banks, and the PIF. The loan program is funded by USD400 million from the development apparatus and USD100 million from banks earmarked exclusively for long-term loans. In Arabic, *amal* means "hope." Nura Treish, who was project manager of AMAL, told me that "the first thing to understand" is that lending initiatives are a part of the PIF's larger affordable housing plan. Much of the funding comes from abroad but local banks will administer it, to support the existing banking system. The loans will begin in the Rawabi and Al-Reehan megadevelopments. The politics of home ownership are a "significant economic objective; a key objective, but not the only one." Home ownership, they believe, will create "community stability," will "give youth a stake," and will "empower people on their own land." Echoing political language that has been a part of the Palestinian national movement for decades, she told me that ownership will "advance the struggle through steadfastness." It will also create economic development through jobs and opportunities for small business; after all, 90 percent of the economy is made up of small to medium enterprises (SMES). Furthermore, home ownership will contribute to "capacity building," to "economic and social stability," and to "security"; it will "build wealth," "create jobs," and "prevent brain drain." AMAL will begin with about six thousand loans, reaching thirty thousand people, and the hope is that if the program is successful, it will encourage the USD4 billion Palestinian banking industry to do more lending.

There is, lenders argue, a lack of affordable housing, a latent demand and potential market, calculated in 2006–2007 as 400,000 units over the following decade. Most of the coalition of organizations in AMAL are Palestinian, other than the Cooperative Housing Foundation (CHF), which no longer works on cooperative housing and was rebranded "Global Communities" in 2012; and the Middle East Investment Initiative, a part of the Aspen Institute.[3] The mortgages rely on the megadevelopments: lenders need borrowers, and developers need buyers. But, given the huge projected housing deficit, Nura Treish argues that large-scale development is necessary, and that AMAL will eventually be able to reach 60 percent of needy households and create a "significant shift in the affordability of housing."[4]

The PIF and AMAL calculate that 10 percent of households can currently afford a home, and the PIF can give loans as low as USD45,000 to aid middle-income families. They say that reaching the rest, given PA inability, would require subsidies and loan guarantees from the Overseas Private Investment Corporation, the World Bank, and others. And as a "quasi-governmental" and "private sector–oriented" organization, they are able to partially fund and administer these loans. They create specific forms of demand that can be met through private development. Loan guarantees insulate developers while incorporating buyers.

They planned to build at minimum thirty thousand units of affordable housing around the West Bank in the coming decade, initiatives that will "encourage and stimulate the housing sector." For PIF, because land is scarce and expensive, long-term mortgage financing is necessary to drive down immediate costs. (Rawabi has managed to ameliorate some of these problems by going far outside of the city where land costs are lower and getting the PA to cover infrastructure and aid in land titling, eminent domain, and reparcelization.) But also, crucially, the people working toward large-scale development in Massar, the Portland Trust, the PIF, and elsewhere envision an ongoing lending and debt market that will be the foundation for a finance sector in Palestine.

One of the primary goals and an important source of appeal for all actors is the idea that thinking long-term can enable stability and aspiration to a better life despite Israeli territorial prerogative and control. If people want to affirm their connection to the land because of the "trauma of diaspora," as then head of the CHF in Palestine, Rami Khoury, told me, then the Palestinian nationalist bourgeoisie see political and capital commitments as increasingly conjoined. What privatization can do is not only create clear titles, but in doing so, also enable ownership and buying and selling—a stable relationship to the land. It is, he said, "fairly universal" that people want to own land, own a house and a part of Palestine. Israel has demonstrated economies of scale with settlement building, and Palestinians have learned from it. Khoury suggests that megadevelopment is a way forward *right now* given the present condition: people will not have to save for ten years to build an extension on their houses.

But because there is no precedent for long-term, fixed-rate loans, many Palestinians will need convincing. AMAL has begun "home-buyer education" that will "make the benefits more visible" to consumers and to banks because, while "nobody's enthusiastic about a 25-year loan, people want to own their own homes." Khoury told me, "The market is a good one . . . there is a good debt service mentality in Palestine." Moreover, people do not tend to move very much in Palestine—while there is already an emphasis on ownership, it is based on expanding existing housing. The PIF believes that young people will move out of larger family homes in order to own something that is solely theirs; the culture of family homes is "diminishing bit by bit," but the PIF and developers believe they need to cultivate those attitudes to have buyers for their apartments. The state, capital, family life, and gender roles are mutually constituted (Anagnost 1997; Brown 2006; Kligman 1992), and while there are still few indications of how successful home buyer education will be, private development is one socially oriented state-building technology of the Palestinian government, local capitalists, and international community. As debt, land, and consumer markets are created, accumulation and family life are oriented around them.

How do these projects enter the government? One of the primary ways is through plans and statistics that circulate. Groups of developers and bureaucrats make their visions authoritative, sensible, and legitimate, and they incorporate people as they shift government priorities and goals. The "national priority to develop affordable housing" emerged on the government side in 2007 in response to its own "lack of capacity" and as an argument for large-scale real estate development.

On the private side, the pro-privatization NGO, the Portland Trust, and the PIF proposed large-scale development. Those groups then created vessels for investment in housing. They elaborated the changes necessary to enable it, and the Portland Trust hired a New York-based architect to design what became Rawabi. Thus, housing is a national priority, elaborated by the PA and representative coalitions of large developers. How does the putative state work toward those priorities?

The PA elaborated the priority in its 2008–2010 national plan, the Palestinian Reform and Development Plan (PRDP), and in subsequent national plans and national program documents with names like "Ending the Occupation, Building a State" in 2009; "Palestine Moving Forward" and "Homestretch to Freedom" in 2010; "Establishing the State, Building Our Future" in 2011–2013; and in 2014–2016, "State Building to Sovereignty." Apparently, the goal has been achieved and subjects incorporated into the state, allowing the PA to move to the "next phase" with its 2017–2022 plan of "Putting Citizens First." Beyond the titles that seem at best aspirational, reports are productive. They represent, describe, and orient government reforms. They elaborate priorities and activities. But they also propose and create opportunities, mechanisms, and justification for aid and private sector responsibility. And they become the basis for the reports and the practical and ideological justifications that follow.

Chapter Six

Public-Private Partnership

SOMETIMES IN PALESTINE, as "national priorities" are established they are intertwined with the institutions and procedures to implement them. Along with the Palestinian Reform and Development Plan (PRDP) and the Constitution, studies, documents, and reports by think tanks and donors are sometimes given significant practical authority (Ferguson 1994). The emergent government, market, and polity do not operate in isolation—physical facts are created with a population in mind, and that population forms in a relationship with them, as do laws and government operations. Developers and ministers talk about working for a future Palestine, for "the day after." That future will emerge in part from the conditions being crafted by development and PA ministries, based on the impediments of the present condition of occupation and imperatives for growth and accumulation. In an attempt to change the structure of possibilities for the future at the political level, real estate developers and the PA are working to stabilize the present.

Afif al-Sayyid at the Ministry of Public Works and Housing (MOPWH) made it clear that, as far as Rawabi is concerned, the government is "working for the public interest of the company." Although there is a proposed planning law that would benefit and further enable private development, "it is stuck," and they are forced to organize planning around the dated Jordanian

Law no. 79. A proposed law that attempts to increase public control over planning had been sitting in committee for two years when we spoke in 2010 and was not likely to emerge; on the other hand, laws at the proposal stage can somehow become organizing principles that through practice, precedent, and repetition start to accrue authority. Sometimes it seems that, with the superabundance of laws and jurisdictions that can regulate the same things in the same places, the Palestinian government is one of the only bodies that subjects itself to law.

First of all, these ideas that are continuously generated really do circulate. They exist in reports and presentations, and they are part of decision-making processes in government and among donors. One can trace them in PA attempts to join the World Trade Organization (WTO) and to make legible reforms, and in the annual reports to the Ad Hoc Liaison Committee—an international working group for "economic peace" set up around Oslo, headed by Norway, and including the PA, Israel, the UN, the World Bank, the IMF, the EU, the United States, and seven other states. Specific ideas take on weight in the dozens of academic and critical pieces written about the PRDP. You can see them taken seriously, for what it is worth, in this and other academic accounts.

In my interviews, ministries and developers very regularly invoked a 2009 World Bank white paper written by a consultant named Richard Martin. Written after the initial housing studies, it argued for large-scale private development. National planners incorporated it into national reports, making it almost retroactive and self-fulfilling. It is only twenty-two pages long, but it accrued legitimacy to the wider project as it circulated. The Martin report also proposes the creation of a new mechanism for disbursing aid through the PA to the private sector—the Municipal Development and Lending Fund, also sometimes referred to as the "PRDP trust fund." As the government and the donor community implement the priority and the trust fund, the private sector becomes a legitimate recipient of foreign aid. This is framed as beneficial for the donors: it will be a "rapid disbursing opportunity" that will leverage "substantial additional investment" (Martin 2009). Housed in Washington, DC, the fund is one way that international finance actors "came to fully oversee Palestinian economic development and policy making" (Hanieh 2013a, 117).

Matthew Hull's study of planning and files in Islamabad is helpful here. With reference to Latour (2005), documents are "constituted by and constitutive of broader associations of people, places, and other things" (Hull 2012, 18). They tie people together through the practices surrounding their circulation, and they bring people into bureaucratic structures. Hull focuses on everyday experiences of bureaucracy, but it holds. Documents are a part of how the private sector and the PA simultaneously produce each other and the contours of the economy. Ideas and documents circulate, but *people* fix ideas in housing projects, the direction of investment, and in laws. They unify and continually produce the sense of officialness. In a context where the state is perpetually forming and the legislature does not meet, that is almost as good as being official.

In the West Bank, laws, like everything from borders to paychecks, are often vague, nonexistent, or malleable. But they reflect specific values, and they can be invoked to direct or regulate practice. And there is precedent in the way Israel legalizes settlements: Israel makes and changes laws for specific past events and eventualities. From the construction of need to a population of homebuyers, through statistics and reports; from forthcoming laws ordering practice in the present, we can see how these ideas come together as structures and to interpellate Palestinians. Stability can emerge out of chaos through the practices around law and regulation, even if laws are never completed and perpetually forthcoming. They do work despite their questionable existence.

Let me return to the question of housing, need, and planning. The current articulated need, at this scale, is new for Palestine. The 1998 National Plan put home ownership at 80 percent, most of it in "acceptable" housing. Unlike today, planners were sure that most needs would be accommodated in existing built-up areas, and the rest would be met through the natural growth of cities once the occupation planning structures were dismantled. If the creation of Rawabi is enmeshed in complicated notions of the future and planning in the present, or new forms of class aspiration, the way it is being built demonstrates how the state is shifting toward localized private governance. In the next chapter, I will elaborate on how Rawabi incorporated ordinary Palestinians and became a vehicle for social change. The question here is how it happened in terms of weakened national-scale rule.

Lack of Capacity and Political Reform

A polity is presupposed in this wider political economic vision, and state actors and the private sector reform one another as well as local capacities through these projects. As a consequence of the privatization of public services and space, local institutions have been strengthened while national government is weakened; even as a state and governance at the national scale are ostensibly emerging. The economist Raja Khalidi told me in summer 2014:

After visits to chambers of commerce in four cities in the north, I am surprised at how strong regional economic, social, cultural, and political differences are, deeply rooted, and as much an obstacle to "development" as an asset for endurance. . . . The point being that the claim that "there is no capacity/there is no will" is accurate in more ways than one: I just don't see any way to stitch this all together, pick up the pieces, or somehow emerge distinctively as a viable nation-state. Much better to aim for federation of Palestinian city states since the municipal level governance and economic development is the only thing we are able to do half completely. Then who needs to care about Area A, borders, or national institutions? Nablus is stronger than Yishar and Eli any day. . . . In fact, if an accountable, elected, public sector remains in the Palestinian body politic, you find it in municipalities and chambers of commerce more than in any PA ministry.

Government itself is increasingly modeled on the private sector, and a private sector is being built alongside and through a state oriented toward private accumulation. For the PA itself, it means a willing and unwilling cession of authority. On the one hand, there is general agreement with the practices, at least at the level of leadership. On the other, a body that already struggles for relevance politically, symbolically, and certainly in terms of its ability to act concretely is shedding parts of itself.

Beyond questions of rhetorical and ideological orientation, authority and jurisdiction exist in institutions and practices governing relationships to the land at the local level. Governing begins to be about creating and distributing principles. The Ministry of Public Works and Housing (MOPWH) is one ministry that has undergone significant change during this time. When I spoke to Afif al-Sayyid about ministry involvement in Rawabi, the stated policy was to "encourage private development and to make a balance between the end users—the public—and the investors." The MOPWH helps with investments, it helps users to get ownership of their homes, and "the policy is to facilitate the business of the private sector." They deal with three areas: aiding the private sector, doing "affordable housing," and changing the law. Rawabi is, he said, "the first experience of its kind in Palestine"; and "it is known" that to make a real town, people must be living there. So, alongside the development process, the MOPWH builds up relevant institutions of governance. There is no local authority there, he said, no local government and, since the town had not developed over time and in a way that would be entirely public, it necessarily brings together the public and the private sectors to govern. "Someone has to do it." Speaking of public works, he said, "in the end, we don't know whose property this will be" as the relationships between public and private form.

On several occasions he referred to the housing shortage and the Richard Martin (2009) document. He gave me some of the higher projections I had heard—a shortage of 132,759 units in the West Bank and Gaza based on three categories: first, the annual natural growth of 57,303; second, the large number of old or vacant units in need of replacement, about 8 percent or 75,456; and the fact that only 40 percent of this need is being met. Nevertheless, the idea of affordable housing is "a kind of illusion"; it is affordable "for people who can pay for housing." With these statistics the government assumes an ongoing need and helps the private sector continuously meet it. To speed development and aid private developers, the government intervenes to change the rental law, laws governing land surveying and registration, the Ottoman land law, land pricing laws, laws protecting absentee owners, and income tax laws. Currently, developers argue that property tax laws disincentivize Palestinians from using their land productively; land is not taxed, and supposedly owners keep it indefinitely, hoping the market will go up enough to motivate them to sell. The idea is that if land were more heavily taxed, owners would either utilize it to generate income or be forced into the market.

Karim Nashashibi, one of Prime Minister Fayyad's main advisors, was with the IMF for twenty-five years and was country director for Palestine for four of those years. He told me that the public sector provides the infrastructure, the literal groundwork to make private activities possible. The West Bank, says Nashashibi, is in a period of growth, but that growth is not sustainable. In 2008–2009, the PA managed to "right the ship" under Fayyad's leadership. It was able to pay wage arrears to the 145,000 workers in the security and civil services, in part thanks to USD380 million in foreign assistance and an end to the international financial boycott imposed after Hamas's electoral victory. (The boycott ended with Fayyad taking office in the West Bank.) This provided "an injection of liquidity," a stimulus that increased domestic demand and spending. And he argues that this was not because of Israel easing restrictions in 2009—the PA had created 6 to 7 percent growth in 2008. Growth and quality of life increased when Fayyad "completely changed the development strategy" from a focus on top-down projects like hospitals, water mains, and big infrastructure to a "ground-up" strategy. He goes to the villages and asks, "What do you need." Thus, the average public project now costs only USD120,000, and includes electrical grids, roads, wells, sewage renovation, and so on.

As villages do indeed begin to see the PA as acting in their interests, the PA localizes and individualizes governance and drives down its own costs. Nashashibi puts the PA "lack of capacity" this way: while these labor-intensive projects use local materials and also aid in economic growth, the problem is that "doing small projects" in a context of "a high fiscal deficit financed by donors" is not sustainable. As a result, the burden for larger projects falls to the private sector, and the government is stripped down to a set of local institutions.[1]

Unlike other contexts where neoliberalization demands the state's dismantlement, here an economic neoliberalization process is forging the state. The push and pull of destructive and creative "roll-back" and "roll-out" practices (Peck and Tickell 2002; Peck 2010) is shaping state governance. Palestine is under Israeli control, has a real and imagined lack of capacity, and is almost entirely dependent on ongoing external aid for day-to-day government operations. In 2013, the World Bank extended its 2008 "PRDP Trust Fund" to aid the private sector, and John Kerry proposed his USD4 billion plan to aid Palestinian private business (perhaps reform started to seem impossible; at some point recently they rebranded the trust fund a "Recovery Program" [World Bank 2020; Gearan and Booth 2013]). With Donald Trump, the situation changed, but new funders stepped in, and the groundwork had already been laid for increasing private investment over international aid. After moving the embassy and openly supporting annexation of occupied Palestinian and Syrian territory and, at times, parts of Egypt, the emphasis on cultivating business stability and developing separate and specific places for Palestinians within Israel/Palestine seems likely to continue.

The idea of a weak central state is framed within and supports the logic of neoliberal rollback as the state is being made. But even in this context, the balance could be different than in a PA with limited capacity and economic intervention reoriented toward funding for private developers. While Nashashibi is clear that growth cannot continue without an end to the occupation, he says that the PA has created transparency, and, "for the first time there is security; one of Fayyad's greatest achievements is security and the rule of law," and the removal of armed gangs and militias. Security, law, and economic growth produce and necessitate one another. Local security remains with the PA and enables investment and coherent property rights, the law crafts the contours of both, and the economy builds upon and feeds back into the wider context. The state-building project is not simply about local institution building with the goal of eventually making a state; it is also about building a privatized state under the present conditions that make such state building possible today.[2]

Localization

Beyond the land beneath buildings, there is a Rawabi bylaw outlining the rules in its planning area. I asked for it constantly but never saw it, and when I last asked after residents had begun moving in, it was still forthcoming. But I know it has been dictating how people in that area use their own land since at least 2010. I have heard of two cases where developers invoked the bylaw and complained to the PA, who in turn stopped individuals from building on their own land. There are probably more such instances. This is another way that ideas that circulate at the scale of government reach the ground. People are brought into private governance in multiple ways: as subjects of eminent domain, as surrounding landowners, as potential buyers and consumers, and as Palestinians partially incorporated by a changing state process.

What does this all mean for the relationship between public governance and private development? What does it mean for potential buyers? And is it sustainable? It is not entirely clear, but according to a 2018 pricelist, apartments in Rawabi range from USD101,000 to USD180,000, and a 2015 BBC documentary put the average at about USD95,000. In that documentary, the reporter asks Masri if "only the wealthy middle class can afford" to live there. The developer replies that "a young couple making a little bit higher than minimum wage *should* be able to afford this." The reporter counters: nevertheless, there could be "an ocean of resentment" if it is not affordable. Masri shifts the blame to the state: "low income homes should be supported by the government . . . usually. Unfortunately, we have not gotten any support, financial support, from the government." He continues to question not only the PA's efficacy, but also its politics: "I think the Palestinian Authority should have done this already and done more than this." And "I'm not saying they're useless, but I think they should have built more, especially around the settlements" (McMullen 2015).

During my field research, I tried very hard to understand to what extent Rawabi was guided officially or by set procedure, and what relationships there are between the law generally, the Rawabi bylaw, planning, and local authority. Planners told me that "there are still a lot of problems" as far as jurisdiction is concerned, and the only actually existing legal framework is the Jordanian law (except for the Egyptian law in Gaza). The Ministry of Planning and International Cooperation (MOPIC) had been working to formalize and rationalize procedures since Oslo and proposed a division of labor between ministries based on the distinctions between local, regional, and national types of planning. I was told "the law should reflect the vision for the future, otherwise it might not facilitate—and may harm—planning." But government planners who wanted to exercise some control were unlikely to succeed, because the current disorganization enabled development, and planning was being rolled back to enable investment and accumulation. Well beyond Rawabi, they worried that the process, and the legal changes it requires, would negatively impact existing cities—Ramallah most of all. Not only would legal change and private planning set the precedent for even greater privatization of services (Jabary Salamanca 2014), it would likely displace many of Ramallah's poorer residents. The old city part of Ramallah in particular is least touched by the housing boom. Many of the same families have rented many of the same apartments and buildings since 1967, at 1967 rents. New pro-owner, antitenant laws that emerge around new debt financing will help owners displace those tenants and extract profit from their property, either by raising rents to market value or by opening million-dollar plots to real estate and commercial development.

In a discussion of just how Rawabi's plans were approved, I told an informant from the Ministry of Planning and International Cooperation that I was trying to get information from developers about the process; the informant told me not to bother. The process was opaque, developers would probably not give me any information, and even when they gave information to the ministries, often "it's made up." Just as the Israelis are "playing with the language of approved and non-approved" to create precedent to enable building, Palestinians are creating legal justifications in various laws, plans, and reports to donors. The practice is widespread: the "whole staff" at the MOPIC was tasked with work on the PRDP, and "this is nothing more than paper." Yet it has real, material effects.

If affordable housing is a national priority, how is it achieved? Rawabi claims that 70 percent of its residents will also work there and that government aid is justified because the town will siphon Ramallah population and ease stresses on the infrastructure there. A government planner I spoke to is skeptical, believing it unlikely that work will move to Rawabi and that it will be little more than a distant suburb of Ramallah. If the government has to support it, his primary concern is with affordability. He asks: What about transportation costs? Are these factored into the equation? What is affordable housing? Affordability obviously depends on the target population, and anyway there is no national housing policy to determine concretely what it would mean. He thinks housing costs will be very similar to Ramallah. For him, the memorandum of understanding between Rawabi and the PA is "unfortunate" because it enables developers to extract funds, concessions, and political capital from the government, to target a very specific population, and it prevents the government from either planning or regulating housing costs. Even the difference between off-site and on-site is vague: when I met with planning officials, Rawabi was in the process of arguing that roads, streetlights, and nonbuilding infrastructure in the city should be considered public and "off-site." Developers were then working to extract government commitments for a further USD30 million to USD40 million.

For public sector officials trying to balance responsibility to the public with the national priority, the clear problem was this: "how can I make sure that whatever figure [will be invested] will be reflected in the price?" They had no possible way to address this and related questions. Another planner asked, When the money is disbursed, how will it affect other areas, given that PA resources are as paltry as its capacity? Frustrated, he brought up the schools and wondered why the ministry would build them immediately, when there is virtually no one living there? Why is it the government's responsibility to make the private development attractive to buyers? For some in the ministry, Rawabi is happening in a place unsuitable for development, in an unplanned and disorganized way, and without proper consultation. But the ideological and material support the state-scale government promised had tied their hands and diverted resources from already-underserved parts of the West Bank. "There is no balance in the public/private partnership . . . but we are still supporting it." Indeed, as Masri complained to CNN in 2013: "We were shocked when we realized we'd have to build the schools." "That is something I didn't plan for. We appealed to the Palestinian government to come in and assist us with at least that, but unfortunately, they're broke and have other priorities" (Carrington 2013). He expressed this surprise as a way to exert pressure through the media, but also perhaps because the government demonstrated priorities different from his firm's. By taking practical authority for planning from the government, the net effect is that the state shrinks.

The Ministry of Local Government (MOLG), unlike the Ministry of Planning and International Cooperation, is trying to minimize centralized, national control in favor of local governance units (LGUs) to give localities increased tax collection capacity, and to use local governmental bodies to engage parts of the private sector. Housing, says the MOLG, is the largest current and potential economic sector; it promotes "Palestinian urban communities in the face of Israeli settlement activity; develops the national economy by employing workforce and reducing unemployment; promotes relevant industries, including stone, marble, bricks, tiles, paints, aluminum, electrical appliances, and sanitary fittings. The housing sector also contributes to incorporating real estate shareholding companies and commercial bands and increasing the types of real estate investment. . . . The sector helps create new real estate patterns" (Palestinian National Authority 2010).

Thus, the relationship of Rawabi to broader West Bank governance takes on a different valence in terms of state-scale rollback—it is one of the LGUs that the MOLG is supporting. It will have substantial autonomy, and many in the national government support it actively. It is enabled by confusion at the PA scale, allowing it to circumvent and ultimately acquire authority. I met with Hani Hroub in March 2011, then the director of public relations and information at the MOLG. He actively supports Rawabi as "a strategic project, a new city" that will provide a new "modern" way of life, and "a modern type of Islamic life." It will have "the feel of Paris . . . you will feel the same as Paris." And this hopefulness about Rawabi culture is one reason that the PA made an agreement with the developers. Hroub would like to see the Rawabi model adapted to other places, other locales, as both a cultural shift and administrative practice. He sees urban planning as a competitive advantage and a way to potentially minimize instability and insecurity in the West Bank.

At that time it was important to the MOLG that the area becomes an official municipality that incorporates 'Ajjul and 'Attara; the ministry prefers a big municipality, so it can bundle and outsource public services. Rawabi developers successfully sought municipal structure because, presumably, it primes the pump for public funds to continue to flow there in perpetuity. The MOLG holds that Rawabi will be "big, strong," and will benefit the villages. On the other hand, village municipalities suspect they will be marginal in the decision-making process. They had already seen lands taken by presidential decree or otherwise failed to benefit from speculation in the area. One MOLG official told me that many villagers would not quickly sell their land when they got wind of Rawabi, hoping instead for a big payoff as the area became increasingly "sought after." In his opinion, the "uneducated" and "normal" villagers think only in terms of the present, not about long-term goals.

However, it seems to me the opposite: villagers who thought they would benefit from an open and free land market knew that if they sold immediately, they would cash out before a spike in land prices. Instead, they were forced into a market at a severe disadvantage; some saw their land expropriated by the government for the benefit of the private sector. According to MOPWH's Afif al-Sayyid, there is a public-private committee to set land prices. The average value was 12 to 20 Jordanian Dinars (JOD) per square meter, and some people got as much as JOD58 per square meter. He thinks it was fair. Villagers were reluctant to cede their political authority to private developers, as they had believed there was collusion in the land acquisition process. In the end, for the MOLG, clearly the public and private sectors must work together: "You need two wings to fly." Rawabi then became its own municipality, and the public itself was subsequently incorporated. At the local scale this public-private partnership is premised on the PA's "lack of capacity," and it enables the PA to shed parts of itself. What does it mean for the PA at the national scale? In the BBC documentary on Rawabi, Saeb Erekat, the chief Palestinian negotiator with Israel, said of the developer, "Those people who will make the investments with high risk, are the ones who are gonna take Palestinians toward independence . . . and in an expeditious fashion" (McMullen 2015).

Like many officials I spoke with who were "totally with Rawabi," one planner saw problems with it—the regulations and the laws are old and malleable, so Rawabi becomes precedent, even though it does not aid the Ministry of Planning and International Cooperation's priorities to encourage tourism and agriculture over the finance sector.[3] Even whether it should be understood as a private project was "a big debate. . . . Everyone had this debate." For landowners, it is a private development, and Massar should not be able to take their land. Developers framed it as a political act, a public good, a job creator. In the opinion of one planner it is "a private project" and that should not be granted ownership or authority over privately owned land. As for the government reparcelization, "most people that know the law think that this is illegal . . . but to do things in this environment you need to compromise between legal issues and your own interests as a new state."

So, what public good does the government obtain from investment in Rawabi? How do ideas at the scale of government affect what actually happens in Palestine? Public aid does not operate to aid the public or as a subsidy to otherwise drive down housing costs. Instead, it alters the structure of governance to strengthen the private sector and ostensibly to provide opportunities to the polity through private development.

Jurisdiction, Assuming a Public, and the Groundwork for Investment

In late 2010, I interviewed a staffer at the Ramallah–al-Bireh local branch of the Ministry of Local Government, one of the people in charge of administering building and development and managing approvals, eminent domain, and public comment periods. Rawabi worked its way through the confusing morass of law in the West Bank by first applying to the Higher Planning Council (HPC) as a "planned region" of 6,300 dunams; this application gave them legal authority to create a large plan rather than submitting applications for each individual plot, and the plan they submitted became known as the "Rawabi bylaw." Under Jordanian law, a public consultation period should follow planning, but it is not clear it happened at that time. Subsequently, developers submitted a plan for only the central 750 dunams of their site to enable istimlak (the eminent domain process mentioned in chapter 1). Through the practical authority under the "bylaw," they were able to determine what could happen in the rest of the area, despite not having an official plan for it. Istimlak took shape in that central area, quickly and with little public consultation. Even though, as an MOLG official said, the Rawabi bylaw had not been made official, it was framing the project and constantly invoked. Under Jordanian law, istimlak requires both the prime minister's and the king's approval, and it is to be used for the public good. The istimlak granted to developers over one area enabled practical legal authority over a much wider swath of land. Commonsense notions of what constitutes the public and public good, law and jurisdiction were reconfigured through practical authority and investment.[4]

In Palestine, "public good" has generally referred to things like schools and hospitals. Typically, the public is made aware of istimlak through advertisement and allowed a fifteen-day comment period. After the fifteen days, leaders of whatever project apply to the Prime Minister's Office with a detailed plan, plot maps, and various other forms of documentation. The office then checks that the project meets the public interest, and the government can afford to pay people for their reparcelized land. At that point they have several options for eminent domain: the state could grant a total change of ownership or a long lease (some in the Land Authority advocated for forty to fifty years for Rawabi), after which point the land will revert to its original owners. The Prime Minister's Office then takes its recommendation to the king of Jordan, nowadays the PA president, and a final public notice is released. The project is forwarded to the Land Authority, which finds all of the affected landowners or, in the case of collective lands, the workers, and alerts them and offers compensation. After that, the Land Authority does the istimlak and begins to meet its responsibility to compensate everyone with a stake in the land, including renters.

There are provisions for a rushed process if one is necessary. In that case a project could apply directly to the Land Authority, which will do the istimlak, set up a trust, and then have experts determine compensation after the fact and on the basis of the market price at the time of the istimlak and the advertisements. Typically, this expedited process happens for schools and hospitals, and this is the first time that a private firm used it. The prevailing opinion in the Land Authority at the time of my research was that no matter the outcome, private investment "is not public use," and Rawabi was generally controversial there. But according to the MOLG, this is specifically why Rawabi organized the istimlak around the central shopping center, an area that it could plausibly describe as "public," despite owning and drawing revenue from it.

There is some confusion about the order in which everything happened: an MOLG official told me that first the developers got the MOU, then they did the claim for 6,300 dunams, after which point they started actively buying land and did the first phase of planning. Then they began the istimlak process under the existing planning laws, but the HPC rather than the Land Authority expedited it. As I will discuss in the next chapter, land dealers claim developers were probably buying land much earlier than is generally acknowledged and were able to extract an istimlak much larger than they generally publicize. In any case, there has been a lot of movement without much public knowledge or consultation, and lands were planned before ownership was transferred. And there was a significant legal procedure that only vaguely conformed to preexisting guidelines. The lack of transparency enables investment and capital accumulation in a context without real oversight or public accountability. Here as elsewhere, actually existing free and open markets require state support, financial and otherwise, and those in first can use that support to erect barriers to subsequent entry.

Parcelization, Ownership, Debt

Previously, almost no reparcelization schemes were allowed beyond the "small-scale subdivision of individual plots as part of the development control process" (Coon 1992, 64). Under the PA administration and through Rawabi, that has changed: large-scale reparcelization occurs to benefit the private sector, and in terms of those "out of date, legally valid" constraints on growth, now defined in terms of capital accumulation and market expansion. Today, housing and planning are parts of a wider class project, the foundation for a more open, less regulated Palestinian economy.

Although it is tempting to see market formation in the West Bank as an outside imposition, or something akin to structural adjustment, it is also an internal question of Palestinian capital and privatizing governance to engage more fully with regional and global state and capital networks. It is both a rationalization and a productive act. The 2008 financial crisis depressed interest rates, and in 2009 the Palestine Investment Fund and the Palestine Capital Market Authority (PCMA) mandated investments in projects had to be minimally 45 percent local and 55 percent international to bring capital back to Palestine.[5] Prior to this, 80 percent of banks' investments were abroad; all of a sudden, capital returned to Palestine, and local investments and sites for fixed capital were needed. This is one big reason why real estate and privatization is growing, why capitalists put capital in motion and park it in loans, and otherwise chase growth and accumulation. The affordable housing initiatives and "national priority" fit into economic and occupation contexts and provide a framework for investment, and the state has a fundamental role in working the idea of general need into opportunities for investment.

Buildings and housing are where multiple scales and logics come together in material, physical ways: government retreat and intervention, along with priorities shaped in part through NGO influence, combined with private development funded by Palestinians and from abroad. All infrastructure is social, and the kind of urban master planning occurring in Palestine today requires people as well as remaking governance at the local scale. Given the income situation and in order to bring Palestinians into this new vision, there is debt. Economic planning and debt are tied to large urban environments with clear title. As Rawabi and places like it are increasingly realized, these confluences of plans can potentially be expanded to incorporate larger portions of the Palestinian West Bank and its population.

From the perspective of lenders, large, long-term loans have always been difficult in Palestine. Banks argue that there is a need to reform the structural conditions that protect lenders, as well as to "teach people to accept" long-term loans. They suggest that doing so requires changes not only in the material conditions of wealth and debt, but also in the political conceptions that govern life and possibilities in the West Bank. If the political situation is understood as fundamentally unstable, people do not think in terms of a given future. It becomes impossible to take on debt that lasts ten, twenty, twenty-five years. Social change at the base is necessary for capital accumulation at the top. Political and economic instability makes Palestinians reluctant to tie up large chunks of money in loans; social preference is to save and to build on existing houses. Moreover, land tenure is complicated, and plots of land can be held collectively. Those ideas mean something different to ordinary people: without clear title, land cannot be used for collateral. But clear titling is difficult: PA law, Israeli civil or military law, Jordanian law from 1967, or Ottoman law can govern what happens in certain places and require legal change to be of benefit for lenders and developers.

The Rawabi process is fundamentally altering the legal structure for how people hold land in Palestine. Stabilization and formalization are happening through economics: the Rawabi project is the first tentative step toward a coherent land registration system, made with the intention of creating clear title and profiting from the land. One of the first attempts toward reconfiguring registration and land tenure was a land-titling project undertaken by the World Bank in 2005. That project stalled specifically because the Palestinians administering it tried to block the open sale of land (Goedeken 2009). By 2008, when the Rawabi idea started to form, and increasingly afterward, it fell to the private sector to make titles coherent, visible, and adequate for sale and transfer (Kohlbry 2018). It is by no means widespread, but compared to 2005, today the rhetoric of free markets and the rhetoric of nationalism are intertwined, and there is far less capacity for non-elites to either object or to do anything about their objections.

The government stepped in to solve the registration problem for developers and lenders. Figure 6.1, submitted by Rawabi's developers for planning approval, shows incomplete titling, but it gives a sense of the large number of plots underneath their site. Developers bought a patchwork of land where they wanted to put the new town. Supposedly they sent teams out into the diaspora: to Jordan, Lebanon, Latin America, and Dearborn, Michigan to track down the families and individuals who owned that land. The government then did a fairly large eminent domain to tie together the site footprint. Typically, eminent domain must meet "the public good." This is the first time the Palestinian government did it for a private entity. As a result, land on a large scale has clear title, apartments can be collateral, and a mortgage market can emerge (map 6.1 gives some sense for the scale of the titling process).

As I had initially understood it, the eminent domain happened using the rush provision in the Jordanian law. The Palestinian Land Authority set up a fund to pay out people who had their land seized and notified them of both reparcelization and compensation. In practice it was both larger and more complicated than I had been led to believe. Compensation was based on prices in the area prior to speculation and development. Owners had two choices: they could take the money, or they could fight it. Either way, their land had already been incorporated. The plan here had accrued legal weight through eminent domain.

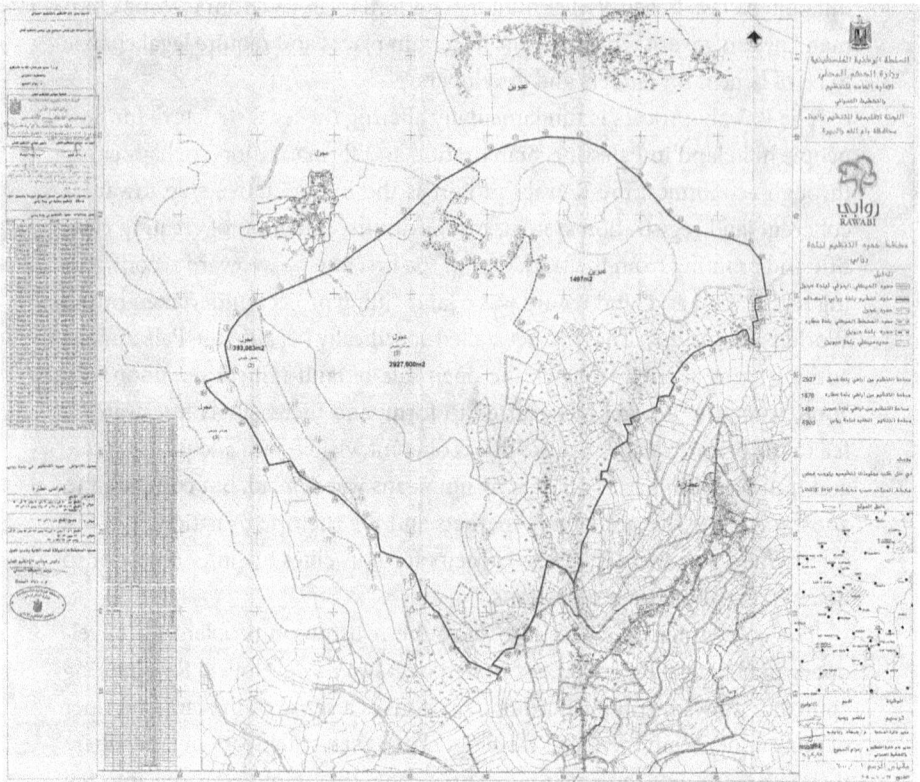

FIGURE 6.1 Private land under Rawabi. Source: Higher Planning Council.

Planning and Process

Under state building, planning became a type of official and legal practice oriented toward concretizing accumulation in the present. Attempts to formalize national governance around Oslo have given way to an emphasis on local government, enabled by the fluid administrative and legal structures that are a part of occupation. On top of the morass of law I outlined in chapter 4, land is governed by various 1996 "regulations" (*nizam*) that the MOLG has worked continuously to update, as well as local municipal and village regulations for density, height, and other practical zoning concerns that are approved by the Higher Planning Council. Originally under Jordanian law, the HPC had between six and nine appointed members. Arafat expanded it to seventeen members including each deputy minister and headed by the MOLG. The effect was to minimize HPC independence and to place national planning un-

British Fiscal Survey

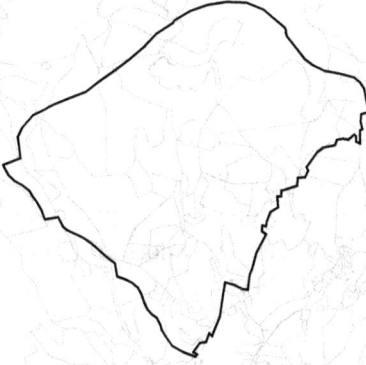

Current Palestinian
Land Registration

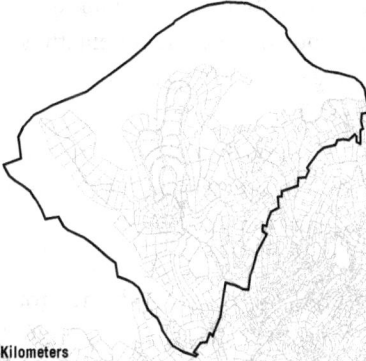

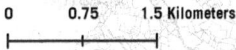

0   0.75   1.5 Kilometers

MAP 6.1 The first image shows plots digitized from British land surveys. Over the course of a months-long process that included petitioning the minister of local government and asking for help from the Prime Minister's Office, I learned it is the only available historical land map for the area. British surveys started from scratch with the goal of making land visible in order to regularize taxation, which had previously been calculated on the basis of cultivation. In some of the areas the British surveyed, titling and registration were done to help land enter the market, and as a way to determine the location of state lands. Surveys contained information that the Zionist movement in Europe was keen to have, and which the British were willing to provide (Gavish 2005). The second map shows the most current version of what formalization and regularization look like and gives a sense of the tremendous amount of technical work needed to draw large numbers of plots into existence, to formalize and regularize them as a basis for market relations. Map by Meagan A. Snow, based on data provided by the Ministry of Local Government and Palestine Open Maps.

der MOLG control. It ensured the conversations there were the same as in the ministries and made planning a question for the whole government. Because Rawabi is part of a "national plan" as far as affordable housing is concerned, and since it was designated as a region, the HPC is the first and final arbiter.

According to people in both the Ministries of Planning and International Cooperation as well as Local Government, the MOPIC is specifically tasked with "national planning" and is supposed to be part of the decision-making process for regional planning. The MOLG does local planning and regional planning; thus it overlaps at the "regional scale." To complicate matters, "regional" is the widest scale of planning under the 1966 Jordanian code, where there is no "national planning."[6] So, as the MOPIC is increasingly tasked with writing donors' documents rather than spatial planning, the highest level of planning and approvals are increasingly being done alongside localization in the MOLG. According to regulations, local committees should have their own local governors, but in practice local representatives of the MOLG head them. And as a result, local committees have less power to articulate or dictate their own goals (even if they have practical authority to do small-scale public works). Both local and national governance are coming under the control of the Ministry of Local Government, which then enables certain large projects in terms of "national priority" and direction, while it rolls back state-scale regulation.

Rules and practices around planning touch the ground through local plans and governance, and private enterprise creeps into the domain of the government and reorients it. Planning interventions are a concrete mechanism for mixing public and private sectors in service of firms' stated and unstated goals for ongoing capital accumulation. Within this form of development, there is no clear separation between material and rhetorical projects: they are simultaneously both. And there are consequences for political institutions and participation. When there are municipal elections, as state functions are outsourced and Fatah often runs unopposed, few Palestinians trust the process.

But precedent marks a path, and it orients future capacities and approaches. Projects intertwine the government, private sector, NGOs, and Israel. There is a push and pull between ideas and practice. If neoliberalism is about making the state in the image of the private sector, this is where capitalist logics around growth and accumulation come together as part of peace and stabilization projects.

Rawabi moved through the convoluted system of councils and ministries and approvals quickly and efficiently precisely because it has never been clear what kind of planning approval it needs. I was told Rawabi was able to utilize ambiguity because of its relationships with the PA and its national-scale priorities. Does it need a regional plan—the type that would probably encompass the placement of a new town? According to officials in the Ministry of Planning and International Cooperation, such a plan was never approved. And there is no provision for the amendment of regional plans (Coon 1992, 47). Rawabi's is a "detailed plan," something typically done to amend use and zoning within preexisting towns. The Higher Planning Council approved Rawabi's plan as a national plan, but it has no authority over parcelization schemes. I tried to follow the process, but it never became entirely clear what happened and why. It is likely clear to *someone* in Palestine, but despite the details, whether something is strictly "legal" is less important than the ways that laws justify and, in this case at least, form to justify the expression of power through simultaneous regulation and deregulation.[7]

Before Oslo, the Israeli HPC was a military body, and its primary role was to plan Jewish expansion (62). Post-Oslo, the Palestinian HPC has similar but subordinate authority, and under the current suite of national priorities, it works to make land profitable and expand the capacity for large private investment and accumulation. Bringing capital in and fixing it is messy, and the HPC is one body that works to smooth the process. Rawabi, through practice, authority, planning, and the kinds of changes it makes for the wider West Bank, is envisioning a frictionless open market as it produces one. First of all, developers articulate needs for development, orient practice around their desires, and contribute to the direction of national priorities. As their ideas circulate and touch the ground, they contribute to institutions and institutional forms that enable ideological, physical, and social change. Second, confusion—or incoherence in the plans and their outcomes—enables rather than disables building on the landscape, planned or otherwise. There is a push and pull, a combination of friction and smoothness, and together interventions cohere around specific visions for the future.

Let me take a step back. Here is how the Rawabi developers, Massar, portrayed early approvals, and the process through which they brought together Israelis, Palestinians, private, and public. Documents and approvals are crucial to creating the shape of intervention. In a presentation Massar made to demonstrate and outline progress to potential investors, the firm described its time line for approval this way:

13 DECEMBER 2007 Founding of Bayti Real Estate Investment Company

20 APRIL 2008 Signing of a Memorandum of Understanding (MOU)
between the Palestinian Authority and Bayti in which the PA commits
itself to facilitate and support critical infrastructure, such as roads,
electricity, water supply, as well as public services

04 MAY 2008 Israeli Civil Administration agrees to the construction of
the Rawabi access road in Area "C"

21 MAY 2008 Qatari Diar joins forces with Massar International to develop Rawabi

22 MAY 2008 The Quartet's Special Envoy to the Middle East, Tony
Blair meets with Qatari Diar and Massar International and endorses
the Rawabi project

06 JUNE 2008 AECOM (NYSE: ACM) is Awarded Rawabi Master-plan
Development Contract

15 SEPTEMBER 2008 RTI International (Research Triangle Institute)
completes Economic Growth Strategy for Rawabi

24 SEPTEMBER 2008 Approval of City Limits by Ministry of Local
Government

02 NOVEMBER 2008 Submission of Masterplan to the Palestinian
Authority

15–16 DECEMBER 2008 Participation and Presentation of Rawabi at
London Investment Conference

25 JANUARY 2009 Palestinian Ministry of Local Government Posts
Master-plan for 60-Day Public Comment Period

05 MARCH 2009 Palestine Cabinet Approval of Eminent Domain.

MARCH 2009 Assessment of local contractors and manufacturers in cooperation with Portland Trust, which included numerous site visits

25 APRIL 2009 Launch of the "GROW for a Greener Palestine"—tree
planting program, which aims at promoting a healthy and green
Rawabi and preserving the Rawabi environment

JUNE–AUGUST 2009 Approval of Birzeit-Rawabi Main Access Road

23 JUNE 2009 Final Master-plan Approval by the Palestinian Ministry
of Local Government.

Only four months after the company was founded, it had formalized PA
commitment, and two weeks after that, it had Israel's compliance and approval. A few weeks later it was able to announce massive Qatari investment
and support from the Quartet. About a year after the initial Portland Trust

meetings, in just five months between June and November 2008, all the planning seems to have taken place, and barely more than a year after the PA was formally brought in, eminent domain was approved on the basis of those initial plans, and tree planting in partnership with the Jewish National Fund commenced. In June 2009, the access road was supposedly approved, although it was still somehow a problem six and seven years later. The early parts of the process were not slow or deliberative or held up by red tape.

In that same presentation, Massar stresses its mutual and beneficial relationship to the PA economic agenda this way:

> Rawabi will be predominately comprised of affordable housing, easing the chronic housing shortage in Palestine and also meeting the steadily increasing demand for affordable homes. In April 2008, Bayti and the PA entered a private-public partnership. Both parties signed a Memorandum of Understanding (MOU) in which the PA commits to financially support the off-site infrastructure and public services in Rawabi in accordance with the "Affordable Housing" program as outlined in the Palestinian Reform and Development Plan (PRDP). The PA further agreed to support an enabling environment for the economic growth of Rawabi.
>
> Economically, Rawabi will help ease chronic conditions of unemployment by generating an estimated 8,000 to 10,000 jobs during construction, and beyond that between 3,000–5,000 new long-term job opportunities within the city. Bayti, in cooperation with RTI international, developed an Economic Growth Strategy that envisions Rawabi as the hub of a knowledge-based economy. Palestine carries great potential for future outsourcing in the sectors of Engineering and ICT, thanks to a highly educated workforce. Rawabi will provide the necessary infrastructure to jump-start development of a knowledge economy as well as essential services and training to strengthen the targeted sectors. Moreover, not only inhabitants of Rawabi but also the 20,000 people living in the 9 neighboring towns and villages will benefit from the construction of Rawabi and the development of a vibrant economy.

Money also enters in other ways in Palestine. Developers have claimed they approached nearly all active international development firms looking for funding for public services; Masri has stated he went to seventy-three meetings before Qatar (Booth 2017). But the majority of the proposals I have seen are targeted. They asked for money from development agencies for areas such as education, roads, and wastewater because they had already extracted public commitments for much of their internal infrastructure. But they also sought international aid for things that seemed smaller-scale. For example, their proposal to the British was for funding for a business center for entrepreneurs, a private school, and a country club.

This is important for two reasons. First, in a context where development aid is a fundamental part of economics, private developers have access to funding sources they would not elsewhere. Second, it creates direct relationships between this city and the network of states and enhances developers' capacity to operate as a generalizable form of governance.[8]

Given the context, clearly Massar has had to work closely with all overlapping governments and authorities. Because of its size and ability to marshal resources, Rawabi has shifted the frame for state-scale politics laterally, into private negotiations centered around different agendas than the PA may have once had. First by becoming a recipient of donor aid, the firm begins to operate at the scale of a state. It has crept into the realm of public infrastructure in various ways. A second, related dynamic occurs when the firm positions itself as a national endeavor, and Rawabi begins to circulate globally as an image of the (potential) nation. As the picture of Rawabi's nation slowly materializes through facts on the ground and international investment, it aggregates support and becomes increasingly real. The strength of the representation as a national endeavor coupled with PA support has meant the PA often directly negotiates with Israel on its behalf.

The Road

The developers designed a road that followed an old path to the existing Birzeit road, circumventing the 'Attara checkpoint, and cutting through 2.8 kilometers of land classified as Area C (see map 6.2). That road was stalled for some time and, as of summer 2017, was still under provisional approval. There are several proposals about what the road would look like, but for years Israel had refused to grant approval on the grounds that it needs to maintain security for Route 465. There were plans to tunnel under it or to bridge above it. The development firm is pushing the PA into negotiations to transfer the strip of land to Palestinian sovereignty. This will then allow the PA to undertake reparcelization for a road on that land.

The developers are adamant that the Israelis not build the road, believing landowners will only be sympathetic if Palestinians reparcelize land for Rawabi. But this push has other consequences at a different scale. Since they have managed to make Rawabi a PA priority, Israel uses the road issue in negotiations to extract potentially painful Palestinian concessions elsewhere

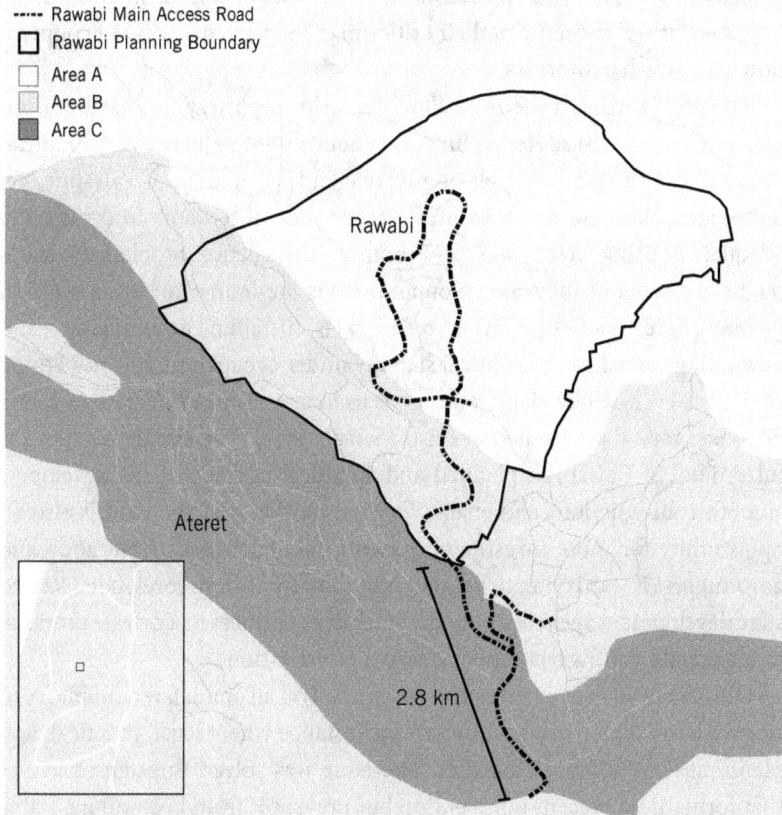

MAP 6.2 The road proposal. Map by Meagan A. Snow, based on data from the Palestinian Ministry of Local Government and Rawabi.

in the West Bank or Gaza. When I asked what would happen if they are not granted road approval, a company official told me, "The PR answer is that it will stop the project, but the real answer is that the company has alternate plans." Despite this and the threat of concessions elsewhere, they are in negotiation.

Although there was a handshake agreement and "preliminary approval" granted by the Israeli Civil Administration in 2008 or 2009, the road issue has been a constant problem for the developers since then, and they have struggled for formal approval. And it is something that has come up and dissipated in various ways and for various reasons related to how developers circulate ideas of politics abroad and at home. The company emphasizes the issue with international organizations that may be able to pressure Israel, while it downplays it with Palestinians in general and antinormalization activists specifically because of their criticism of Rawabi's narrative of cooperation with Israeli authorities.

The problems with the road allow the firm to portray itself as both political and nonpolitical depending on venue and on audience. It is political because it is subject to Israeli prerogative and occupation of Palestine, yet nonpolitical because it can plausibly argue that all it wants to do is build adequate housing, create jobs, and promote coexistence; problematic states ought to get out of the way.[9] "Nonpolitical" is the framework for a political ideology here about establishing free markets, sustaining accumulation, and promoting some kind of political stability under occupation. It is something capitalists everywhere claim, and it has as long a history in Palestine as everywhere capital accumulation exists (Seikaly 2015). The circulating, powerful symbol of Rawabi as planned and apolitical is one way the developers smooth contradictions and enable forward motion. But the road is also an opportunity for more investment; Rawabi internal reports from 2009 and 2010 suggest it was trying to get USD31 million for it from foreign banks and state development agencies. Funders enter in as partners in a private proposal to make public infrastructure that serves privatization.

Ultimately, in 2013 permission was granted on an annual, renewable, contingent basis. The road is an important instance where legal, practical, and planning regimes come together. The issue was solved through measures that formalize a present intervention but prevent it from becoming a stable political precedent for the future. The road solidified the act of private development, weakened the PA elsewhere, and oriented priorities for international aid.

Localization, Regulation, and Deregulation

The scale of national politics has become at once international and local. It is international insofar as it looks outward and is premised on enabling flows of worldwide capital and produced by reoriented international aid. And it is local because it is practiced through specific sites for specific people, for the benefit of even fewer people. The Ministry of Planning and International Cooperation and the national plans that it has produced both indicate and demonstrate the changing approach to planning in the West Bank. Rather than planning for the future, staff plan in spite of it. In the current context and the widespread belief that the PA "has no capacity," the international community and Palestinian capitalists further erode capacity by siphoning investment, localizing and privatizing the national organizing structure, and limiting the power to accomplish anything.

The same peace process that ceded authority from the PLO to the PA has aided the free reign of private developers; the weakened government barely even controls development in Areas A and B. Because there are no coherent plans or planning regimes and no areas allocated for housing development, something like Rawabi can be built where land was empty thanks to the long history of occupation spatial organization. According to one national planner, "unfortunately the private sector is in front of us," while it should be the opposite. They told me Rawabi is probably "value added" for the economy, and the ministry is officially in support of it, but that "I have to cope, for the time being" with poorly planned projects. Poorly planned due to a top level of planning consisting of aspiration and reports rather than the details that are left to private developers with their own priorities and goals.

Through documents that accrue evidence, expertise, and precedent to specific goals and practices, and through the creation of local sites of governance, the national government decentralizes itself as it empowers local units. Private sector and pro-privatization NGOs are pushing the government to reform laws and establish an atmosphere friendly to investment. Given how the PA has operated since the late 2000s, it is impossible to talk about it without talking about the private sector: their goals are in concert, and many of the leadership roles are filled by people who go back and forth. Although there is pushback, it is mostly specific to mid-level technocrats who emerged as part of the Oslo process and who share a vision of a functional national public sector—an idea increasingly marginal to the PA.

On the one hand the PA is a massive employer with reach into many localities. On the other, it is the body that works to shape national priorities and overcome the many internal debates. In the contemporary period, when economic and political development is being led by privatization efforts—and despite changes such as the last few prime ministers, the head of the reconciliation portfolio, and others—large-scale development becomes an object of national-scale political negotiation. It is a national-scale public-private partnership.

Since Oslo, if not before, the Palestinian government and economy has depended on the scaffolding of donor aid, and the PA and aid subcontractors have long been engaged in generating evidence that circulates to sustain and frame continued aid intervention. Sometimes it seems everyone in the West Bank has some kind of an aid project, projects that are oriented around aid, the requirements that come with it, and the imperatives for obtaining more of it. The PA, too, is dependent on aid, and it continuously produces reports and principles for donors that emphasize aid successes and elaborate conditions that necessitate further aid. The imperatives of aid and local market and political stabilization are primary reasons why the West Bank comes to be seen as and operate as a distinct entity from Gaza. And as the political economy of aid shifts from humanitarian development to direct and indirect support of the private sector, so necessarily do the structures of government and polity in the West Bank.

Chapter Seven

Buyers
and Villagers

FOR CERTAIN INDIVIDUALS among certain classes in the West Bank today, a tension is emerging between the desire for normalcy and stability, new sites that offer the image and promise of normalcy and stability, and instability and unease under Israeli control. Structural conditions there make politics and the occupation a necessary consideration in virtually every decision. These conditions explain why developments like Rawabi that explicitly model Palestinian autonomy are crucial for enabling new kinds of economic calculations and practices among West Bank Palestinians. New developments give Palestinians a form and context to reimagine personal relationships to place and to wider politics. Rawabi is a private firm, circulating in public discourse, that engenders state reform, localizes government in a large semipublic city, and has social effects not least because it is dependent on consumers buying their own private space within it.

Rawabi has successfully entered public discourse in the West Bank and abroad. In Ramallah, where the image and idea circulate among potential buyers, employees, and people otherwise affected by it, it is a topic of conversations in coffee shops, homes, in taxis, and online. As the idea travels, a multiplicity of perceptions and analyses of it emerge. Whether it is clean and *mrattab* (tidy), and a nice place to live; or if it is representative of a final Palestinian slide into comprador status, a "dystopia" in one conversation I overheard while writing some of this in one of Ramallah's most upscale coffee shops, it is fully a part of public political discussion, despite the firm's efforts to manage its image in the media. These accounts and arguments build the image and practical reality of Rawabi—the image of land is, after all, as important as the land itself in conceiving of space (Soja 1996)—and are a part of the process to interpellate or exclude people from a future premised on their abilities to identify or change themselves through it.

Private development is important beyond housing as a result of the process of its creation, and arguments it makes about the future become politically relevant as it jumps scales and reshapes governance. What does it mean to craft a future within the terms, ideologies, and geographies of the present? What can get made, and what kind of future is implied? On the one hand, history cannot be solely determinative. On the other, critics see Rawabi as a fantasy based around neglecting history as well as present realities rather than as a utopian promise.

The circulation of images and ideas is of primary importance to process here, and Rawabi's delays, funding disputes, and issues with the water and the road are less of an impediment to its success than they might be in other political situations less defined by deferral. Those problems feed directly into the broader narrative of antioccupation economic aspiration. Process is part of public discourse and has been instrumental in allowing people continual opportunities to craft relationships to the idea and meaning of the place, as well as to the place itself. In Palestine, where the whole political arrangement since at least 1967 has been to hurry up and wait, a project that is simply moving along can be politically relevant. Just like the peace process and its endless networks of institutions, funding structures, and employment opportunities, real estate development works on the long term by extending the present.

When an ambitious project is jump-started by a single-minded man and is joined to the question of state politics through ideological, government, and cultural support, it becomes clear that the goal and the capacity for change go beyond the city boundaries. In this chapter I try to understand how people conceive of their relationship to Palestine and to their futures in terms of the changing built environment. Drawing on a handful of exemplary interviews, I ask: How do different people participate in new visions and places in different ways? How are they incorporated? And if Rawabi represents one possible direction that Palestine is moving politically, nationally, and socially, how does that vision diverge from and converge with others? What are the local and universal dimensions?

Potential Owners

Nisreen Shahin of the Portland Trust reiterated much of the content from the Martin document, the widely invoked 2009 World Bank brief emphasizing large-scale private development to meet housing needs. She told me that "the culture of ownership has always been here" and that 40 percent of Palestinians own their homes. As such, the market should target nonowners on the basis of affordability and accessibility. New forms of mortgage financing would enable the construction of new housing—financing will aid people and meet their needs for homes and stability. Financing is a main barrier for housing, and the existence of things like the Affordable Mortgage and Loan Program (AMAL) will "encourage low- and middle-income people to approach the banks." And the demand—generally high—is latent because of increases in population growth and artificial scarcity based on the limitations of Areas A, B, and C.

This description raises questions about the differences between Ramallah and other places—if there is scarcity, is it everywhere? How does migration to Ramallah affect it? What are the housing rates in Ramallah versus elsewhere in the West Bank? I asked why the current practice of Palestinians living in housing owned by a family member and expanding on family homes is unsustainable. She replied that the number of households in total is increasing, but the market is also based on the assumption "the mentality is changing" and people are more satisfied with single-family, smaller housing. That assumption becomes fact when it is encouraged and used as the basis for subsequent material action, and when it supports the specific types of housing they already work to build and sell. Developers and the PA construct the idea of need, problems, and solutions simultaneously, and they incorporate Palestinians into new facts on the ground.

Saleh Numan is a potential Rawabi buyer who has been an active participant and informal booster since nearly the beginning of the project. Numan met market researchers at Bravo, one of the upscale supermarkets in Ramallah, in 2005, and during the course of my research, he has worked with and participated in focus groups every few months.[1] Developers introduced me to Numan in 2010, when he was an IT specialist with the Cooperative Housing Foundation (CHF), an NGO that, at that time, worked on housing issues and homebuyer education in the West Bank. He is thus well-versed in housing politics and supports new forms of development. "It all comes down to the necessity to own," "to stop renting," which he understands as an indicator of, and contributor to, his personal instability. For him, owning in the West Bank is "essential" both because rents in Ramallah are high and because he wants to stabilize as many aspects of his life and work as possible. He tends to work in three-month, project-based contracts, and he believes that new loans will give him, his wife, and his six children the ability to own a home, which, in turn, will insulate them from economic instability and rapid changes in the rental market. Mortgages against the new apartment will allow them to occupy it immediately. Borrowing gives Numan security in a home that would otherwise come at the end of years of saving. It is a logical response to his situation.

Despite his short-term contracts, he barely mentioned the potential complications that could emerge from taking on massive debt; he wants a change that is both immediate and lasting, and accumulating debt gives him both. The mortgaged apartment will bring him stability: he feels it is time to move out of Ramallah and away from "no system and chaos" into a "new, modern" house in a place without Ramallah's disadvantages. Ramallah, he says, has not been able to cope with growth after Oslo, with the proliferation of NGOs and PA ministries and in-migration of Palestinian workers like him. A move to Rawabi will be a move away from crowds and to good, functioning services in a "neighborhood." He currently pays USD400/month to rent an apartment in a building with five floors and twenty units. His building is already large and cumbersome, on its own almost like a neighborhood, but one that is severely underserved. It was built in an area "without planning and zoning," and the roof leaks. He endures these conditions because finding another rental in the current market would be "a financial catastrophe."

He continues, Rawabi will give him a bigger, cheaper place with a "modern layout," public space and greenery for the kids, strong IT infrastructure, schools, hospitals, easy movement, and "calmness and quietness." His neighbors—and the prospective consumers for Rawabi—will be engineers, doctors, and the middle to upper classes. And the infrastructure will be superior to Ramallah's: the transportation and the streets will be better, and there will be better distribution of services *within* Rawabi; developers claim that it will have functioning water, sewage, electrical, and communications systems. And, while there are "a lot of obstacles," "if it is done as planned, it will be excellent." From an IT perspective it will be "just delightful." He is already thinking about the potential for change, for a different life, and Rawabi is giving him a framework to imagine it. He is so enthusiastic about Rawabi that he plans to move even though he had yet to visit the site when we spoke in 2010. His ties to the firm, his excitement and his kids' are the result of the Rawabi commercials and advertisements, 3D renderings, and so on. He knows the political climate is uncertain, but he insists that this is not a political project because it is a private initiative.

Although he is "politically neutral," he has worries—will he be an "ongoing customer" rather than an owner? Will the Israelis stall the project? But in the end, the draw of individual stability, the desire to extract stability from an unstable situation, is strong. He imagines Rawabi will be durable, wealthy, and also part of the nature and specific character of Palestine. He believes that it offers potential buyers an alternate future. Or at least it offers them a long-term commitment and an orientation toward politics of the future by ameliorating the conditions in the present through nonpolitical means. Housing debt is a form of aspiration and deferral, but it is also about forms of consistency in new spaces. It is an attachment and a promise quantified (Harker 2014b, 2017). And it can bring an aspiration to bear much sooner through new developments. Tying Palestinians to new spaces changes the nature of ties to family and to place in the West Bank, and has bearing on what happens in areas that are not actively being developed.

The time line has changed from when I interviewed Numan, and it could complicate matters, although it may not significantly alter calculations for people who are planning to buy. People may not want to enter into Rawabi because it is still in progress, but for those who see it as the future, it remains productively in the future. This is perhaps also why the developers rushed to open the Q Center shopping mall: it gives residents of the West Bank a reason to come see Rawabi more specific than curiousity; it shows off the town; it allows them to engage; and it demonstrates a small part of its promise.

According to one young marketing engineer and former Rawabi employee, Rawabi will provide "the most current thing" in terms of services. And it will help toward the political goal of "saving the hilltops" from settlements. But she is clear—"this generation's requirements are high," and Rawabi must meet them. No one, she says, would move there solely for national or antioccupation reasons; those politics are a secondary motivation to developers and potential buyers alike.

She became visibly emotional when describing Bashar Masri, Rawabi, and her work there: Masri was a micromanager in the extreme, but "a perfectionist." And because of his strength and his vision, "it is like a dream come true." If it works out, there will be "no disadvantages" to the project. She is not only a supporter, she loves the idea and clearly imagines a Rawabi-inspired future for herself: a normal, well-provisioned new lifestyle in Palestine. Ideas of individual normalcy contribute to and are shaped by the dynamics of capital accumulation, Palestinians are said to desire certain kinds of services that do not yet exist there (3D cinema, American franchises). For her, it is a benefit of privatization that services and distribution systems can be built and centrally controlled by developers in the town. In a broader environment subject to political instability and disorganization, a driven, wealthy individual can establish the precedent for stability.

Everything, she told me, is subordinate to Masri, who is "an amazing person." "It has to be perfect," and everyone is working in service of "his dream." The planning firm AECOM institutes his demands; market surveys are conducted to support his ideas, and *he* will provide the services she dreams of. There is sort of a hierarchical cooperation in the vision, and she shares a similar individual and personal aspiration: although for Masri "the return will be huge . . . not twice, not triple, even more," it will also be a "good investment" for buyers, and prices will only go up. She believes—contrary to the firm's surveys—that people do not *need* Rawabi; they will desire it. "People will come to prefer Rawabi" because "it will look like a new place like in Dubai." "*Anyone* would prefer a good environment . . . and would like to have buses, public Wi-Fi, parking. Just look at the UAE." It will be so successful that it will prove to be a new model for building in Palestine. She is certain that there will be "a Rawabi 2, 3, 4." If available land is combined through political will, capital, and a vision that brings consumers in, land rent and ongoing accumulation becomes possible.

When I asked that former employee about the critiques of Rawabi both generally and in terms of normalization, she said, "Palestinians only like whining," suggesting that, instead, they should "go and do something" rather than criticize. For her, the national dimensions of the politics in Rawabi are about the ability and individual responsibility to do something, rather than doing nothing, and, she says, the wider occupation does not necessarily play a role in the development. Masri "doesn't care about [Areas] A, B, C." He wants a road, and "he will get it." Masri is presented as a hero in ways that make complete sense given the individualist economic ethic that emerged out of the real lack of capacity in the PA, the dissolution of the national movement, and the absence of cohesive politics within the West Bank (let alone between the Occupied Territories, Palestinian citizens of Israel, or Palestinians in the diaspora).

In this conversation and nearly all others, there is a tension between support and critique: it is not and cannot be simply a housing development. Rawabi had almost immediately been embedded in a series of conversations and critiques and a narrative about modernization and promise. Potential buyers want change toward normalcy, and this is giving them a vessel to determine what it might look like somewhere down the road. The image projected into the future combines with ideas about the land, potentially in lasting ways for buyers and nonbuyers alike. But that image not only supports the consumer side in this instance, it has also aided investment and been used to gather support from donors. It describes and enables the Palestine in which they would like to intervene. The image is adding value to the land, a competitive advantage alongside eminent domain and investment.

For the developers, Rawabi constitutes politics because it refuses to concede the occupation and will materially benefit investors and target populations alike.[2] Rawabi is framed as nationalist investment in Palestine. According to both developers and potential buyers, it will resist the occupation by giving people a "normal," "better life," presumably within it. Because of Rawabi, Numan can be certain when he leaves his home in Rawabi at 7:00, he will not encounter checkpoints and will arrive at work at 7:30. Antioccupation politics are transformed into support for privatization. Privatization promises new geographies and ways of being that offer a chance to overcome the contradictions between the realities of the present and "the day after." In both cases, aspiration is shaped in relation to the choices available to individuals and families. Thus, social and geographic stratification is, in part, occurring on the basis of class through those populations consciously targeted, rearranged, and incorporated as potential buyers.

New Ways to Profit from the Land in Palestine

As value from industry declines (value in all senses—labor, monetary, and time), value from real estate and construction increases (Lefebvre 2003). Real estate is a solution to wider economic issues around value generation, wage distribution, and market expansion. Land is an object of market relations. It is not just another name for nature, but a social relation affected by law and custom (Polanyi 2012). This brings the question of land price, industry, and profitability to the forefront. Land prices do not determine house prices; it is the opposite (Haila 2015). Clearly that is the case for Rawabi.

As the agricultural economy dissipates in the West Bank, peasants have to become consumers; generalized markets, production, and circulation present as problems for household production (Luxemburg 2003). The consequence is that, viewed from a distance, Rawabi is part of the mechanics of incorporating noncapitalist places (such as fallow land) into capitalist social relations, markets, and practice. The groundwork was set well before 1948, and real estate investment today is part of an ongoing dynamic accumulation process, an aggregate relation and urban totality (Lefebvre 2003).

Capitalism emerges in part as a series of practices of categorization as well as a kind of social penetration that can appear as quantification (Mathew 2016). Real estate development has relied on categorization to enable visibility and valuation of land. This is especially relevant in Palestine, where market logics and relations enter into the context of Israeli territorial control. Boundaries are constitutive of markets themselves; land in the occupied West Bank is specifically suited to some forms of development and integration and profitability but not others. Not only is integration crucial, *expulsion* of certain trades and forms of economic and social life is vital to market creation. Large-scale private housing development is a process to remake, consolidate, and incorporate land into profit- and rent-generating circuits.

Many critiques of Palestinian privatization have productively explored the intricacies of the rent question (Khan 2004; Hanieh 2008; Haddad 2016); I supplement them with an anthropological description of the social relations embedded in and fundamental to markets. Prior accounts capture how big capital and class politics are intertwined with nationalist politics, diaspora, and shifting ideas of national priorities. It is not only a question of inside and outside or imposing an order on Palestine and its markets, but of remaking internal dynamics so that Occupied Palestine generates profit and stability continually and expansively for its capitalists and funders-turned-investors.[3]

If Rawabi is the kind of economic practice that makes sense for profit generation in this place and this time, questions of nationalism, of the occupation, and areas A, B, and C are incorporated within it. Political concerns about the occupation are not ancillary but intertwined. Developers lead with their capital and orient it around a sense of economic national politics. Rural areas and lifestyles provide an idea of foundational Palestinianness, but they are increasingly targets of private development by NGOs, the private sector, and the PA. UN-Habitat, as part of its directive to improve housing in Palestine, pledges first and foremost to implement the Palestinian Reform and Development Plan (PRDP) and to work on "strategic formulation cover issues like: introducing efficient mortgage finance mechanisms, regulatory frameworks for public-private partnership, incentives to the growth of a rental market, review of standards" (UN-Habitat 2009, 12). Its first assumption is not the need for affordable and universal housing, it is the need to utilize land to build a market out of the rent gap.

Part of the foundation to validate such an approach has to be categorizing culturally and economically "appropriate" standards for low- and median-income housing, and land use and density regulations to optimize utilization of scarce land. UN-Habitat argues for a planning approach based on the current and already-existing area and colonial planning systems that prohibit villages from spreading (12). UN-Habitat proposes granting substantial support and authority to the Ministry of Local Government, the ministry that is most invested in privatization and decentralizing government.

> The Municipal Development and Lending Fund (MDLF)—established jointly by three Ministries, MOPIC, MOLG, and the Ministry of Finance (MOF)—avails now of capital funding from the World Bank and seven bilateral donors to finance projects of infrastructure, basic services delivery and housing for which technically and socially sound proposals need to be formulated. The MDLF will also support the development of local physical plans, working with the MOLG, and needs support to build capacity in the private sector. (UN-Habitat 2009, 13)

The MDLF will give the MOLG a great deal of control over aid distribution, and it would be able to efficiently funnel capital to private developers and support the privatization of public services. Privatization, "adequacy," and housing needs are all bound together here. Large development and investment will be a path to modernity. For Raffie Samach, Rawabi's one-time main planner, there are two "old ways of life": the village life that no one wants to return to and the current urban life that needs to be fixed. "Ramallah has no urbanism, Ramallah is chaos," there is no place to walk, to park, to engage in "the urban experience." And this kind of "chaos" is a "universal problem." "What is needed is a move from the street life that is not urbanism" to a "flowing" kind of urbanism in the new town. To make problems solvable though private investment, they are conceived as resulting from the present urban form rather than Israeli planning or the absurd Oslo categories. Money is distributed and funneled in specific ways, and investment, privatization, and economic interventions have a material, geographic kind of fixity.

Bringing Palestinians into this approach requires a "cultural" shift, and Rawabi represents a concerted series of interventions to target the middle class, to create a specific type of urban middle class, and to consolidate the cultural and economic ties among the one that exists. Once again, as Jamil Hilal told me in an interview, "the middle class is not unified." This is not because of social or economic position, but because of the diversity of positions: they are part of the PA, of political parties, of NGOs, of the private sector, and there are a wide number of political affiliations within the class: national, pan-national, socialist, liberal (P. A. Smith 1984, 1986). Today, the thing that defines and—to the extent possible—unifies the middle class is that it is, by and large, dependent on "installment aid" such as PA wages, according to Hilal. For Hilal, the development of a middle class can only occur through the development of shared culture. But forms of shared culture have emerged in specific ways and, as the Rawabi case shows, they can be encouraged and cultivated. If there is a shared outlook and type of dependence but a diversity of opinion among the middle classes, the confluence of aid, administration, and privatization works to create places in Palestine where shared outlooks can be encouraged—and, potentially, where older forms of national and antioccupation politics are less present in daily life. This cultural conception is crucial to understanding how the contextual forces—the existence of debt, PA wages tied to politics at the scale of negotiation, and so on—are also part of how class is formed. Social reproduction contributes to, and emerges by and through, relations and modes of production.

How Are Other Publics Incorporated?

Rawabi is, at least in part, organized around the idea that middle-class and putative middle-class Palestinians will modernize out of the political context in ways that are uniquely Palestinian but not constrained by Palestine. They are offered the freedom to have class aspiration within such projects. However, Palestinians in the villages surrounding Rawabi understand its potential and their own present and future differently. Three villages surround Rawabi and have had land recategorized as part of its planning unit: 'Ajjul, 'Abwayn, and 'Attara. I focus here on 'Attara and on how its villagers see their lives and culture changing because of the development. Villagers I interviewed might have had specific positions and relationships to Rawabi, but they nevertheless understand its mixture of aspiration and nationalism. Simultaneously, they are subjects of intervention, aware of how that intervention is framed, of what it purports to do versus what it achieves, and of the ways it targets and tries to bring in different types of Palestinians.

Dominant Palestinian national narratives center on the idea that Palestinians are, at heart, a rural population, living in villages and experiencing a long dislocation as a result of Zionist colonization. Bracketing what exactly is meant by "rural" and "urban," the Palestinian Central Bureau of Statistics states that at the time large development projects began to take off, in the Ramallah/al-Bireh area, nearly 55 percent of Palestinians lived in urban environments, nearly 40 percent in rural environments, and slightly more than 5 percent in camps (Palestinian National Authority, Palestinian Central Bureau of Statistics 2009). These categories are defined by population density and access to hospitals, schools, and other public services, and they might tell us more about occupation planning and occupation geographies than about labor or ties to the land. 'Abwayn and 'Attara have populations of 3,496 and 2,492, respectively; 'Ajjul houses 1,402 (State of Palestine, Palestinian Central Bureau of Statistics 2018). These small towns are hooked into electrical and sewage grids, and by and large they have indoor kitchens and bathrooms and access to local schools and clinics.

This is the framework in which private development is being substituted for public housing. *Rural* is assumed to mean *poor*, and it is clear that the categories of appropriate housing are more than a description of a place or a style of life; they are organizing principles, terms defined by cultural and class character and then operationalized. When developers and NGOs talk about the appropriateness of housing, they mean specific, privately funded homes. And the category frames both the question (Do people live in adequate housing?), as well as the answer for how to make it so. Distinctions between public and private life are complicated in Palestine, as Sandi Hilal and Alessandro Petti have argued (S. Hilal and Petti 2018). They suggest that for refugee camps, and in other places under occupation or repressive regimes, the public sphere is closed, living rooms become a kind of commons, and privacy may have a larger political function.[4] "Public" and "private" are not easy to separate analytically; they are techniques of state that emerge around liberal ethics and ideas about liberal individual subjectivity (Asad 2003). The question Hilal and Petti raise is something like, What happens to collectivity when private home life is no longer a means to hold space for politics or resistance but provide the chance for individual distance from them? In the case of new housing, for individuals these questions are arranged around class and opportunity. This class question, tied to massive changes in political economy and intervention, works to reform both public (as governance, as the public sphere), and private (as the home, as developers taking on governance).

In late 2010, near the end of my longest phase of field research, and sorting through a huge amount of data, proprietary information, and the beginning of an argument about economic and physical restructuring in Palestine, I spoke with Rawhi 'Aql, then the mayor of 'Attara, and his friend and colleague Zaki 'Awda at the municipal building there. The building stood as a dusty reminder of a fading era of international aid for public works—big, empty, and funded by USAID. When I first described my research, 'Aql told me about how Rawabi is a "national project" that will be good for job creation, for encouraging foreign investment, and for providing good housing. Then he clarified—that is "the PA perspective," the position shared by the president and the Ministry of Local Government and the one they implement. He reiterated that this was "the position of the government," both to make clear that it is a decision that has been made elsewhere and to feel out my own position on the topic. He continued: the PA, the United States, and Israel support it. Americans come to visit it all the time. Tony Blair came. Americans keep coming. Longtime Israeli politician and founder of Birthright Yossi Beilin came and said it showed him that "the Palestinians are starting to think correctly." The visitors all believe it is and will be good for peace and the economy.

Multiple forms of development intervention—state, nonstate, infrastructure, economic peace, liberal, neoliberal—have come together in Rawabi. It is part of the wider shift in types of government and Palestinian relationships to the state. But it is also indicative of the ways this housing has become public in terms of government practice and discourse. Rawabi is the form of practice that makes logical sense in terms of desire for capital accumulation on this land, in this political situation, and in terms of the specific types of investment that can come in from overseas. Its vision is not simply local. I asked other members of the 'Attara municipality if locals were getting jobs. "There is not one job." "When the project started developers promised jobs . . . then they stopped talking about it." Really? Not one single job? "Actually, there is one. A driver." Villagers in 'Ajjul speculated that, because they put up a fight against land expropriation and projected municipal incorporation, their village was being punished. One suggested that workers were being hired from more compliant nearby villages. Another disagreed—the contractors all come from Nablus. The second man was right; none of the surrounding villages were especially acquiescent, and none are well represented on the enormous construction site, at least not in 2010 when work was just beginning, or in 2013 when it was happening on a huge scale. 'Aql says that the villagers assumed from the outset that Rawabi would subsume them, and they tried to exert influence on planning and administrative changes. But despite the company's assurances, the councils were not consulted, and whatever information they have about Rawabi, they usually find on its website.

Land as Patrimony and Commodity

In 2015, a knowledgeable land dealer told me that, indeed, more people were hired from 'Attara, but it was because constant turnover forced the firm to seek out new labor pools. Rumor has it, the firm cycles through contractors, firing workers before they become vested or eligible for benefits or raises. Local populations can serve as reserve labor from time to time but are not as relevant to the financial aspects of the development. What the villages gave was their "land in the middle of Palestine" and their vistas looking out as far as the sea, "as far as Syria some days." They gave their "healthy, good air" and their part of Palestinian nature. But they do not anticipate much in return. The hospital and schools "will be private and unaffordable." If the villages are subsumed within Rawabi's municipality, "we will be zero."[5] But just as important, the privatization and recategorization of the landscape "is taking them out of history." 'Aql could not bear to see the name of the area changed: "'Attara is a Palestinian name. I'm a son of 'Attara, not of Rawabi. It says 'Attara on my ID, on everything. *Even the settlers* chose the name 'Ateret' to incorporate themselves into the area's history." The kinds of dispossession and stratification that they experience have been material, physical, and political as well as cultural.[6] And unlike potential buyers, they do not engage development as individuals but experience it as subjects of much larger phenomena.

'Aql's constituents in the area have mixed feelings. "They support [development], but not in this way" and not at this scale. They hold out hope that there is a better, more widely beneficial way to develop. The residents experienced reparcelization and incorporation into Rawabi's planning zone firsthand. 'Attara fears this will make their area more open to speculation and a combination of state and market-based land seizure. They repeated stories of homeowners who were ordered to stop building extensions on their houses, within the Rawabi planning zone but quite far from the site itself, because they were not designed in accordance with Rawabi's master plan or the still-undetermined rules of the Homeowners' Association. In one case in which the owner appealed the order based on distance and his private ownership, the Ministry of Local Government revoked his building permit altogether.

Other landowners were brought into the housing market and had their participation limited to two bad options: they could sell to developers, or they could receive payouts from the government. Villagers who owned land in the site footprint were given offers. Those who refused were told they could receive fair compensation from an istimlak fund, in an amount determined by the PA based on pre-Rawabi, prespeculation land prices. The process supposedly happened very quickly, land was bought, the reparcelization was expedited, and villagers lost control almost immediately after offers were made. According to village residents, compensation averaged around JOD8 per square meter, and shortly thereafter market prices nearly tripled. Afif al-Sayyid from the Ministry of Local Government told me the public-private committee set prices at an average of JOD12 to JOD20/square meter, while some people got as much as JOD58/square meter (JOD12,000 to JOD58,000/dunam).

This account was supported by a few interviews I did with land deal- ers in the area, although the figures they gave differed. I was told real estate brokers started working in the area around 2004, for a pre-Bayti company that involved people from the Portland Trust. One broker told me he was charged with buying up land, mostly from local sellers. That land—years be- fore Rawabi was announced and when only rumors circulated about sales and consolidation—was not ordinarily profitable. It was cheap, little was us- able for agriculture, and "the area was dead." When it became clear what was happening, villagers supported development on the grounds that it would increase their property values, local infrastructure, and so on, not realizing the scale of capital and state intervention and consequent friction. It turns out, a broker told me, that "Bashar took it for profit, not only for the nation."

Another broker described how he believes sales were consolidated in a Masri-owned firm—Palestine Real Estate Co., or something similar—pre- Rawabi. When he founded Bayti as a 25/75 partnership with the Qataris, Masri sold the first firm's holdings to the second at a profit. The large-scale istimlak, this land dealer told me, drove the costs of the surrounding land downward because it became clear that people would not be able to hold it and would be forced to accept nonmarket prices. Istimlak rates were JOD12,000, 14,000, 17,000/dunam, when previously they might have gone as high as JOD50,000/ dunam. This broker believes Masri started buying land at low prices four years before the firm was announced and selling it to the Qataris at a high markup, and through the political process was able to drive down prices for additional land within and around the development site. Part of the reason this is difficult to track, according to that broker, is because it happened before Rawabi was starting to materialize publicly, but also because at least one broker was forced from the company in 2006 over a dispute about the possibility of istimlak and others shortly thereafter, when Masri cleaned house and brought in new staff.

Although nothing was public until Bayti was formed, Masri had the idea and the vision for the land well beforehand. "He was ready with contracts for equipment and materials from day one." Once it became public as a mas- sive, well-formed endeavor, with Masri as a large landholder, he was able to pressure local governments for support. For example, he was able to secure a low rate to buy water from a spring in 'Attara that he trucks in at minimal cost. I asked one land broker about low numbers of istimlak; he speculates that Masri purchased outright about 3,500 dunams and was able to otherwise procure another 2,500. That is far more than what I had been told by develop- ers: that they were granted reparcelization on bits and pieces of land within a 750 dunam area. The broker told me one family alone had 117 dunams taken.

Moreover, the complicated legal issues surrounding land titling are relevant here in a practical way: different villages and areas are subject to different regimes. While some lands are officially registered and visible as *tabu*, a form of land registration dating to the Ottoman period; others were more informally registered as *maliyya*, a Jordanian system where lands are determined in part by neighbors agreeing on boundaries. This system was beneficial for villagers during the period of Jordanian control over the West Bank—they could underreport their cultivation and holdings and pay fewer taxes. But it also gave developers the opportunity to take advantage of landowners who did not know the precise boundaries of their lands or their neighbors'. Supposedly people who did not actually own land sold a lot of it. This practice is not uncommon in Palestine and other contexts where settlement, property, and land rights form alongside one another—this is seizure and consolidation to transform land into something visible and movable into land markets.[7]

More importantly, according to one broker, the legal confusion benefits development. All of a sudden Masri became the landowner of large numbers of neighboring plots. He was his own neighbor for the purposes of drawing boundaries, for istimlak, compensation, and intrafirm land sales. I was told large swaths of land were redrawn into Rawabi in this way—one land broker claims that some villagers received as little as JOD1,000/dunam for plots with borders adjacent to those he sold to developers for as much as JOD40,000/dunam. He believes Masri sold that land to the firm he started with the Qataris for as much as JOD75,000/dunam.

As Rawabi establishes itself in contrast to an existing Palestine and Palestinians, the 'Attara experience suggests that many Palestinians will be left behind. The Palestinians who represent an important form of shared Palestinian identity and live on the land that is fundamental for Rawabi and its self-image, and who are its neighbors, are excluded. Rawabi is forcing villagers into a truncated market relationship where their only choice is to receive minimal or no compensation for their property. They are not participants in the labor market, and they have long had trouble provisioning or relying on older sources of income derived from the land—"I used to sell [olive] oil. Am I supposed to start buying it now?" Moreover, privatizing the image of Palestine makes the whole nation unstable: Why would they knock down old houses? "The trees, the songs, the olives are Palestinian, cultural, part of our heritage. . . . Why change the name? Why uproot the trees, the symbols of *sumud* ['Palestinian steadfastness']?"[8] Developers are targeting Palestinians based on certain ideas about tradition and modernity, and rural and urban, in the context of the privatization of the state. Increasingly, villages provide that vision, a shared memory of Palestine and a disappearing reference to it.

One politician made the distinction between economic development and investment. Rawabi, he says, is about investment. It does not help locals. "Why build buildings that may remain empty? Why not build factories? Or support agriculture? Why not help olive farming instead of uprooting trees to build?" And, in contrast to the potential buyers I interviewed, ʿAql, of the ʿAttara Municipality, suggested that the process of financialization and subjecting things to the market makes them less stable. The public-private land sale process dispossessed villagers as it enabled opportunities for mobility and long-term participation for potential buyers. If everything is consolidated and can be bought and sold, he asked, what would prevent another company from coming and buying Rawabi? What if an Israeli company buys it? The company owns only the site footprint but has administrative control over privately held land far beyond it. If there were new ownership, what would happen to those village lands? Interviews with villagers demonstrated a real anxiety about the conflation of capitalist and nationalist goals: "They took so much."

Market Creation and Social Integration

Who is going to move into Rawabi? The question of affordability is still "the million-dollar question" according to Rami Khoury of AMAL. Who is the middle class that is being imagined and projected into existence; who can both choose *and* afford to live there? Developers work hard to integrate economic and individual political and social concerns, and Palestinian desires for stability and a life beyond the occupation are critical to privatization. Developers say that a cultural shift is needed, and they target middle-class, urban populations to create a new buying class moving out of family homes, changing their expectations of what housing should be, and entering into mortgage and land markets as nuclear families and individuals—markets that they may have previously engaged in more collectively or markets that did not previously exist.

When I spoke to him in the summer of 2010, the president of the Bank of Palestine, Hashim Shawa, told me that the economy is still developing. There is a need to actively bring in new industries that will contribute to large-scale economic development. In particular, he said that Palestine needs a finance sector: the two cornerstones of a new economy will be housing and a private pension system. Housing will provide "equity in brick and mortar," jobs, an increase in consumer spending on white appliances, and so on; a private pension system will provide long-term financing and funding for banks. Eventually the goal is to create a high-tech sector, "to follow the Israeli [economic growth] model hopefully."

Palestinians, according to Shawa, are now willing to pay down debt monthly, but they are still reluctant to do long-term mortgage financing. They do not understand that they "are paying into their own bricks and mortar, that there will be capital appreciation . . . there is a strange" resistance due in part to "the lack of awareness, and people feeling like they're being ripped off." One of the primary goals of AMAL, the mortgage financing program, is to "shift the culture" and convince Palestinians to equate long-term debt with stability and regularity rather than uncertainty. AMAL has already grown the mortgage market in Palestine fivefold, says Shawa. But the banks need to "be a part of the shift" from "traditional" family housing that "should be phased out," at the same time as they cultivate that shift, and integrate people into debt relationships—debts that are in many ways also moral obligations and social relations (Graeber 2011). In the absence of wider political economic stability, or wage stability, people have increasingly felt that they are getting richer as property values increase. And they maintain their standard of living and liquidity through debt. Such a situation could be understood as a bubble waiting to burst, but with loans guaranteed from outside and the political environment producing land scarcity, risk is situated with individual consumers but not necessarily among lenders and big capitalists.

At least in the short term, there is a mismatch between the growing availability of housing and the pool of willing buyers. Developers chip away at the idea that Palestinians are predominately homeowners; most young people, according to market research carried out by the Palestine Investment Fund for its Al-Reehan development, do not consider themselves to be homeowners, and would move out of family compounds if there was affordable, adequate housing available. Again, the PCBS reports that more than 80 percent of Palestinians are homeowners (Maan News 2011; State of Palestine, Palestinian Central Bureau of Statistics 2018). Normalcy is powerfully appealing to many Palestinians, and in this case, normalcy is increasingly framed in terms of class aspiration, consumerism, and property. This is the market gap formed out of class consolidation and aspiration. These ideas are given shape in the developments, while at the same time they fix and distribute capital investment to make different and previously unprofitable parts of Palestine profitable.

That mismatch is why continual process is important to this development—market creation is ongoing. But capital and investment are not new for Palestine. Political power determines, and is determined by, market forces, and both form the context for social ideas, life, and reproduction. Today, under post-Oslo occupation political economics, real estate development is making communities for debts, generating capital from land within the area system, and integrating Palestine into regional and global economies. On a political level real estate development is enabled and justified by the ideas of a "housing shortage" and "national priority" for affordable housing. Class itself is shifting, cultural, and situational.

Chapter Eight

Critique, Capital, and the Landscape

THE IDEOLOGICAL PRACTICES mobilized as part of the Oslo accords—the PA and the symbols of self-rule, the idea of an open market under occupation, the internalization and formalization of a land regime—and the contemporary state-building project operate on the premise that the economy can be decoupled from politics and administration. Not unlike other representations that preceded it, Rawabi and its international backers have a vision of a Palestine that it is open—open for business, open for building, and open for habitation. This is a "green," "ancient" Palestine that, with some prodding and economic initiative, will be transformed along with those Palestinians who are stuck somewhere between modernity and poverty. This vision of progress through development, planning, and urbanization lies in direct contrast to both the lives of the rural laborers and the long history of Palestinian urbanism.

In chapter 4 I discussed some of the ways land in Palestine has been kept empty through Israeli control, planning, and practice. In this chapter I describe how the idea of the land, and the people and buildings on it, is tied to relations of production that have given nature an identity separate from politics and history, and beyond human relations (N. Smith 1984). Palestinians are well aware of how the political situation is inscribed in the landscape, yet by placing rural life outside of discussions of political economy, even critical discourse reshapes it in ways that may enable privatization and development.

As one architectural critic and planner told me, "Palestinian society is small-scale, family driven," and Rawabi is an "external import of a global phenomenon." This is one of the more salient critiques of Rawabi in Palestine, and it sits atop a framework in which present relations are understood through dead reckoning. Rather than a unidirectional import, I believe private development is emblematic of much wider processes of neoliberalization and simultaneous state building and state dissolution—Rawabi is a site where Palestinian politics and general forms of state-economy relations are visible. Moreover, it might also represent greater integration of Palestine into global markets by accommodating the current conditions of occupation with the imperatives of global capital. This is a Palestinian capitalist project that requires imagining, making, and growing a middle class of potential buyers, encouraging certain kinds of economic and political aspirations, and integrating them into an alternate political economic vision of Palestine. This project has the potential to create widespread and intertwined political, cultural, and economic shifts.

Anthropological approaches to international development (e.g., Ferguson 1994) describe how that endeavor imposes its own worldview on problems and solves those problems rather than the ones that may exist. The development situation in Palestine is related but further along: interventions, local governance, and state building are made in a dialectical relationship with changing ideological and political economic contexts. Interventions and their targets change together. Development and investment are not neoliberalizing Palestine in any single or straightforward way; they demonstrate the specific ties between Palestine and the rest of the world, even while circumscribed by and suspended within Israeli territorial, political, and economic imperatives. In my framework, Oslo is not a moment of rupture that opened Palestine to new forms of intervention; it is embedded in a long history of political economic control in Palestine. It marks one moment of transition when the dynamics between Palestine's uneven integration into regional and world markets changed and when Palestinian capitalist actors became more fully empowered to manage them.[1]

Discourse and Imposition

Palestinian commentators and critics aim directly at the distinction between an urban future and a rural past and present. But unlike NGOs, the government, and private developers, they seek not to build upon and transcend that tradition, but to strengthen it in the face of encroachment. For critics like Raja Shehadeh (2012), the famous Palestinian human rights attorney and essayist, the changes that something like Rawabi brings are an imposition and distortion. Shehadeh is one of the most prominent Palestinians critical of Rawabi, and I quote him here at length. He describes his first experience of Rawabi like this:

> We passed by the area where the new Palestine city of Rawabi is to be established. When there are over a hundred villages around Ramallah, what is the point of establishing a new one? Why not expand existing ones, keeping the development in line with the contours of the hills? By acquiring land, chopping off the tops of hills and destroying the landscape, we are only mimicking the Israeli ways, which for decades we have been criticizing. (Shehadeh 2012, 93)

He continues:

> Only after seeing the new city of Rawabi being constructed in the hills north of Ramallah did I understand the full ramifications of our defeat. Rather than struggle to gain our own space and assert our own way of life, we seek to copy the colonizer and use the same destructive methods that damage our land and natural heritage . . . . Yet rather than fight the battle to lift the restrictions on building in the confined villages spread throughout the West Bank, a group of local and Qatari investors set their sights on one of the most attractive hills north of Ramallah which rises 780 meters above sea level. Two and a half years ago they began buying terraced land cultivated with olives, from unsuspecting farmers for knock-down prices, in order to build the new city of Rawabi . . . . The land they were unable to buy had to be confiscated by the Palestinian Authority. . . . Qataris don't know the terrain. Most of them have never visited . . . . [How could Rawabi's environmental rhetoric be expected] to convince anyone when we could see the attractive village of Ajoul close by and contrast it with the sterile monstrosity that was being erected on hills destroyed for that purpose. To get to this artificial creation more roads will be needed. All this to house 25,000 middle-class Palestinians who could easily have

found homes in the villages surrounding Ramallah had an effort been exerted by the Authority to pressure the Israelis to loosen their control over land-use planning . . . . The hills are now cluttered with piles of rubble from new construction work and roads being built as Ramallah expands. Our guide pointed out two housing projects that looked exactly like Jewish settlements, with rows of identical houses one next to the other, totally alien to our traditional way of building. (Shehadeh 2012, 157–62)

Shehadeh outlines the intertwining arguments that form the prevailing critique—that Rawabi mimics Israeli settlement, that it is somehow external, and that this imposition is an unnatural form of development that not only contrasts with but in fact destroys traditional ways of life. Shehadeh's arguments cohere around specific assumptions about Palestinianness, nature, and Palestinian history. Others have suggested Rawabi represents an "architecture [that] will suit the needs of colonial invaders" (Yehya 2012) and that it demonstrates how "Palestinian nationalism is being transformed into a zeal for real-estate deals . . . rather than a focus on liberating human beings and giving them the chance to decide for themselves how they want to live and what they want their communities to look like" (Abunimah 2011). Critics are mindful of the effects that colonial planning has on Palestinian vernacular and the need for community autonomy but sometimes minimize how development is a Palestinian class project.

If villages are circumscribed and produced by political forces, so is the nature around them. Shehadeh asks why the developers build a "sterile monstrosity" instead of conforming to the hills; yet the Palestinian developers and Palestinian bureaucrats are explicit about the ways they see their development as built upon and working in concert with both Palestinian vernacular and those exact same hills. Both are rooted in political images of timelessness and forms of landholding that in fact have a more recent genealogy. Without an emphasis on internal differentiation and class, critics and developers share assumptions about nature, and about architecture's relationship to the land, but they propose different approaches to them.

Part of the reason discourse and critique around development have been narrowed is practical: developers work to shape public debate, and news organizations, especially Palestinian Arabic-language outlets, are said to be afraid of litigation after the row over the report from the Bisan Center for Research and Development. Raja Khalidi's Rawabi op-ed proposed a way for development to aid national and pan-Arab goals. Arguing that private class aspiration represents a general failure of the national movement, but also specifically with respect to questions of land defense, widespread imprisonment, and national self-determination, Khalidi suggested that there might be opportunities to combine the tracks and strengthen nationalist politics. The newspaper where Khalidi had been publishing articles on the economy for a few years rejected the op-ed on the grounds it could not contractually publish a piece critical of its advertisers; others were similarly disinclined.

Like the media practices I described in chapter 3, Rawabi also attempts to throw its weight around in more private conversation. Around the same time as the conflict around the Bisan report in 2014, Rawabi threatened Palestinians for their posts on Facebook. In summer 2017, in response to critiques of Rawabi, an ostensibly grassroots organization called the Rawabi Owners' Union issued an Arabic-language statement on social media defending Rawabi, themselves, and Bashar Masri from attacks (Rawabi Owners' Union 2017). During a moment of extreme Israeli repression and violence against nonviolent protests in Jerusalem, the owners worried about "a systematic campaign of defamation and abuse . . . beyond rumor to curses and accusations against the city's residents and developers." Those slanderous insults, they maintained, are based on "foreign agendas" that "aim to discredit the pioneering national project . . . and undermine social unity at a time when we desperately need it." They said they were proud of the project and of the planning, and they claimed to represent a large portion of Palestinian civil society. They were protective of Masri and his "remarkable national achievement" and denounced the "organized campaign" against him. And they rejected the occupation, the treatment of Palestinian prisoners, and the Israel Defense Forces (IDF) closure of al-Aqsa. The union threatened to prosecute anyone who slanders, or insults them, Rawabi, or Masri. Instead of hoping to sway critics directly, they instead invite media to visit the city, learn the facts, and convey the true image and message of the city and its population.

Several things are important here: first, that they felt the need to issue such a statement about national politics and allowed it to circulate; second, that it is not obvious who wrote the statement or why (given the small number of residents at that time); third, that they threatened to prosecute; and finally, that they invited people not to discuss Rawabi critically, an action they equate with slander, but to see the city. They worked to funnel and control the narrative as they tried—with limited success of course—to quiet online discussion. And unlike other authors, they were able to get their piece published in newspapers. Despite the obvious impossibility of shutting down private conversation on a huge public topic, developers can go a long way in determining which parts of Rawabi are integrated into authorized public discourses. Palestinians are treated as and assumed to be abstract, a target population, so the image they want to circulate has an outward orientation. They emphasize a peaceful polity waiting to be activated by peaceful investment. The consequence is that structural critique is funneled toward individual experience.

Clearly Rawabi has received a lot of attention in the international and Palestinian media and is very well known in the West Bank. But it is not as important as all the attention would imply.[2] It is important for different reasons than are generally assumed—it is not constitutive of Palestine, nor is it an outside imposition or a "Palestinian settlement." It is a large, public indication of one direction in which Palestine is moving, and it will continue to require a huge number of political, administrative, and practical shifts in Palestine and between Palestinians. As the Rawabi construction site becomes a physical place and a conceived space, accounts that are necessarily narrow aggregate to contribute to the way it is described, understood, and received. Here, I hope to shed light on the space-making process in Rawabi through the elaboration of the site; its political economic origins; broader relationships; ramifications; and the legal, political, and material changes that it requires and that form around it.

Rural Past and the National Narrative

In nationalist and political rhetoric, Palestine is often composed of a dignified rural peasantry that toils thanklessly, steadfast against Israeli colonization, dispossessed or bamboozled into selling the land that provides their livelihood. But population in the West Bank is distributed in very specific ways by blue line plans, general harassment, Israeli designs on certain parts of the West Bank, and economic restrictions, that were exacerbated by Oslo's categories of A, B, and C. These Palestinians are not backward, traditional, unconnected to Palestine, or immune to politics: they live in difficult circumstances because of clear, recent, political phenomena.[3]

Across the West Bank, fewer than 12 percent work in the agricultural sector, and more than 50 percent in the service sector (Palestinian National Authority, Palestinian Central Bureau of Statistics 2009). In 'Abwayn, 5 percent of the population works in agriculture, in 'Attara 15 percent, and in 'Ajjul 20 percent (Applied Research Institute-Jerusalem 2012a, 2012b, 2012c). The importance of small-scale agriculture is as much rhetorical and cultural as economic.

In many ways, that cultural prominence emerged as a *consequence of occupation*. The historical record has been stratified due to a clear focus on the wealthy Jerusalem families who left behind libraries and archives, while everyday forms of Arab urban life in Jaffa, Haifa, Nazareth, and Jerusalem were among the first casualties of the foundation of Israel.[4] Moreover, "the loss of metropolitan centers through war also meant the loss of urbanism as a cultural product of big cities. Small towns became the arena for the formulation of the ethics of political resistance, but also for the restructuring of normative behavior. In this sense the values of small towns became the values of society in general" (Tamari 1988, 55).

Palestinians have long identified with images of rural life based on their precolonial history and the steadfast persistence of some Palestinian villages. The national narrative centers claims of authenticity and autochthony, and in the present it operates to bind together different classes of Palestinians through a shared cultural history. The image of the peasant has been a national organizing principle, a signifier of struggle and a central character in the national and nationalist Palestinian self-image. The *fallah* is a "symbolic site of unity": "As nationalist discourse remolds memory in order to turn the peasant into a unifying symbol, it sheds the *fallah* of its distinctive class features, rough edges, subversive capacities, and past treacheries. The *fallah* is able to serve as a signifier that unites and mobilizes by virtue of the fact that it dissimulates past and present differences within the national movement, in the interests of a leadership with particular class interests" (Swedenburg 1990, 19).

The figure of the fallah is used to naturalize Palestinian links to the soil and to permanently link Palestinians and Palestinianness with Palestine. "The overwhelming cultural presence of the *fallah* flows from the endangered status of the Palestinian nation. It is a nation imagined but unrealized, a people whose relation to their territory has been severed again and again, whose identity is tenuous and constantly under threat. The figure of the peasant serves as a crucial ideological weapon in the Palestinian confrontation with Israeli colonial policies" (Swedenburg 1990, 19).

Elements of the cultural projection of village life clash with economic history. Large-scale, mechanized agriculture began in the West Bank more than a century ago in citrus production, and the occupation had a major role in shaping Palestinian political economy. Labor and economics have never been external to Palestinian vernacular, space, or politics. The colonization of Palestine preceded the occupation, and Palestine has long been integrated into world markets and politics.[5] Moreover, small-scale agriculture in Palestine has diminished for some of the same reasons it has diminished around the world: industrialization and technological inputs, especially in transportation; labor transformation; and the concentration of capital in urban centers. Relationships to the land have historically also been political economic questions.

In the pre-1948 period, Ottoman reforms not only spurred out-migration, in part as a result of new laws about conscription, but also made land visible in new ways through one of the first projects to regularize title and integrate land into a functioning market (Norris 2013; Rabie 2018). Changes in tenure created owners for collectively used lands and the possibility of a land market, and that market expanded rapidly as a result of European—Jewish—immigration. Prior to the foundation of Israel settlers, lacking a state that could manage expropriation on their behalf, had to purchase land and did so at rather high prices. These phenomena gave Palestinian *ownership* a political valence in the face of market-based dispossession (Mousa 2006, 299). In urban areas, barriers on labor immigration to Palestine marked certain labor pools as Arab and racialized class structure (Banko 2019). At the same time, the globalized Palestinian merchant class brought ideas and practices from abroad that were integrated into Palestine as culture, practice, and vernacular (Norris 2019). Other parts of Palestine experienced proletarianization and dispossession as a result of British prohibitions on land rights and attempts to privatize common land, and terrible harvests and debt conditions in the 1930s. This too made land available to Zionists to purchase as they began colonization in larger and larger numbers (C. Anderson 2015). In part because of those land sales, Palestinian landlessness meant the intermixing of economic and political dispossession. Obviously, it was not ameliorated by "settler developmentalist ideology" (C. Anderson 2018). Moreover, there was a downward pressure on elite Palestinians and Palestinian capital, and as a result of conflict, bank holdings became suspect. The Arab Bank, founded in 1933, called in its capital in 1936; British banks became unsafe and were seized by Zionists (Mitter 2020). By the time of the Mandate, some of the foundations for racializing class had been established, and the British sought to encourage a specifically Zionist industrial sector that further separated Arab and Jewish people and economies. British monopoly protections for Zionist firms and permissiveness toward discriminatory hiring practices in turn encouraged the importation of a Jewish working class, which increased cost of living for Arabs in mixed areas and excluded them from participating in new labor markets—creating the economic basis for the pre-Israel Zionist "state within a state" (B. J. Smith 1993).

All of this contributed not only to rural radicalization and the Revolt of 1936–1939, but also to the radicalization of the wider Palestinian movement. It is a backdrop to narratives of Palestinian resistance to Zionist settlement and occupation that begin with 1948.

The historical development, class position, and radical lineages of the Palestinian peasantry (as peasantry) do not neatly fit a contemporary nationalist and developmentalist narrative. Rural-urban division and the figure of the fallah was held out as an opposition to the problems of modernity, and aspects of that identity were selectively cultivated and incorporated into ideas about modern subjectivity (Selim 2004; Gasper 2009), as well as into scholarship that presented peasants descriptively but with little engagement with the context or real contours of everyday life and labor (Mitchell 2002).

Salim Tamari complicates the picture of how the figure of the fallah was flattened and brought into the national imaginary. Historically, an urban intelligentsia morphed contempt of rural Palestinians into identification with them for political reasons. In the first phase of the national movement, the fallah was the

> Cannon fodder of the movement, mobilized for the national cause, but left out of its leadership. In the second phase, they became its hallowed subject: sentimentalized and elevated, but rarely the object of its organizational network. In both cases the tillers of the soil were perceived as the True Palestinians, the spirit of the nation and the *raison d'etre* of the national movement. What unites the ethnographic content of these two periods is an obsession with peasant lore seen as embodying the spirit of national culture, and being undermined by external forces: the City, modernization, and colonialism in the 1930s, and dismemberment and Zionism in the 1970s. (Tamari 1988, 77–78)

So, in the political imagination, these urban intellectuals will "objectify the [fellah] into a faceless collective identity, whose function is either the justification of relations of exploitation ('the [fellah] is extremely backward') or the elevation of peasantry to a condition of uncontaminated purity. In either case the peasant is rendered an *object*, and not the *subject*, of nationalist ideology" (82).

Idealization and affirmation of Palestinian presence was a response to 1967 that led to a specific version of village life becoming sanctified in the political imagination. Lisa Taraki has described forms of cultural politicization that emerged after 1967 and the various revivals and cultural festivals that contributed to the "museumification" of Palestinian culture (Taraki 1990). She describes a Styrofoam Palestinian village built in Birzeit in 1984 and quotes an onlooker complaining about the absurdity of a festival explaining village life or traditional foods such as *musakhkhan*, and *za'atar*. Consequently, other ways of life, labor, or understanding of dispossession were less relevant to shared national narratives.[6]

Culturally and politically, the idea of occupation as a moment of rupture has meant that much of our history has been infused with national commitments organized around ideas of an agrarian, prelapsarian peace disrupted by the impositions of Zionist colonial modernity. And when critiques assume a stable fellahi identity as the basis for both identification and stratification, they carry some strange baggage. Nationalist folklore revival as a form of cultural resistance in the 1970s was based in large part, as Tamari demonstrates, on the Palestinian orientalist and salvage anthropologist Taufik Canaan's work. Through readings that were "hagiographic and uncritical," Canaan provided the basis for an argument for reactive nationalism and self-evident autochthony in the service of national struggle (Tamari 2004, 39).[7] It is not difficult to sense a contradiction behind the historiography when we are talking about some of the longest-inhabited and most world historically important cities on the planet.

Because of the emergence of this image as a political claim, consistently reiterated and made self-evident through the national movement and the resilience of both the occupation and resistance, it has not only persisted but has become a node of shared Palestinian cultural consciousness everywhere. And it has returned to urban populations who identify with it not on a class or material basis, but as part of the foundation of a national political identity. At the same time, the villages and villagers experience ongoing change as a result of "the two countervailing trends of urban peasantization and rural suburbanization [that] have narrowed the disparities in the habitat conditions . . . both in terms of class diversity and in terms of the cultural distinctions that separate villages from townships" (Tamari 2008, 50). Ideological, practical, and geographical distinctions between peasants and nonpeasants are dissipating in some ways. But despite shared cultural ideas, the West Bank is seeing a high degree of middle-class growth and consequent class stratification as a result of private initiative, presented as modernization.

Developers stress that they have planned Rawabi in ways simultaneously suited to Palestinian life and "ancient" existence on the landscape, while "[taking] cues from international contemporary practices" to "transfer expertise" and "build a city which will become a model for future development in Palestine." Many Palestinian critics of privatization mourn the loss of the land, national patrimony, and tradition. Both proponents and opponents of development rely on a version of Palestinian history that has obscured class and economic change.

Agriculture in Palestine is invoked as a cultural narrative, a way to identify Palestine before colonization and to remain Palestinian against change. But the rural imaginary of Palestinian life prior to 1948 is in fact one of unequal market integration; political and economic pressure; proletarianization; dispossession; and insecurity along racial, ethnic, and national as well as class lines. Peasants endure hardship and humiliation as agricultural laborers subject to debt, landlords, and seasons. After Oslo carved up the landscape, they tend to live in places where they more directly experience Israeli prerogative. They are laborers who, like "the peasantry" everywhere, are highly stratified and who are being negatively impacted by privatization and market-based dispossession.

My goal here is to situate the town-country distinction in a discussion of both the Palestinian political context and the global political economy. Critical discussion of privatization and political change has emphasized the *imposition* of something on a stable Palestinian nation. But it has also demonstrated the widespread and shared ideological assumptions around development in Palestine.

Although both developers and critics share an attachment to rural identity and agree that the fellahi way of life is being destroyed, they believe it is happening for different reasons. Both counterpose privatization to tradition, and in doing so they render class stratification and the consequences of privatization exogenous. This framework obscures the relationships between Palestinian capitalists, market logics, settler-colonial political-administrative imperatives, and real work done in Palestine. And if development and its critiques are based on different relationships to the same ideas and language of agrarianism, then both contribute to make the development narrative viable. Critics see modernization as a threat to an imagined past; they see encroachment.

Conditions in villages are difficult, and few urban critics seriously imagine reverse migration there. At the same time, the PA and developers offer a corrective that—even if fantastic and unrealized, and even if unavailable to the villagers themselves (whether they can be defined as peasantry or not)—is based on a shared conception of Palestinian identity. Because of that fact, it is increasingly legible and appealing to many current and future middle-class Palestinians.

Land and Capital

Real estate development is better understood in its wider context and as a consequence of how Palestinian capitalists are benefiting within the political situation; how settler capitalism unevenly develops environments, forms of accumulation, subjectivities, and cultures; and how a state is being produced today in ways that are likely to maintain the present context. Cultures change over time, and countless colonial and postcolonial critics have insisted that colonialism and the unequal relationships that emerge under it are primary agents of social, economic, and political change. What does the romance of the peasant, landscape, and past enable and disable? In terms of Palestinian state-building today, that romance makes it difficult to see what Palestinians are doing to build Palestine and forces analysis into a binary: Palestinianness versus the occupation-capital nexus. But the latter produces and is inflected by the former, and the forms that economics take under settler colonialism and occupation produce dynamics of market integration and exclusion, shifting rural-urban distinctions as well as ordering social relations.

Like all markets, land markets are not just about circulation and profit; they are also geographical, productive, social, and cultural. They interpellate subjects into broader politics and networks and, in this instance, ideas about political development and the future. They are relations. This distinction is of course not unique to Palestine. In England, says Raymond Williams, there is an "idealization of a 'natural' or 'moral' economy on which so many have relied, as a contrast to the thrusting ruthlessness of the new capitalism. There was very little that was moral or natural about it" (1975, 37). The idea of a happy rural past—neglecting the hard labor conditions, brigandage, poverty, and generally terrible situation of farmers in precapitalist England—was "an idealization, based on a temporary situation and on a deep desire for stability, [that] served to cover and to evade the actual and bitter contradictions of the time" (37). In *Culture and Imperialism*, Edward Said (1993) correctly critiques Williams for not adequately taking account of colonialism and imperialism. Williams is right that the romance of agriculture mystifies economic change and class antagonism, but neither can be understood without reference to British imperialism. If *The Country and the City* is "[mainly] about how English culture has dealt with land, its possession, imagination, and organization" (82), then the ideas of land and nature need to be situated in political and economic contexts in order to adequately base political critique. Whether in British novels or in a national movement, culture and cultural production emerge from existing dynamics and circulate back into the ways that politics and possibilities are understood.

Palestinian history is too often understood through contemporary narratives. The task here is not to "refute a fallacious proposition in its own terms [but] to combine a critical attitude to the facts as presented with the employment of an alternative method which can be used to provide a systematic and coherent account of the available evidence" (Owen 1993, 2). Much of the narrative around the rural versus the urban, progress versus backwardness, and mechanisms for political and economic integration into worldwide networks are neither new nor reflective of the present realities. Many forms of economic behavior in Palestine reflect the local and present situation but have analogs, build upon the past, and can tell us something about tendencies at a greater geographic and political scale.

Back to the Land

As former mayor of 'Attara Rawhi 'Aql suggested, when a place is bought, sold, and renamed, then the ideological, political, and memory ties to land can come with it. One land broker told me that developers "bought the land cheap because it wasn't useful for agriculture. They sold it, they mined it, they sold the rocks, they sold the land itself. . . . It's treasure. It's like gold." Developers have managed to engineer growth by titling, consolidating, and putting land into a new market. They have figured out how to sell parts of it off, to sell parts of it back to themselves, and to integrate meaning as added value. The threats to Palestinians living outside of cities are not simply the imposition of a new vernacular or the loss of an old culture; they are about a growing land market and, for many, the commodification of national symbols.

Political and cultural ties to land might be abstract, but they are the clear outcomes of dispossession by market and colonial relations. Rawabi exists in the context of a preexisting settler-capital land market, in a shifting legal terrain used to consolidate control over the land. [8] If there is anything new here, it is not the dispossession of owners from their lands; it might be, however, the Palestinian/PA formalization of consolidated, large-scale ownership against old ideas and narratives of steadfastness. The PA actively supports the private sector by changing the legal and administrative framework for land ownership and does so with the intention of integrating the West Bank into global markets and encouraging investment alongside specific ideas of stability, autochthony, and unanimity among Palestinians. The political context, shifting and overlapping jurisdictions, and the land market orient practices and means of control over large pieces of land in Palestine.

Ideas that inflect the land shape it and are reintegrated into ideas about it. In *Uneven Development*, Neil Smith (1984) argues that capitalism has produced unequally developed landscapes that contain both poverty and wealth, industrial urbanization and agricultural diminishment; and this culminates in the processes of imperial capitalism that classify and commodify space in its relationship to the metropole. Accepting the premise that Palestine is unevenly integrated rather than separated means the relevant questions, at least for the West Bank in the contemporary political economy, become about localized underdevelopment (Rodney 1982) as the framework for understanding de-development (Roy 1999). Ideas about nature and human relationships to the land are part of how capitalism comes to seem universal—Karl Marx calls the production of the idea of a separate natural world "second nature." And this second nature is the basis for arguments that both support and resist capital investment and development in Palestine. Smith suggests that "to the anti-imperialist imagination, our space at home in the peripheries has been usurped and put to use by outsiders for their purpose. It is therefore necessary to seek out, to map, to invent, or to discover a third nature, not pristine and pre-historical . . . but deriving from the deprivations of the present" (N. Smith, quoted in Said 1993). Privatization seemingly would conflict with territorial collective ambitions previously understood as national liberation. I think Rawabi aims to accomplish both, and that collective national logics with shifting referents have *enabled* market relations. Both capital and settler-colonial administration are premised on the theoretical, and real processes to create social relations and make them seem common sense.

The next chapter expands this discussion of land outward toward the state scale and examines law, rights, and land claims to ask how the state form can emerge through legal reform and market relations, within an occupation. Of the bodies of law that can determine rights to the land—Ottoman, Jordanian, PA, Israeli military law—not one is tied to a specific or currently existing territorial state. What might it mean that they are being used to incorporate land and differentiate people and produce legal authority on the state scale?

Chapter Nine

Settlers and
the Land

IN THE SPRING AND SUMMER OF 2010, during the "settlement freeze" announced by the Netanyahu government under pressure from the Obama administration, Israeli settlers in the West Bank began mobilizing against Rawabi. Right-wing members of the Israeli Knesset joined in protest with residents of Ateret and representatives of various settler organizations—most notably Regavim, The National Land Protection Trust—in the media, on the web, in the courts, and at the site. In March of that year, a handful of settlers attempted to set up an outpost in an empty Palestinian housing development near Birzeit. (The Israeli military had seized the area during the second intifada and declared it a closed military zone, and construction was brought to a halt.) The outpost was supposedly a response to the existence of Rawabi and an attempt to "create a Jewish territorial sequence from Ofra to Ateret, [because] the Palestinians plan to create a similar building sequence" (Grossman 2010). For a short time, settlers held regular demonstrations near the 'Attara bridge, and on one or two occasions marched toward Rawabi from Ateret. An inflammatory website went up at www.rawabi.co.il. Perhaps designed to trick googlers, it was nearly identical to www.rawabi.ps, save for the blood red background, invitation to witness Israel's failure to stop 24/7 Palestinian construction, and fantastical descriptions of how Palestinians planned to launch missiles from the development.

Security was the settlers' stated goal for these demonstrations and land seizures: even prior to completing the building sequence, they believed Rawabi would be a source of potential infiltrators in settlements (U. Baruch 2017).

That particular outpost was short-lived, but some of the main tactics that right-wing Israeli civilian settlers use to extend their territorial claims in the West Bank were visible. First, they presuppose a Jewish right to all of Historic Palestine and draw a false equivalence between state suppression of Israeli and Palestinian land rights. Second, they illegally occupy land in response to legal activity by Palestinians in areas under Palestinian control via the Oslo accords. The next step is to operationalize the idea of the law, legal classifications, and many "temporary" legal measures while arguing that the law is subjective and discriminatory. Settlers strive to shape law in the wake of their activities and to make Jewish Israeli presence in and political control over the West Bank permanent through practice and, ideally, retroactively under Israeli jurisdiction and law.

At different times, in different places, and for different legal categories of people, the bodies of law that overlap and apply to the West Bank include Ottoman, British Mandatory, Jordanian, Palestinian law post-Oslo, the Oslo regime, Israeli civil law, Israeli military law, and Israeli de facto control. In this context and absent a constitution or a bill of rights, the Israeli Supreme Court is empowered to rule—or to refuse to rule—on settlement practices and, thus, state jurisdiction and borders. The court is an important site for settler movements to make and elaborate claims about rights and legal practice, formal inclusion, equality, and citizenship. Israeli settlers bring civil law and jurisdiction with them to places that might have been previously been covered by international law.

Regavim demonstrates two parallel tracks of activism in the courts. First, it uses the language and idea of equality to reform legal practice to maintain race-based and discriminatory enforcement. Second, it strengthens Jewish legal and human rights to aid the slow creep of Israeli civil jurisdiction and control into territories previously outside of it. These are practical applications of persistent and notable trends in recent Israeli law and jurisprudence including continually shifting that legal precedent, the uneasy relationship between the 1948 and 1967 territories under Israeli control, the role of both civilians and the military in maximizing Israeli territory, and the settler-colonial logics that exclude the indigenous population from the protections of local or universal rights. International discourse, jurisprudence, and law are subject to the particular conditions and forms of liberal human rights practice in Israel and the territories it occupies.[1]

As it relates to state form, I take Zionism here to be an ideology and movement for colonial settlement that incorporates Jewish people of European, Arab, and other origins into an ethnically exclusive nation-state. Although many early thinkers in the Zionist movement sought a kind of racial emancipation, through the state and on the basis of rights and inclusion in civil institutions, Jewish Israeli citizens become opposed to Muslim and Christian Arabs living beyond its internal borders but within its jurisdiction. The act of settlement expands legal jurisdiction for Jewish citizens of Israel in the West Bank and, consequently, pushes de facto borders. Colonization with the goal of permanent settlement—settler colonialism—presupposes the need for generational stability and formal, enduring institutions to maintain status and hierarchy.

Practically speaking, settlements "have operated in three major ways: (1) they have restricted Palestinians' movement and development; (2) they have been used as tools for surveillance; and (3) they have served as an ethnic policing mechanism" (Gordon 2008, 118), and they have necessitated a system of ethnic jurisdiction. In sum and alongside the military and police, settlers are part of the web of control over the subject population in the West Bank. Settlers use legal claims to pull the court to the right and solidify Jewish privilege, rights, and law, and to limit both Palestinian jurisdiction and recourse. This brings more of the land in the West Bank under Israeli legal authority while excluding Palestinians from its protections. Here too, separation and "occupation" are insufficient descriptions. In a nonstate situation like the Palestinian West Bank, where state sovereignty can barely intercede, international law bears more weight than it might elsewhere. As Palestinians create quasi-state institutions of small-scale governance with international ties, settlers and their constituency in the government struggle to define what those international relationships can look like; and then to subordinate those relationships to expanding civil law and limit possibilities for Palestinian sovereignty.

When it comes to building and defining which groups of people can live in which parts of the land, practices around the law separate groups by race and consequent relation to different bodies of law, even in the same place. In a situation where precedent is constantly shifting, the law—the idea of it, settler and state practices of land control and dispossession, the definitions of rights to the land, and jurisdiction—and the elaboration of settler human rights bind civilian settlers to their state through the control of the West Bank. Malleable relationships between people and territory in that rights framework make meaningful distinctions between settlers and the state, or between the

1948 and 1967 territories, impossible. Settlers are enacting Israeli civil and civilian control over the West Bank by invoking different combinations of settler and liberal discourse, Jewish rights, human rights, and Israeli legal rights against Palestinian presence and, often, the signs of their existence. Settlement activity brings the law into territory, and precedent is enabled by the elaboration of civil jurisdiction over settlers themselves in territories under military control. Land, titling, and laws form a framework for practice that is both fluid and opaque, but that enables and disables certain types of people from holding land or making legal claims. Jurisdiction over the West Bank has covered Jewish Israelis, and subsequently/retroactively the land where they reside, but has excluded Palestinians who may also be on that land. At the state scale, Israeli imperative has been to control but not to annex, to exercise power over Palestinian land without conferring rights to the people there.

Regavim uses the language of universal human rights to spread an exclusionary nationalist agenda into the Israeli legal system and onto the West Bank. Settlers are moving from fighting Palestinians directly through intimidation, harassment, violence, graffiti, and arson to fighting them in the courts and by demanding state enforcement. Violence is increasingly abstract and depersonalized. Legal activism is productive regardless of the outcome of individual cases: whether the court rules or postpones right-wing filings, settlers use them to formalize claims against Palestinians, to assert expansive rights on the basis of their Jewish identity, to minimize Palestinian presence on the land, and as part of their larger reform agenda. Human rights claims are the vehicles settlers use to enter into occupied areas from which they have been formally—although not actually—excluded. Simultaneously, the Knesset continues to pass laws to regularize, formalize, and normalize settlement practice on the West Bank.

Through the new technique of petitions that mirror those of "leftist" human rights organizations, settlers critique the system, make arguments about the unequal application of laws, and use those arguments to extend Jewish privilege and dispossess Palestinians. A contradiction necessarily emerges here between whatever forms of international law govern the occupation, a discourse on the universality of rights, and a settler-colonial regime in which a privileged group is empowered to act on behalf of the state. In practice this is similar to the production of physical "facts on the ground" by Israeli citizens' active colonization—the "civilian occupation" (Segal and Weizman 2003)—and formalized by military orders that happen in local-scale settlements throughout the Occupied Territories. As a right-wing nationalist technique, litigation has the effect of legalizing and instantiating prior Israeli practices. International law is subject to local jurisdiction, and liberal rights discourse is bound to its illiberal Israeli context. Settlers are going to the courts to extend jurisdiction and administration far into the West Bank. This combines to rationalize de facto control of the West Bank, as part of a practical, implicit annexation process.

Regavim v. Rawabi

In 2014, Regavim sued Israeli officials responsible for the West Bank over Rawabi, in a case that brings together the logics of rights claims in Israel and the West Bank today, the mushy institutions that comprise the privatized state, and two of the main characters in this story (H.C., 3355/14, *Regavim v. Minister of Defense et al.* [not published]). By 2014, many of Regavim's techniques had been honed, in particular the use of satellite, aerial, and on-the-ground photography and mapping of various plans and existing work onto the area system. In this case, given the scale and scope of Rawabi, Regavim made claims about the infringement of Zionist national rights in order to target and "reverse" building, and minimize Palestinian rights to the land. That work to reverse Arab presence operates as both specific barrier and as a larger legal reform project.

I became aware that Regavim had sued Rawabi when the first news reports emerged about a year later, and Regavim asked the government to enforce regulations around road building (Lazaroff 2016). Plaintiffs argued that roads would be built on private property and that property issues ought to be resolved prior to road construction. Those filings have not been published publicly and Rawabi developers could not share details, so I hired an Israeli lawyer and a translator and petitioned the court for access. It turns out that the case builds on a previous set of claims—Regavim first argued that Rawabi is illegally dumping small amounts of construction waste nearby in Area c, amounting to a steady "creep" and encroachment into an area where construction is not permitted and closer to Jewish presence. This is a literal pile of dirt that, "beyond the illegality of the works . . . also creates a strong sense of insecurity amongst the settlers." The danger posed by the dirt was quickly resolved, and Rawabi stopped dumping. They did so even though the Israeli Civil Administration asserted it had been done in Area b and that the two parties are in "constant contact" with one another (see figure 9.1).

So Regavim moved on to the road issue. Through photos and maps, they used planning as a tool against building.[2] They argued that there was no plan for Rawabi and that it lacked a "holistic logistical solution" already, even at

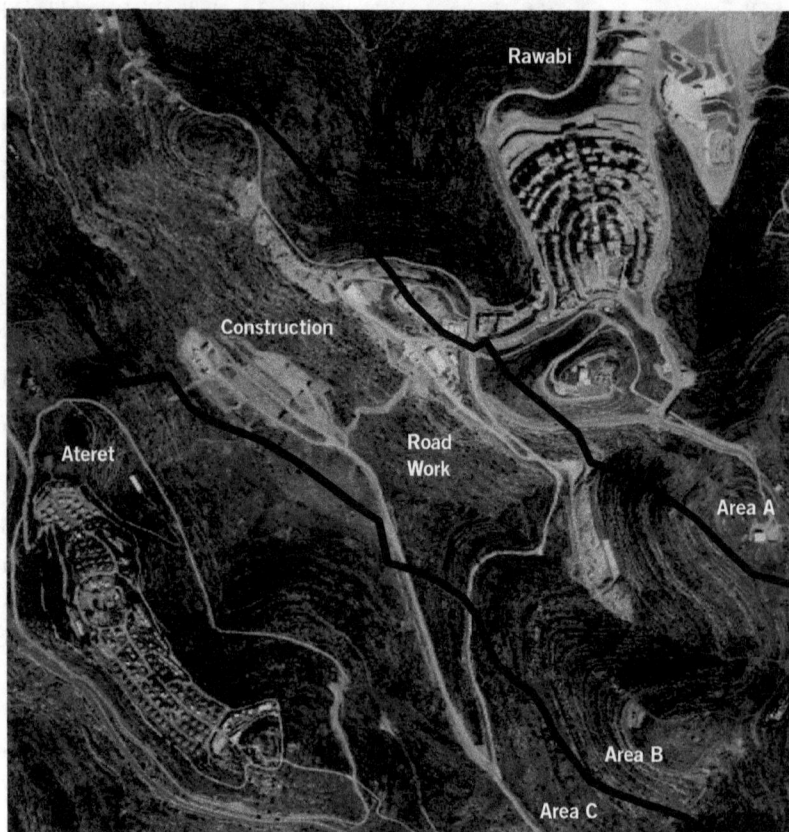

FIGURE 9.1 Rawabi, Ateret, and the location of slowly creeping evidence of Palestinian life Regavim is suing to regulate: construction, mounds, transportation systems, and so on. Image by Meagan A. Snow, based on Esri World Imagery, data from the Palestinian Ministry of Local Government, and the various legal filings.

the beginning stages. And this is just "the tip of the iceberg." In its own defense, Rawabi argued (with potential consequences for discussions of the PA, istimlak, and opacity) that it did not have easy contact with surrounding landowners, that the Israeli Civil Administration would not help them locate owners of disputed plots, that problems had arisen due to powers of attorney being signed either overseas or in PA embassies. "The problem is that some of the landowners live in Palestine, and the Civil Administration refuses to accept power of attorney ratified by the 'State of Palestine.'" The idea that something discernably objective governs what happens in the land is vital to making sure that is not the case, hence the curious situation in which settlers argue for planning on behalf of Palestinian private owners, or a military apparatus refuses to accept Palestinian authority over areas it ostensibly covers. All of this raises questions not only about what governs the processes through which developers have acquired land, but also about the creeping Israeli civil jurisdiction over the landscape and the "State of Palestine." Finally, Regavim argued that demolition orders were being unenforced. Through complaints about land ownership and building, modeled on claims against settlement construction that imply Rawabi had been built with similar disregard of the law, Regavim first attempted to stop Rawabi and, if that proved to be impossible, to draw out the process endlessly.

Rawabi's counterarguments speak mostly to the factual basis of Regavim's claims—whether or not the dumping was in Area C and whether or not works conform to the law. But later they go on the offensive and argue, correctly, that Regavim's claims are openly "political" in ways that contravene the assumed objective character of law. Regavim's suit is "harassment from a plaintiff that has decided to become a nuisance to [Rawabi] and prevent it in any way possible from finishing its flagship project, the construction of a modern city in the Palestinian Authority. This is of course due to a political agenda." The filings are "not the first plea from these plaintiffs, and probably not the last"; the plea is "a tactic, a tool for the political agenda of the plaintiff, and should be treated as such." That political agenda, Rawabi argues, drawing from Regavim's own website, is a "Jewish and Zionist agenda regarding land use and the environment," the goal being to force "all parts of state government to work according to Zionist ideals." Regavim asserts the Israeli state "should work to prevent foreign bodies from taking over resources such as Jewish land and natural landscapes."

According to Rawabi, that settler agenda is obscured by abstract and "laundered language" but is in fact one element of an "extreme political agenda" in which plaintiffs also "organized a protest march against the paving of an access road to Rawabi; organized a demonstration of hundreds of settlers against the road; organized boycotts of Israeli companies that are assisting with the construction of Rawabi; and more." They mention Rawabi.co.il, attach a 2010 letter they sent warning the plaintiffs to remove it, and list various threats to Rawabi and attacks on workers by settlers. These attacks have always gone unanswered (H.C., 3355/14, *Regavim v. Minister of Defense, et al.* [not published]).

Against Regavim's exclusionary politics, Rawabi self-presents as a huge nonpolitical and nonboycotting project concerned with worldwide goals and universal aspiration. That it is, in essence, not only based in equal rights to the law and the land, on the ostensibly objective character of the law, but at that point also too big to fail. It is an undertaking of "over a billion dollars," the success of which

> depends, among other things, on the initiators' ability to create job opportunities for the people of the city. This is why the city planners saw great benefit to building a logistics park and light industry area in Area B, as close as possible to Area C and road [Route] 465. This is in order to allow Israeli companies that collaborate with [the defendant] easy access to the city and the site. This proximity and the ease of access it creates will encourage Palestinian-Israeli collaborations. [Rawabi is] "motivated by economic goals and has no political agenda, not against the plaintiffs nor anyone else. [Rawabi] can happily state that their actions advance collaborations with Israeli companies and hopes in the future to help with the economic growth of both sides, Palestinian and Israeli." (H.C., 3355/14, *Regavim v. Minister of Defense, et al.* [not published])

Beyond the specifics of the conflict over the land and the language of cooperation, this case, in all of its weird details, is the logical outcome of the forms and ideologies of territorial control in the West Bank today. Claims and capacities are crafted on the basis of the rule of law, but with little reference to its shifting content. Like the state in the West Bank, these cases use universals in ways that purposefully or unintentionally obscure the real and illegal violence of Israeli control and land regimes. The arguments made here are also intelligible in terms of the longer-term practices of right-wing legal activism, the role of the court in Israel, and the work being done to legalize settlement, expand the reach of Israeli civil law and practical control into the West Bank, and compel certain forms of behavior to reform the entire judiciary rightward.

The Supreme Court and Elon Moreh

Why legal activism and calls for stronger enforcement? In Israel, the Supreme Court and High Court of Justice enjoys unusually high prestige and power—something Regavim finds troubling. In a situation that is sometimes politically unstable, and in a state context where ideological extremism is often unobscured and mainstream, the Supreme Court is widely believed to be one of the only objective, even activist parts of the state. Built upon colonial-era

British Mandatory Law, the Israeli Supreme Court has "a dual function as the final court of appeal and as a court of first, and last, instance in petitions to the 'High Court of Justice'" (Kretzmer 2002, 10). Indeed, in the absence of either a constitution or a bill of rights, the High Court of Justice has enshrined a "judicial bill of rights . . . a central element of the country's constitutional system" (13). Its position creates three characteristics for the court as far as the Occupied Territories are concerned: First, a primary role is to enshrine the relationship between the international law of belligerent occupation and local law. Second, without a constitution, clear territorial boundaries, or a bill of rights, the Supreme Court must rule—or choose not to rule—on the nature of rights accorded by those laws within Israel, the West Bank, and Gaza, and thus on the outlines of the state itself. And third, somehow the Israeli Supreme Court is both an "objective" and an "activist" court. For rightists that means it is leftist, subjective, unjust, and contestable; a "threat to democracy"; and the site of struggle over the implementation and character of state power (Arutz Sheva Staff 2017b).

I focus here on the West Bank. In 1967 the political geographies of the war took on symbolic, historic weight, and the settler movement emerged at that time, under a Labor government. From that moment, civilian control of occupied land, litigated and clarified by the court, entered into the structures of both Israeli colonial control and rights in Israel. Two relatively recent legal mechanisms that I mentioned earlier, the special outline plans (blue line plans) and the Oslo accords that carve up the West Bank into Areas A, B, and C, have given the force of law to restrictions on Palestinian building and use of private land. But it was the landmark 1979 Elon Moreh case that opened the West Bank to more or less legal widespread Jewish Israeli settlement.

Elon Moreh was an outpost established on seven hundred dunams of privately owned land in the West Bank requisitioned by the IDF "for the needs of the army." Under pressure from the militant Gush Emunim settlers' movement, the government initiated the requisition and pushed it through as a military matter. Palestinians fought this land grab and received a favorable judgment, in part because rightist settlers petitioned the court and made highly ideological arguments that the court could not abide, and because "the political echelons had initiated the settlement and only then had the military given its approval. This provided the court with a formal basis for deciding that the dominant reason for requisitioning the land had been political, rather than military" (Kretzmer 2002, 89). In pushing back against the use of military justification for settlement, the court forced the government to shift tactics from military requisition to recasting settlements as "state land," a category of Ottoman Land Law. Land was declared fallow and thus open to seizure. According to Neve Gordon, "the acrobatics Israel was willing to perform after the Elon Moreh petition in order to 'legally' seize land reveal just how important it was for the government to portray its actions not as the suspension of law but as acts that abide by and follow the rule of law" (2008, 129). The executive and judicial branches worked together to ostensibly restrict seizure by making it into a legal question and to expand legal justification and capacities for seizure.

This is the same body of law used to establish settlements today. And it accounts for Regavim's insistent focus on enforcement and rights, and likely also Rawabi's references to the right-wing politics obscured with seemingly objective language. For rightists, the entirety of Israel and the Occupied Territories is understood as "national land," in the law it is all potentially "state land," and "the illegal overtaking of land" consists of all forms of Palestinian existence. The Oslo accords and any human rights initiatives intended to help Palestinians encircle them—as Regavim's Meir Deutsch has said, "A is for Arab, B is for together, and C is ours," reframing a formal legal categorization into one practiced on the basis of nationality or race. But more importantly, the High Court, the law, and civil legal practice are the central battleground for the character of Israeli territorial ambition in the Occupied Territories and the ease with which it can continue. For Regavim, the court is where the boundaries of Israeli jurisdiction and the character of Zionism and the nation in the state are determined.

Palestinians are allowed to petition the High Court on the basis of "good will" rather than any legal right (Sultany 2002, 51). As such, legal arguments about rights are necessarily and primarily about the ways those rights are granted to Jewish Israelis, even when on ostensibly Palestinian territory. For example, in late 2013 the Israeli High Court ruled that there can be no "Israeli nationality" or form of citizenship that trumps Jewishness, keeping in place both identity cards and the centrality of the Jewish nation to the character of the state (Gross 2013; Cook 2013). Citizenship, which can be held by non-Jewish people, is subordinate even inside 1948 Israel, where it is possible. Still, Israelis across political affiliation tend to hold the court to be a liberal institution because of its capacity to review military activities (Kretzmer 2002). However, as Sultany argues, review is not novel, and the idea of an activist court is "more perceived than real" (2014, 316). Because of those perceptions of checks and balances, court review often legitimizes military rule. Sultany refers to the processes of "decontextualizing" and "recontextualizing" military activities into civilian bodies of law. He discusses the fluidity and "indeterminacy of rights," which enables states to use rights as weapons against populations as it defines and orders them through those rights. It is "inclusive subordination" (318). If the occupation is reframed as a humanitarian question (Ben-Naftali and Shany 2005), then recontextualizing rights within the occupation narrows them drastically, even while claims are carried out using language of objectivity and universality.

Finally, what is happening in the West Bank remains a *colonial* conflict (Kattan 2009). Zionists and Israeli institutions gained legitimacy over land through international law and agreements, Balfour, the Mandate, and the United Nations Partition Plan for Palestine. Those were also malleable: the British believed in a "national home project" as a solution to the Jewish question at home, and ignored international law when it clashed with Zionism (Kattan 2009). But they did not entirely abandon international law, they folded Zionist imperatives into it—they made Balfour part of the Mandate so as to recontextualize the Zionist colonial movement as governed through existing and prevailing legal norms (Kattan 2009). The law has also shaped the context, form, and limits of contestation; it has been difficult for Palestine to establish alternative legal and political legitimacy using those same mechanisms, to say the least (Erakat 2019).

Where does the authority to change law come from? In part through jurisdiction, "the authority to have authority" (Pasternak 2017). Jurisdictions bump together and produce and map onto "the shared space of our societies" (or races or nations). Jurisdiction precedes law—states and laws categorize people, express control, and establish order and regularity. The law as a body of rules is less important here than the practical processes of extending jurisdiction in the West Bank and changing those categories governing relationships between the West Bank and Israel. States project an image of homogeneity within space while at the same time being based on, and busy maintaining, categories of people and land in part through the law (Pasternak 2017). This is one way it produces undifferentiated legal space in practice and is able to reorient the practical meanings of international law and human rights. These procedures legalize violence, operationalize legal nonviolence as violence, and enhance hierarchies of people and populations.

Legal jurisdiction is fundamentally a question of land control; it maps, limits, and defines social and political life in space. Whether serious or frivolous, rightwing Israeli legal activism is one of the most important ways jurisdiction is established in the Palestinian West Bank. Two overlapping and concurrent trends—jurisdiction by the act of settlement and jurisdiction by petition—reform the way law is practiced, create precedent, and enable ongoing settlement and legal change.

Legal practice around something understood to be objective, or universal, or democratic, has consequences for the kinds of state institutions that can emerge for Palestinians in accordance with law in the West Bank. Right-wing human rights groups demonstrate the limits of analytically separating the Occupied Territories from Israel, and at least in this instance, human rights are a form of discourse and argumentation that frames what happens in a contested territory as much as an institution that governs it. If there is a tension in terms of translating international law into local norms (Merry 2006), here an Israel-specific idea of discrimination against Jewish people is used to crowd Palestinians out of the discourse on legitimate victimhood and deny them access to legal recourse. I do not believe these settler groups are being infringed upon; the settlers' innovation is not to ignore human rights as is typical in Israel but to use universalist ideas about legal protection under the law to enhance discrimination. All sides organize claims around an idea of law as though it were objective and the content of justice were stable.[3]

Discrimination and Human Rights

Two events in recent history are important for understanding settlers' arguments about insecurity and the need for reform: the Gaza pullout and the so-called Amona Pogrom. In 2005, when Israel withdrew settlers from Gaza, the country plunged into a national argument about what to do with the remnants of the Jewish presence there. The architectural components of colonization, practices, and the structures and infrastructures of settlement were under threat. Israeli, American, and Palestinian officials debated the options for reuse or demolition of settler homes. Benjamin Netanyahu, at that time the minister of finance, left the Ariel Sharon government in protest of the potential image of "Palestinians dancing on the house roofs" of Gaza, a scenario that would have mirrored the foundation of Israel in 1948 (Weizman 2007, 225).

As the evacuation came to be understood as a collective trauma for settlers and Jewish people, it was brought into the present as a crime against the humanity of settlers in the West Bank and Jewish people everywhere else. Terms like expulsion, deportation, demolition, and destruction entered public debate in Israel, and this discursive form helped settlers produce symmetries between Palestinians and themselves. Those symmetries were adopted by settlers in both their resistance to evacuation and attempts to push the state to the right (as well as to the east) through the courts. The destruction of an individual settlement did little to scale back the wider movement, but these shifts gave rise to this settler-colonial human rights movement. The settler movement and the opponents of disengagement adopted a perspective that located the evacuation within a chain of collective Jewish tragedies. But opinion pieces and calls for civil disobedience against the army and the police also situated the expulsion within a much larger framework of international human rights violations.

The Wallerstein Declaration, a 2004 open letter written by settler leader and member of the Binyamin Regional Settlement Council, Pinchas Wallerstein, invoked legal rights and made comparisons with Palestinian expulsions as he called for civil disobedience against the state: "If someone were to try to pass a law for a transfer like this of some Arab village . . . all the knights of justice and civil rights would immediately protest and scream their hearts out to the heavens. . . . There is no justice and there are no rights?" (Perugini and Rabie 2012, 42).

The shock of Gaza was reiterated in another node of dispossession mobilized by the settlers: the Amona Pogrom in 2006, soon after the Gaza disengagement. In Amona, nine houses were evacuated, and settlers fought back against the kind of disproportionate military mobilization Israel usually deploys only against Palestinians. Settlers explicitly referenced the Holocaust in the images and descriptions they used, and scenes of Israeli police on horseback beating settlers shocked Israel.[4] Both settlers and human rights activists on the left discuss Amona constantly, and it gave rise to particular uses of the law and human rights claims to extend settler privilege in the West Bank. For settlers, a moral question emerged in legal terms: whether or not the Jewish state can discriminate against Jewish people, and the courts became sites where ideas of historical persecution, Jewish privilege, territorial rights, state politics, and the local understandings of social justice were contested. The violence of Amona is a foundation for the practice of false equivalence between peoples with very different relationships to the law and to the land.

Within this context, around the time of the settlement freeze in November 2009, a new practice of exacting revanchist, retaliatory, retributive violence on Palestinians as the "price tag" that must be paid for Israeli state action against settlement became commonplace. The freeze announcement had little consequence for settlement building, but it served to further radicalize the already-radical settler population in the West Bank and gave shape to arguments about state persecution. In September 2011, the Israeli military enforced a court order to evacuate houses in the "illegal outpost" of Migron.

In response, settlers retaliated not against the court or the IDF, but against the nearest Palestinian village, spray-painting "Mohammed is a pig" and "Migron = Social Justice" on the local mosque. The suggestion is that Palestinians and the state are together persecuting Jewish settlers. Settlers made themselves into victims of the state and have carried out resistance to it in part through aggression against Palestinians who they represent as having the favored, protected status that the settlers themselves actually enjoy.

Court decisions like Migron bring together two of the main bases of the ideological settler population in the West Bank: far-right secular nationalists and messianic Orthodox practitioners.[5] For ideological settlers, "Migron = Social Justice." That is to say, *this* is what justice looks like in Israel: a state actively persecuting them and reiterating historical collective trauma. The ostensible oppression of Jewish settlers by the Jewish state helps those on the right to distinguish themselves from the parts of Israel that they feel must be reformed; but the extravagance of the claims also help liberal Zionists to imagine the right and the West Bank away, beyond the boundaries of Israeli democracy. To most clear-eyed observers, the state of Israel presents problems to settlers only to the minimal extent it restricts the rights of Jewish individuals to freely, forcibly remove Palestinians and occupy the entire West Bank. For settlers, Palestinians are the problem, albeit one that can be partially ameliorated by reforming Jewish rights within Israel and extending Israeli civil law, attached to individuals, into the Occupied Territories. They wish to create a space in which Palestinians are invisible and formally excluded. Present, but not granted rights; ultimately, perhaps, settlers hope to reverse Palestinian presence altogether.

In September 2010 my friend and colleague Nicola Perugini and I met with a representative of Regavim, Meir Deutsch, in a West Jerusalem coffee shop. (At the time Nicola set up the interview he would give only his first name.) According to Meir, he and his friends started Regavim in 2006 as a result of time spent in the south of Israel—Area C—where they saw "tons of illegal housing" and came to the conclusion that "the state does not enforce the law." They began an advocacy campaign and reached out to Jewish Israeli mayors and Knesset members. At some point that year, Yehuda Eliyahu, a settler activist and member of the Binyamin Regional Settlement Council, became involved. They registered Regavim as an official NGO and began scouting work under its auspices. One of Regavim's primary activities is monitoring the land: using techniques they learned during compulsory military service, they surveil building in majority Arab areas in the north, the south, and the West Bank ("the Galilee, the Negev, and Judea and Samaria"), identify and map potentially illegal building, and provide information to the Israeli Civil Administration.

For Regavim, Palestinian building—and Palestinian presence—is out of control, and the state is failing to adequately monitor or minimize either. Regavim utilizes the language that emerged around the Gaza pullout, violence at Amona, and the settlement freeze, about unfairness and inequality under the law, and to make the claims that they are being persecuted and prevented from building on the land that is their birthright. This is the rhetoric that they began to take to the courts and the ideas that persist in arguments that seizing Palestinian land and dispossessing Palestinians is a "humane response" to ameliorating settler "distress" (Berger 2017c). By litigating narrow Zionist moral claims in the courts as questions of universal rights, they reference and enact the repetition of historical suffering at the same time as they integrate the substance of those beliefs into legal practice.

Settlers are surely not fighting for inclusion and representation, nor are they on the margins of the state. These settlers are actively supported by the government through military protection, infrastructure, and funding. The state encompasses the West Bank through administrative and military practices and through the legal system. Israeli citizens are subject to civil law wherever they are, and jurisdiction follows them. Even though the settlers are subject to Israeli civil law, it is not worthwhile to think of the Israeli military governance as separate from it. There are two primary legal regimes distributed along national lines within the same territory, and the settler administration is closely tied to the military occupation. These settlers are not radicals trying to dismantle the state of Israel; they are citizens using the techniques of Israel's liberal democracy to reform it and orient practice and legal precedent around settlement.[6]

Israel has numerous internal borders, none of which present barriers for Israel's Jewish citizens; civil law supplants military law for them. Israel, like other settler-colonial states, relies on its civilian population to do what it may not be able to do openly or legally. This not only enables a kind of governmental plausible deniability, but it allows laws and extralegal prerogative to work together as jurisdiction and precedent. Israel gives the appearance of operation within international and moral norms for the treatment of its citizens. Yet as an ethnically exclusionary state, its Jewish citizens allow it to operate in an illiberal fashion toward those subjects who are denied the benefits of citizenship on the basis of race or origin.[7] Israel's settler population—with legal, material, and ideological support from the Knesset, the military, and the polity—actively dispossesses the Palestinians while the courts create legal, and sometimes ethical, precedent around them. The state is always, and has always been, helping civilians to seize land: "The Israeli government frequently depicted the Jewish settlers as defiant citizens, even as it transferred millions of dollars to support their 'recalcitrant' behavior. The appearance of being unable to control the settlers allowed the state—when criticized—to absolve itself of responsibility by attributing the confiscations to illegal initiatives carried out by ideological citizen groups" (Gordon 2008, 117). Categories of racial, ethnic, national, and geographical exclusion are relations, and the artificial distinctions made between Israel's 1948 and 1967 territories and between settlers and the state obscure these practices. The main territorial and racial imperative of settler colonialism—the necessity to control the maximum amount of territory with the fewest number of indigenous inhabitants through expulsion and violence, but just as importantly by recategorizing and otherwise eradicating the category of indigenous and making life impossible for indigenous people (Wolfe 2006; Kauanui 2016)—is the operating principle here.

The overlapping jurisdictions and different forms of governance for different types of people in the same place mean, concretely, that the interplay of various laws work to categorize people, practices, and restrictions. This system results in government by confusion and prerogative—Palestinians appeal to laws without enforcement capacities, and Israelis legalize once-illegal activities after the fact. Palestinians' lack of coherent political or territorial control creates an environment where laws are built around precedent created by people who have the power and ability (if not necessarily the authority or prior jurisdiction) to do something. In a settler-colonial administrative framework, space-making is part of the process of othering races and populations. As Sherene Razack (2002, 1) puts it, "place becomes race," and laws that govern what happens, what is built, and how movement between places occurs become about the geographic arrangement and maintenance of race and racial categories and onto the contours of life.

Regavim and the State

Regavim is an active, taxpayer-funded organization (Berger 2018), modeled on "the left" and primarily concerned with "writing policy" (Goldman 2016). Regavim activists work to enhance their public stature as they make claims against Arab land use and the state. In 2018 they began work against what they think of as Arab trees—a fascinating inversion in a context where Jewish National Fund tree-planting was an explicit part of Zionist diaspora identity and colonization of Palestine—and have begun to support "Bedouin" crime victims in the Negev against "Arabs" and an uncaring state (Rudee 2018; Arutz Sheva Staff 2018). Furthermore, they comment not only on settlement and legal issues but on matters they find politically and culturally important. For example, at the time of the Brexit referendum, Regavim released a satire terrorist's video in support of the Leave campaign. Remaining in the EU, actors costumed as masked terrorists argued, benefits Palestinians and pays for building "European colonies" while preventing Jewish construction (Rudee 2018; Arutz Sheva Staff 2018). The video was bizarre and somewhat racist, and the humor did not land. This state-supported organization has also spoken strongly against camel ownership (Sones 2018a) and the dangerous incursion of an Arab tractor into a Jewish area (Sones 2018b).

Regavim works to write its threatened status in the landscape and create the structure of possibilities for state enforcement. One of its primary activities is monitoring Arab Palestinians using drones and mapping supposed illegal building and changes to the built environment over time (Fendel 2016). Although Regavim argues that buildings in close proximity make Jewish residents of the West Bank unsafe, it seems just as concerned with the ephemera of Arab presence everywhere, from Rawabi's construction materials to camels and tractors to Arab garbage (Arutz Sheva Staff 2017d). Regavim mapping is important for arguments about the objectivity of law and subjectivity of enforcement—it claims that the law is constantly being ignored, but law can also be revitalized, reoriented, and utilized against Palestinians. Indeed, Regavim is proud of its work helping the Israeli Civil Administration's reformed "blue line team," charged with redrawing those lines using new technology and with greater precision, so as to reclaim territory for the Jewish nation. In protecting West Bank settlers from Arab crimes both real and imagined, Regavim circulates and gives authority to claims about settlers' threatened status at the hands of Arabs. Each time Regavim files a claim and the state rules against it is another example of discrimination on the basis of its members' Jewishness.

In the final newsletter for the 2017 year, Regavim proudly proclaims that it filed eleven new petitions in June and July alone and had begun researching eighty-four cases of various Arab malfeasance, amounting, in sum, to a "quiet occupation being carried out by the Palestinian Authority through gradual, uncontested population transfer from Areas A and B into areas under full Israeli [control], in accordance with the Fayyad Plan to create a de facto Palestinian state in Area C." An "occupation." For the rest of that summer Regavim filed fourteen official complaints over construction and five over dumping, worked to pressure the state to enforce Supreme Court orders, politicize activists and journalists, and publicize its work (Regavim 2017).

Tracking Regavim and its approaches to the land illuminates shared and overarching contextual land logics linked across geography and agenda; legal confusion enables opaque land deals and subsequent formalization. Right-wing practice materializes politics into structures. In the case of settlements, it works to regularize and formalize them and fill them with legal subjects. Arab buildings, on the other hand, are to be emptied and reversed. Land deals utilize opacity: "almost all" settlement land transfers are based on improper contracts and forged documents (Levinson 2016). Regavim's first imperative is to make Jewish Israeli settlement acts appear legal, and second, to retroactively legalize them. The violence of land seizure is abstracted into forged documents and legal claims. As I show in the next chapter, the liberal left in the form of Yesh Din and Peace Now insist that this is about violence, seizure, and actual victimhood. The right wing represented by Regavim already presupposes Jewish rights to the West Bank. It argues that law ought to treat matters objectively and without reference to race or colonization. It concentrates on objects and inanimate structures, mounds of dirt and buildings, objective issues of planning and enforcement.

In an op-ed accompanied by a photo of Israeli police on horseback attacking settlers, the head of Regavim proudly takes credit for the work he and other "Blue Liners" did to help pass a 2017 "Regulation Law" to remap even more land, in part as a result of threats to Jewish presence by "extremist anti-Israel NGOs" (Hasten 2017) such as Peace Now and Yesh Din. In 2015 alone, the Civil Administration team remapped more than 62,000 dunams they claim were incorrectly characterized as state lands, in part because of 1980s–era mapping technology. Thus, these plans are still living documents, and Israeli reinterpretation has opened huge amounts of land to different jurisdiction and potential settlement (Berger 2017a). Regavim and Israeli occupation authorities work together to orient and give new life and character to existing law and enforcement.

Alongside mapping and regularization, settlers also work toward government localization; the Israeli right attempts to strengthen municipal control and the power to enforce and, presumably to interpret, state civil law (Arutz Sheva Staff 2017a). So, when the Regulation Law encountered judicial review in late summer 2017, Regavim responded that the courts were not respecting the Knesset's lawmaking function. A far-right Knesset member made this claim: "Again, we see how the Supreme Court is destroying the boundaries between the lawmaking authority and the justice authority . . . . The fight against Jewish settlement in Judea and Samaria, and against Israel's existence, is not just fought by terror and incitement. It's also fought by abusing Israel's justice system . . . . If the Regulation Law is rejected, we will have to pass a different law, one which restricts the Supreme Court's authority, to the dismay of its princes and knights" (H. Baruch 2017).

This is not simply a politically motivated appeal to abstract equality under universal ideas of humanity enshrined in law. Those claims are based on strategic arguments, beliefs, and rhetoric about settlers' unequal and subordinate status in the West Bank. Moreover, Regavim attempts to block all Palestinian building on the grounds that any and all of it threatens the Jewish people. For example, they describe a school for civil service training as actually a "megalomaniacal" intelligence base and military outpost (Ben-Porat 2016). Making claims that are at turns nationalist and historical or racial or paranoid, but with objective legal language, the content of those claims is obscured as they are integrated and abstracted into contemporary legal practice.[8]

This occurs continually and in concert with legislative attempts to solidify and expand Israeli control over the West Bank. While the Regulation Law stalled, a new "expropriation law" was passed, but it was subsequently held up in response to a petition by Yesh Din, Peace Now, and others (Berger 2017b).[9] In the midst of this slow process, the government countered with a legal brief and an entirely new interpretation of rule in Area C. While the High Court has tended to treat land claims there using international law of belligerent occupation and has ruled against Israelis living on Palestinian land, arguments on the legislative side increase the possibility of formal Knesset legal authority over Area C.

Such authority would imply that land is Israeli, subject to Israeli law, and thus land claims ought to be adjudicated not by international law but with mechanisms like eminent domain. They are using civil jurisdiction in an attempt to strip Palestinians of international protections and to retroactively legalize expropriation. Finally, this would extend to Israelis living beyond the green line and classify them as part of a "local population" that has rights against displacement and to ameliorative compensation, creating precedent for local law to be used in new ways to dispossess Palestinians, and pushing international jurisdiction from the West Bank (Berger 2017c; Lazaroff 2017).

According to human rights attorney Michal Sfard, the state's argument is a "100 page legal fantasy in which confiscation of land from Palestinians to benefit Israeli settlements and settlers is legal, and in which the settlers are considered protected persons," formally extending rights to one group in a territory but not another (Lazaroff 2017). The end goal, according to Regavim? To "reorganize" the Civil Administration due to the "scandalous" "discrimination against Jews and lack of demolition of illegal Arab housing in Judea and Samaria" (Arutz Sheva Staff 2017c) and to reform the regulations and institutions of occupation. This is the work being done to bring Palestinians' land into a civil legal system that is openly discriminatory, while watering down or transforming the protections Palestinians might enjoy through international law. Appeals to law—regardless of the claims being made—extend Israeli sovereignty onto people who can move through land, and subsequently onto the land, keeping the Arab parts of the West Bank and Palestine fluid and malleable. Even when settlers make arguments opposing the state, the end result is to strengthen Israeli legal control in the Occupied Territories and apply it unequally to its Jewish citizens only. Israeli legal activism makes up much of the context in which Palestinian forms of landholding solidify. Here too there is constant movement but little change for Palestinian life.

Chapter Ten

The Law, Mirroring, and the State

ACCORDING TO LEFTIST and liberal Israeli legal activists I interviewed, "Regavim was established because of Dror Etkes" and "in response to the relative success of his petitions." Etkes is a former staffer at Peace Now who began its Settlement Watch Project and, around the time Nicola Perugini and I interviewed him, had just established Yesh Din to carry out similar work and actively block settlement construction through litigation. A Peace Now staffer told me that Regavim only really started to talk about enforcement and the illegality of Palestinian building when it began to feel court pressure toward its own illegal outposts. After Amona it formulated an approach that would use existing legal processes to punish Palestinians and the courts, and push the state rightward—mirroring the petitions filed against settlements.

In this case, as is usual in Israel, there is no clear distinction between public and private, civil and military, state and civil society. Although it is an NGO, Regavim cannot be meaningfully understood in isolation from Israeli state administration of the Occupied Territories. Its longtime director Yehuda Eliyahu serves on the Binyamin Regional Settlement Council, Regavim gives its research to the Civil Administration, and Etkes has seen Eliyahu directing Israeli military bulldozers during Palestinian home demolitions. Although the system of funding is murky, nearly everyone I interviewed who had interacted with Regavim believes it is covertly and illegally funded by the Regional Settlement Councils, the municipalities that encompass and serve settlements.[1]

These civil "copy/paste petitions" enact false equivalence to decontextualize and recontextualize legal rights in two ways: first, by claiming that Palestinians are favored by Israeli law, and second, by equating and overwriting Palestinian dispossession with the consequences settlers have occasionally experienced at the hands of the Israeli state.[2] Etkes argues that, for the settlers, Amona was an unjust but rational application of law. By comparison to the fact of Palestinian building and the presence of Arabs in the West Bank, Amona brought about the idea that *enforcement* was unequal, that the human rights regime that allowed the Gaza withdrawal is inclined toward the protection of Arabs at the expense of the truly dispossessed class, Jewish Israeli settlers. In Amona, the state was compelled to enforce the law against settlers, laws that it generally avoided, ignored, or changed, and it engendered the settler movement's Zionist rights and legal reform project. In Regavim's mirroring, universal rights are protection from suffering at the hands of the state. Ironically, settler human rights become both protection from law enforcement and the mechanism through which civilians work extralegally and in concert with state colonial imperatives to reform law and compel the state to exact suffering on others.

Through the courts, Palestinian homes become "settlements" and "illegal Palestinian construction"; battles against the environmental effects of settlement expansion become claims against the "Wild West" of Palestinian home-building in the West Bank. Amir Fisher, Regavim's attorney, explains the technique in an interview with a settler newspaper:

> Unfortunately, Defense Minister Ehud Barak does not permit Jews to build, even in places that have certificates and outline plans, which actually forces people to be criminals. . . . The use of petitions is effective, because it brings the true facts before the Court. Until now this method was only used by left-wing organizations, and it is time that we change the hearts and minds of the judges. We show them that the Palestinians are building villas, castles and huge schools, and all without a permit. (Benari 2012)

They are, Etkes argues, "a copy-paste of our petitions. I am not a lawyer and I am not the one writing the petitions, but they were copy-pasting parts of the petitions, changing names" in order to authorize settlement. Etkes told me:

Yeah, they are basically using the same language . . . a mirror picture of what Yesh Din is doing, [they are doing it] a lot. What is striking is that, for example, they have a petition in Yitma, about an unauthorized outpost. . . . What they say, what they write in the petition is against [Palestinian] houses built out of Area B [defined by the Oslo accords as subject to Palestinian civil control and Israeli military control], out of the plan approved [by the Civil Administration] for the village, and they call these houses "illegal Palestinian outposts." They say that it [the "outpost"] is only 400 meters from the settlement. . . . They don't call it settlement, they call it Yishuv. Yishuv is just a community. What they are trying to do is just to reverse the reality. Yishuv means something that is there legally. There are phrases in this manner all along their petitions. They are taking the petitions of Yesh Din and they are reversing them.

This is borne out in the documents themselves. The case file for Regavim's petition against construction in the South Hebron Hills is awash in references to "illegal building" and is explicit that, on law itself, "the petitioners will refrain from repeating what has been said beyond the necessary minimum." The petition focuses on the need for state intervention: "The petitioners know that this court has said multiple times that it will not issue declaratory rulings saying that the law should be enforced. However, the petitioners' request is for a specific order requiring the respondents to engage in concrete actions in a specific case" (H.C., 6068/12, *Regavim v. Minister of Defense, et al.* [not published]).

Both Yesh Din's filings and Regavim's petition cite similar statements by the president of the court on the ways that "illegal construction not only undercuts proper planning of construction, but its implications are wider-reaching: it is among the most prominent phenomena that damage the rule of law. People who make their own law damage, in a clear and obvious way, the rule of law" (H.C., 4475/09, *Village Council of Dayr Istiya et al. v. Minister of Defense et al.* [not published]; H.C., 6068/12, *Regavim v. Minister of Defense et al.* [not published]).

The key issue here is enforcement, but without reference to the context for the offenses. It is the state's practical relationship to the law. Both sides use the same law, the same arguments, and the same precedent to seek opposite outcomes. Through the idea of enforcement and the fluid ways that the law touches the ground, competing visions about Zionism, the state, and the land are articulated, contested, and formalized. Mirror petitions aim to bring Zionist, exclusionary human rights into the law through its practical application. Regavim also works to equate Zionist and Palestinian dispossession so as to redefine abstract human rights and victimhood. By focusing on enforcement, Israeli settlers argue they are themselves victims, and they ignore the extremely visible power dynamics and legal and political infrastructures of Israeli control over Palestinians. For these settlers, "human rights is both a political tool and, just as importantly, an *epistemic framework* that shapes the way different actors conceive their own position within social space and the political significance of events they witness or are concerned about" (Perugini and Gordon 2015, 12; emphasis in original). Within the language of politics based on weakness and strength, settlers are aware how weakness can be strength—how victimhood leads to empowerment. Whether they succeed or fail in court, Regavim's arguments successfully alter legal and police practice; their object is not really to force the law to line up with universal rights principles but instead to reorganize universalist principles so their articulations are exclusive and particular.

Mirror cases help illuminate the limits and boundaries of this contemporary rights practice in Israel and Palestine. In Historic Palestine building—and the laws around land tenure, ownership, and who can legally or illegally build—shape wider politics and capacities for holding that land. Law, and its different applications for different categories of people, contributes to the dynamics of state, what it is, who it is for, and what it can accomplish. In very real ways, Regavim utilizes the idea of legal objectivity to force the question, What character can laws have outside of the power and racial hierarchies in which they are practiced?

Below, I look at a Yesh Din case on behalf of the village councils of Dayr Istiya and Kafr Thulth against the Israeli minister of defense, the IDF Central Command, the Civil Administration, the police commander of Judea and Samaria, and the Samaria Regional Council and compare it to Regavim mirror petitions against the minister of defense, IDF Central Command, the Civil Administration, and villages in the South Hebron Hills. These arguments overlap and map their shared framework for claims, language, and the extralegal implications in land claims.

In both instances, petitioners primarily argue about enforcement against illegal building, about the force of law and the state, and the various threats that the presence of another group presents for the plaintiffs. Plaintiffs agree that the law is not being enforced, but they believe it serves different goals. Both assume the law offers protection and ask for the same remedies: stop-work orders and the enforcement of existing stop-work orders. Regavim more often goes one step further: it wants the courts to make a formal declaration that laws should be enforced, and it wants enforcement to extend to dismantling illegal buildings on the grounds that leaving them intact will encourage subsequent law-breaking settlement expansion or necessitate expulsion.

The Yesh Din files against the illegal Israeli outpost El Matan ask for the enforcement of a stop-work order against it on the grounds that the building is large and being hastily constructed without proper oversight. Yesh Din also points out that settlers typically try to populate buildings quickly in order to make enforcement difficult without expulsion—extralegal or illegal action that makes it more likely courts will retroactively allow the settlements. It cites the State Investigative Commission's "Shamgar report" on the Assassination of Yitzhak Rabin, an important precedent for questions of enforcement:

> Failings in enforcement of the law have been revealed. . . . Our accepted point of departure is that without effective law enforcement there can be no effective government. In an environment where every person can do as they please, without any tangible risk of bearing the responsibility for deviating from acceptable behavior, the authorities charged with effective governance on the ground suffer. The High Court commented years ago that the rule of law is not created ex nihilo and is not an abstract concept. It must have tangible day-to-day expression in the existence of normative and obligatory arrangements and their practical operation with respect to all people. (H.C., 4475/09, *Village Council of Dayr Istiya et al. v. Minister of Defense et al.* [unpublished])

Yesh Din continues to assert:

1 The Israeli police will be responsible for the enforcement of law and order in Israeli towns. The IDF will be responsible for taking care of the area surrounding the towns. (This applies whether or not information about the event was known ahead of time.)

2 For all other events where advance information enables organization ahead of time, the Israeli police will be responsible for the enforcement of law and order at the event itself, and the IDF will assist them in the surrounding area. (H.C., 4475/09, *Village Council of Dayr Istiya et al. v. Minister of Defense, et al.* [not published])

The basis for Yesh Din's claim is that police have responsibilities and obligations, that there ought to be more state intervention and that thus civil rule and policing carries in these areas, even if they are surrounded by Israeli military-occupied Palestinian areas. It also asserts that the situation is "severe and outrageous," and the policy of turning a blind eye amounts to "giving unspoken permission to crimes on public land, and all this for the purpose of expanding an 'unauthorized' and 'illegal' outpost that lacks an outline plan or building permits" (H.C., 4475/09, *Village Council of Dayr Istiya et al. v. Minister of Defense et al.* [not published]).

The government has abdicated its responsibility to operationalize the rule of law, to the benefit of settlers:

77 This order is requested due to persistent, wide-ranging, ongoing, and therefore unusually severe, refusal on the part of the authorized governing authority to fulfill its legal duty by enforcing the law. This order is necessary because the extent of the illegal construction on the one hand, and the complete lack of enforcement (which cannot be interpreted as other than deliberate) on the other create the threshold set by the ruling for court involvement in law enforcement policy—total abdication of the authority's responsibility to enforce the law. (See H.C., 6579/99, *Amichai Filber v. The Government of Israel*; H.C., 4475/09, *Village Council of Dayr Istiya et al. v. Minister of Defense et al.* [unpublished])

Even though it understands state policy to generally mean "giving unspoken permission," Yesh Din must argue for state intervention and enforcement:

72 In the absence of any remedy of the issue or step toward enforcement on the part of the authorities, the petitioners are left with no choice but to request that the honorable court assist by forcing the authorities, respondents 1-5, to fulfill their legal obligation and implement their obligations as established by international law, military legislation, constitutional law, and the Israeli administrative law. . . .

76 We knew, and considered before submitting the petition that the honorable court has repeatedly stated its practice is not to issue declaratory rulings saying the law should be enforced. The petitioners request an order requiring the respondents to enforce the stop-work order and demolition order for particular buildings that are being constructed in violation of Israeli and international law, and in complete opposition to government decisions, on state lands entrusted to the respondents and that have been used by the petitioners and the people of their villages for years, use that has been prevented as a result of ideological greed on the part of the people of the outpost. (H.C., 4475/09, *Village Council of Dayr Istiya et al. v. Minister of Defense et al.* [unpublished])

Here Yesh Din is doing two things: separating "the law" and its institution, the court, from mechanisms of enforcement, and appealing to the court to compel adherence to the law. Yesh Din is clearly aware what happens in a frontier zone and the ways that people operate against, through, or without reference to the law.

Yesh Din assumes that the law is designed to govern and protect equally—or at least asks it to try to act that way. Regavim's goals are the opposite yet its claims are the same. Yesh Din believes that by working in the courts it can strengthen the law and the state and articulate civil jurisdiction over settlement activity. Regavim must know that it can rely on the state to at least implicitly enable settlement expansion and that victimhood is just as discursively useful as real. Enforcement is both insufficient and only one goal here; the aim is to bring in and strengthen civil jurisdiction, make human rights and humanity an intra-Israeli question, and open more Palestinian areas to new forms of public/private repression. They want to treat military occupation as a matter for both the Israeli state and civil society.

Unlike Yesh Din, which stops at enforcement, Regavim believes that stopping building is not enough. It was the settlers who pioneered the approach of populating outposts to create facts on the ground; Regavim wants to dismantle buildings and Palestinian presence and make sure it can expand civil jurisdiction to fill empty space as a precursor to Jewish settlement.

In a suit over construction in Yatta, it argues that the Israeli authorities are abdicating their undeniable responsibilities to monitor and govern Palestinian building in Area c: "In Judea and Samaria there are thousands of construction and work sites without the permits necessary for their implementation, carried out by Palestinians in Area c, in which both civil and security authority falls undeniably on the respondents" (H.C., 6068/12, *Regavim v. Minister of Defense et al.* [unpublished]). But that is not just a matter of permitting; it amounts to a holistic threat to Jewish safety and presence:

33 In order to be brief and to save precious judicial time, the petitioners will refrain from repeating what has been said beyond the necessary minimum. It will be noted only that in the region of Judea and Samaria, there is "deep trouble" in the form of thousands of instances of illegal building that are not addressed as they should be by the authorities, as the neglect in addressing them has influence in a variety of ways over what is done in the area.

34 Among others, the authorities' failure damages a number of different areas, as briefly detailed here.

a The Urban Planning Sphere—when every person can do as they please, without planning or forethought, as part of establishing facts on the ground in a way that does not enable proper planning or providing minimal utilities.

b The Criminal Sphere—when anarchy and failure to obey the law and contempt for law enforcement authorities continue to spread in ways that seriously damages the ability of the authorities to govern in the region of Judea and Samaria, not only in the areas of zoning and construction but also in other areas, including transportation, property, and even in areas that border on physical harm. It should be stressed that this applies not only in the area of security, but also in that of basic criminality—which everyone agrees should be enforced for the welfare of all residents of the region.

c The Environmental Sphere—when anyone who wants can build and demolish without planning or forethought and hurts the environmental fabric in a way that will certainly constitute a calamity for future generations.

d The Commercial Sphere—in a place where illegal construction activities fulfill their goal of establishing facts related to claims of rights over public land, whether on state land or abandoned land.

e The Security Sphere—when even in places where the zoning laws were designed to protect the lives of Israelis in the area there is no proper enforcement, such as cases of building adjacent to major transportation routes or adjacent to towns etc., or, as in the case of illegal building that is the subject of this petition, that is taking place within a marked firing zone.

35 The violation of zoning and construction laws has already received a variety of epithets and denunciations from this honorable court and other courts and has been called such names as: "deep trouble," "national calamity," "anarchy," "neither judge nor justice," and a variety of other sayings, all meant to describe the court's dissatisfaction of the various courts with what is happening on the ground in this area. (H.C., 7121/12, Regavim v. Minister of Defense et al. [unpublished])

Finally, Regavim uses similar precedent as Yesh Din to demonstrate the negative consequences of a lack of enforcement, and argue for its necessity and equal application everywhere and to everyone encompassed by Israel:

21 It will not be superfluous in this context to cite the words of the Honorable President Shamgar regarding the enforcement of zoning and con-

struction laws. The following was said regarding violations of zoning and construction laws that are almost comical compared to what is happening in Judea and Samaria—building enclosed porches without permits, putting up fences without approval, etc.: "Illegal construction not only undercuts proper planning of construction but its implications are wider-reaching: it is among the most prominent phenomena that damage the rule of law. People who make their own law damage, in a clear and obvious way, the rule of law." (H.C., 6068/12, *Regavim v. Minister of Defense et al.* [unpublished])

Justice, Equality, and Expanding the Rule of Law over Territory

Under the post-Elon Moreh land regime and the use of "state land" in order to bypass it, Regavim has several larger goals. According to Etkes, they are to "limit the possibilities for Palestinian existence," to serve "as a counter-weight to Yesh Din's work" by "winning in the public by losing cases and showing that the legal system and Supreme Court are moving to the left," thus creating a false symmetry "in a situation where there is no legal, philosophical, ethical, or other comparison." Or else, by winning cases and enshrining false equivalence in the law and at the level of individual buildings by saying, "What is the difference between this and an Israeli building? Illegal is illegal. You have to demolish." And, either way, Regavim floods the courts with so many cases they come to a standstill—paralyzing the threat to the settlements.

In late 2010 Regavim published a report titled, "On the Perversion of Justice: Is Israel's Supreme Court the Last Refuge of the Citizen?" The report clearly argues its position and elaborates this form of equivalence. On the cover of the report (figure 10.1), two images are placed side by side: a large "illegally-built" Palestinian home under construction and the rubble of Amona (Regavim 2010).[3] The message is clear: this is the extent to which justice has been perverted in Israel. Palestinian building continues unabated while the Jewish people are being persecuted in their homeland. The pictures, it is implied, should be reversed (Perugini and Rabie 2012). The report accurately characterizes Regavim's approach, how it understands and portrays what it is doing, and the structure of beliefs about the law and the Jewish state that animates both the mirroring and the cases themselves.

In the report, Regavim presents itself as "a social movement for preserving Israel's land and national properties" in accordance with a Zionism that is "first and foremost a Jewish vision . . . that, in part, expresses itself through virtuous behavior and the rules of proper administration." Regavim's Zionism

FIGURE 10.1 The Regavim report "On the Perversion of Justice." Source: www.regavim.co.il.

holds that the land belongs to all Jews, that those lands should be properly and equitably administered, and that Jewish individuals are being persecuted—being made to feel unequal—through unfair treatment by a court that does not adhere to its liberal principles. I quote from the Regavim report at length:

> Equality is a basic value in democratic society, "that the legal system of every democratic state, by virtue of justice and fairness, aspires to put into practice. . . ." The necessity to ensure equality is natural to man. This is based on considerations of justice and fairness. One who wishes to have his rights recognized must acknowledge the right of others to similar recognition. The need to uphold equality is vital to society and to the social contract upon which society is built. Equality guards government from arbitrariness. Indeed, there is no more destructive force in society than the feeling of its members that they are being treated unfairly. This feeling of inequality is among the worst of feelings. It harms the ties that unite society. It injures the individual's sense of personal identity. Equality touches upon all areas of life and of government. Therefore we should maintain equality among people of varying religions, nationalities, ethnic groups, races, parties, viewpoints, bodies and groups. . . . We learn about the need to uphold equality in Israel from a number of sources. The first among them is Israel's Declaration of Independence: "Complete social and political equal rights will prevail for all citizens, regardless of differences in religion, race or gender." (Regavim 2010, 2)

The report outlines how the court treats Regavim's mirror petitions and evaluates that treatment. Without reference to context or the occupation and unequal power relations, Regavim makes the claim that the petitions fail because of subjective and discriminatory treatment by leftist courts. Whether a bogus, time-consuming petition is treated as such, or if it is treated seriously on its merits and thrown out, each instance constitutes bias for Regavim.[4] Moreover, petitions do not simply demonstrate the courts' bias; by repeating the process and the results, Regavim produces it. Regavim's legal filings, like other documentary claims, circulate to accrue weight and authority to Regavim's legal strategy. The responses and practices around the petitions become facts that have to be worked around, incorporated, or dealt with in some other way.

"On the Perversion of Justice" argues that the court is creating a false distinction between Israel and the West Bank, and in doing so, neglecting its responsibilities to its Jewish citizens in the West Bank, acquiescing to liberals and Arabs, and opening itself to attack. Indeed, the settlers feel that they are being treated unfairly, and they put the court on notice that the court's failure to protect Jewish privilege in the West Bank amounts to denying the promise of democracy to all members of Israeli Jewish society.

The prerogative that the High Court has taken for itself to arrive at a judicial decision regarding the attitude of the State of Israel towards the territories of Judea and Samaria, and to set a legal attitude towards the petitions that are presented before it, removes it from the national consensus and transforms it into an institution that is subject to debate and a political weapon. . . . This causes indescribable damage to the rule of law and the central position of judicial institutions in general and that of the Supreme Court in particular in democratic society. . . . *"Equality guards government from arbitrariness"*: When this principle is violated arbitrariness overtakes the enforcement authorities, and the rule of law is transformed from a supreme value into a political club, from a foundation stone of proper government into an empty, worthless idea, a spade with which to dig in order to advance a particular political agenda. *"Indeed, there is no more destructive force in society than the feeling of its members that they are being treated unfairly"*: If the findings of this report do not show "unfair treatment" we have no idea what "unfair treatment" is. If that is truly the case, how can we complain about the collapse of the stature of the High Court and of the loss of the public's faith in this institution? The members of Israeli society, those that belong to one side of the political divide, feel discriminated against time after time, and indeed, there is nothing more destructive than this. *"This feeling of inequality is among the worst of feelings"*: And it is seven times worse when combined with a feeling of powerlessness, since we are speaking of the Supreme Court whose decisions cannot be appealed and it[s] arbitrary rulings cannot be held up to criticism of any other institution. . . . *"It injures the individual's sense of personal identity"*: Since we are not dealing with one private individual here, this injures the identity of the entire Israeli society as a democratic and equal society where each individual has the right to stand up for his opinions in the court of public opinion without being discriminated against when he demands his day in court. (Regavim 2010, 15–16; emphasis in original)

Yet the ideological bias in the courts is not only about the denial of rights to individuals in ways that harm democratic society; Regavim attacks laws they believe are not sufficiently Zionist, that are undemocratic because they do not adequately protect the rights of the Jewish people and their historical redemption through settlement in Historic Palestine. By making arguments they claim are objective, liberal, secular, legal, and *democratic*, they utilize and slowly reorient the supposedly leftist parts of Israeli democracy in line with their territorial and exclusive ambition.

> The only motive that we can provide to explain this gap is an ideological-political motive, that sees the Judea and Samaria regions as "occupied territory" and not parts of the Homeland, that sees the State of Israel as an "occupying power" and not as a nation returning to its land . . . after two thousand years of exile and redeeming it from its desolation, and sees the Palestinians as an "occupied and oppressed people" instead of as [an] enemy that desires to destroy us and expel us from our ancestral home. . . . The fact that not one objective parameter [has] been divided over these issues for over a generation. However, it is wrong for the High Court to take for itself the authority to bypass the nation, to rule and make decisions consistently favorable to one side rather than the other. (Regavim 2010, 14)

In the conclusion to her reports on the Eichmann trial, Hannah Arendt describes the process of mystifying identity and trauma into the nation. Here, we can see Israeli practices that operationalize nationalism as human rights within the framework of the nation-state. For the settlers, like the Israelis trying Eichmann, there is the problem of "the legalities that stand in the way of justice" (2006, 266). So rather than working from a universal or universalizing the definition of justice, they redefine it to bring the practices of justice and democracy in line with nationalist and geographic imperatives of the settlement project and under Israeli law.

Law, Humanity, and the State

In 2010, Hagit Ofran, then head of Peace Now, told me she thinks all of this legal activism is working. While the assumptions Regavim makes are a gross "distortion of facts," she believes that judges may now try to keep "the appearance of balance" by taking Regavim seriously and, I believe, integrating the beliefs of those it represents—the settler fringe that populate outposts—into the body of law and legal practice.[5] Regavim operates through abstract legal claims and as a human rights organization, although one with a narrow definition of who constitutes a "human." It uses the language of shared rights and the institutions of a liberal democracy to make false analogies between the demolition of settlements and Palestinian suffering to exert pressure on the Israeli court to allow further building, further settlement, and a stronger system of control. As the Israeli Human Rights attorney Michal Sfard says, it is "a stunt" designed to cause "havoc," but it is also a "revolution in the use of the legal system."[6]

Even though such appeals to universality and liberal law are not designed to expand rights and equality, they are not a perversion, and they are not new to liberalism. Rather, they are embedded within it. Liberalism emerged historically as a way to enhance and enforce privilege (Losurdo 2011), and colonialism is, in part, a process that defines humanity and excludes the colonized from it (see, for example, Césaire 2001). Humanity itself emerged as a juridical category shaping social relationships to the law as it places people under its authority (Esmeir 2012). Within a settler-colonial state in the period of globalization, liberal democracy is oriented around racial and colonialist imperatives. Neither Israel's liberalism nor its ongoing occupation are cohesive wholes, but they interact as a series of piecemeal fixes to keep the other intact enough to coagulate as jurisdiction. Law shapes the relationships between place and race—through restrictions on what sorts of things happen in specific places and through the transfiguration of indigenous claims, activities, and disputes into crimes governed by the settler system (Razack 2002; Ford 2010). Moreover, the idea of human rights has been tied to market fundamentalism and does not seek formal equality but rather the unequal distribution of rights (Moyn 2018). These are rights practices premised on the *idea* of abstract, generalizable law (Asad 2000).

Conversely, specific settler laws target groups based on race, implicitly and explicitly. This process demonstrates both the universalisms ambient in and around liberalism, and the local imperatives that determine the contours of nonuniversal application of liberal practice, law, and rights. Rights discourse assumes the law to be objective and universally applicable, but laws can be simultaneously just and intolerable (Asad 2000), and this gives Regavim an opening for its particular type of reform. In the case of the West Bank, in a territory subject to overlapping legal frameworks, changes to laws amplify their social character and role in maintaining Israeli control. Regavim's multiple forms of activism produce practical jurisdiction—legal authority—over people and places and extend Israeli sovereignty. Shared language shapes the limits of claims both sides make, but in doing so, it creates a kind of clear title over the patchwork of state and legal systems and is thus part of the solidification and regularization of the legal regime in the West Bank: "only the state can enforce norms as *the law*. . . . States can and do use human rights discourse against their citizens—as colonial empires used it against their subjects—to realize their civilizing project" (Asad 2000). Mirroring implies, holds up, and strengthens Israeli jurisdiction first, and sovereignty second, diluting content in rights claims and enhancing the state's status as final arbiter of justice. The parallel move—to try to push the court rightward—is part of a reform project to overwrite international frameworks and exclude Palestinians from legal protection. But for the arguments to be legible (and follow precedent), those politics must be obscured, a process fully consonant with liberal democracy and its central assumptions about equality under the law.

This kind of legal practice has other consequences for Palestinians living under Israeli control. Palestinians have long been engaging with the courts to fight the occupation and during the post-Oslo period, the language of "national liberation" and "self-determination" has been oriented toward a rights- and court-based approach. Palestinians are aware of the contradictions of participating from their subordinate position, as well as of Israeli political deployment of legal logics (Erakat 2019). Examples like the High Court ruling against the route of the wall were controversial in Palestine because the end result was to bring the wall into the body of law, to say that one particular route was illegal, that remedies could be offered, and that there could be a more just path for it. It did not challenge the existence of the wall, widely viewed by Palestinians (and outside Israel and the United States) as illegal, unjust, and punitive. And, anyway, Israel simply ignored the International Criminal Court advisory ruling that demanded its dismantlement. This is perhaps why Palestinian international and legal activism, necessary components of the fight against Israeli encroachment and military/state violence, increasingly rely on universal claims about justice rather than protections granted by law through enforcement.

Regavim's legal activism is the outcome of working within a legal system premised upon the idea of a neutral state: even when the state is clearly neither neutral nor truly democratic, the idea and appearance of neutrality can be operationalized as a form of power over its subjects. The rule of law legalizes and obscures violence and enables violence to secure territorial ambitions toward total Israeli control. Alongside the consolidation of Palestinians through planning, the area system, and "inwards and upwards," the operation of liberal law and creeping Israeli jurisdiction orders violence, space, and daily life for Palestinians and Israelis on West Bank land.[7]

It is no surprise that a shared settler colonial state and its legal and ideological context shapes practices, conceptions, and forms of dispute. Like capitalist development and modernization, the perceived universalism of rights and the rule of law does work here. Universals produce and enhance existing forms of jurisdiction and sovereignty. In Israel and the West Bank, the rule of law is part of how colonial domination deepens. But it is also a form of regularization in which the entire situation becomes legal, formal, and translatable across states and networks of states. The West Bank state process and the abstraction of settlement, exclusion, and violence into law enable the forms of dominance and colonial imperative not only to exist, but to persist.

CONCLUSION

ON MY FINAL RESEARCH TRIP for this project in summer 2017, I visited Rawabi several times. It felt somehow like being on a movie set or like looking at a trompe l'oeil. It was all surface, all new, and smelled like paint. From up close it was quiet. But the place is enormous and widely known: the private developers, representatives of finance capital, Israeli and American supporters, and Palestinian government officials that are producing Rawabi know how to draw attention. Rawabi is not something that has to be explained to most West Bank Palestinians, yet it is still after all of these years unclear what it will be or what it will mean. It is not directly important for the broad range of Palestinians, but it is massively relevant for the future it is helping to produce for their homeland.

For over a decade, the idea has circulated, accrued press, and aggregated authority through sheer repetition of stenographic accounts written in hundreds of outlets. For the past few years, public relations officials at Rawabi have been cold-calling universities—departments of design, development studies, and economics—pitching their city as a potential case study and working to create more expertise, seriousness, and authority. In 2018, developers funded a "Rawabi Fellowship for Leaders from Palestine" at Harvard's John F. Kennedy School of Government (Chaidez 2018). With only a few exceptions, all are welcome to come and witness Rawabi. And they are quite open when it comes to bringing in potential supporters they believe can amplify their agenda: from potential buyers and bureaucrats to liberal American community groups, rightist Knesset members, Thomas Friedman, Ban Ki-Moon, and Coldplay. It is likely a large reason why Palestine has gone up twenty-six places in the World Bank's 2018 Ease of Doing Business Index

FIGURE CONC.1 Rawabi in July 2017. Photo by Léopold Lambert for The Funambulist.

FIGURE CONC.2 Rawabi in July 2017. Photo by Léopold Lambert for The Funambulist.

(World Bank 2018), a fact proudly advertised by the Israeli military in charge of the West Bank Occupation (Coordinator of Government Activities in the Territories).

But this is not a business book or a work of Rawabi studies. Whether this particular real estate endeavor succeeds or fails in achieving its stated goals is less important than the unintended and intended consequences of its production. This is a snapshot of a time in Palestine, of a place in which phenomena are materialized, made visible, and produce a future orientation for Palestinian political economy. That future is based on ongoing processes to formalize and extract profit from the present. Concretely, the area surrounding Ramallah is one of fewer and fewer explicitly Palestinian places, as Ghada Karmi (2015) has written. It is comparatively visible or open to the rest of the world, a rarity where a Palestinian polity can express some kind of a future. As Palestine collapses into Ramallah, and Ramallah is given an outward orientation, forms of social life, liberation politics, and aspiration are foreclosed throughout the West Bank, Gaza, Israel, and the Palestinian diaspora. Building for relative freedom in Ramallah is the flip side of policing elsewhere; it is one of a shrinking number of places where return might seem possible. Interventions around Ramallah are enabled by occupation barriers and Oslo categories of A, B, and C. Real estate development happens within a geographical project to limit other kinds of growth, a project that consequently structures contexts in which social reproduction occurs and common sense emerges.

I hope that I have presented an analysis that engages indirectly with assumptions that Palestine and Israel can be studied in terms of their uniqueness and exceptionality, an approach that renders private housing development and capital accumulation new and unprecedented. Too often Palestine is understood through the separation between it, Israel, and the outside—a kind of reading that seeks out and emphasizes micropolitics and resistance to a cohesive colonial power. Yet I believe those readings are often disempowering for Palestinians and orient politics narrowly against occupation. They sometimes feel based on assumptions and imaginaries beyond what is warranted by histories of political life, class stratification, and practice among ordinary Palestinians, whether activists, scholars, workers, compradors, the bourgeoisie, or otherwise. And they counterpose Palestinian national political aspiration to Israel's colonial occupation, a term that does not capture the complexity, geographies, time horizon, or actors complicit in Israeli control over Palestine. As Gary Wilder put it for the case of French decolonization, "to presuppose that national independence is the necessary form of colonial emancipation is to mistake a product of decolonization for an optic through which to study it" (2014, 4).

It is vitally important to look at what Palestinians and international actors are doing to shape and structure Palestine under conditions of Israeli territorial and political economic control, who benefits, and how. The occupation not only shapes what is permitted or punished on the landscape, it can also shape business and growth—for those positioned to benefit. In that sense, the area system is in part about land value and rent and can be a market force as a barrier or determinant for demand. The pervasive sense of political instability has inflected economic activity and created a market that is just as dependent on artificial land scarcity as on the political imperatives among NGOs tied to capital growth. The West Bank state today is not a territorial state so much as a state-scale market and a form of long-term management.

What possible futures can emerge from this context, and how are those possibilities structured if the future is composed within the ideologies, practices, and geographies of the present? I want to suggest that Palestine has been linked to the rest of the world and unevenly incorporated into regional and international economies, and in doing so I hope to contribute in some small way to a change in the geographic and political orientation and objects of Palestinian studies.

Part of the blame for the narrow approach in Palestine has to fall on academics and the imperatives of our labor. Consistent needs for production and growth sometimes force us to seek out moments of rupture and to generate language for old categories: to locate, claim, and name newness. New types of analyses are carried out to create and spread into new markets, and Palestine is rendered unlike anywhere else. Consequently, so much of the framework for understanding Israeli control and Palestinian struggle looks inward. I have done my best to avoid this problem, and I have sought somewhat more clarity locating structural continuities evident in contemporary Israel and Palestine. I hope this ethnography can circulate among social histories of political economic change in Palestine, and I hope to have traced out some of the dynamics of those changes on political and social life. This is necessarily a partial story but one that tries to illuminate some wider aspects of the state and politics today.

Like the Oslo accords and Fayyadism as their logical outcome, Palestinian actors today work to implement ideologically coherent practices and to craft stability without sovereignty. In part they do it by producing spaces and places and ideas about new forms of housing that assume and incorporate Palestinians. Capital investment is one mechanism for stabilization, and capitalism is not new for Palestine. Oslo and the PA—or the area system, the language that Oslo has given for political stability, limited self-rule, occupation, and territorial control—obscure structural continuities. The so-called neoliberalization of Palestine is not a new phenomenon or a sudden change in occupation; it is a complementary reorientation and redistribution of its effects.

Method, Structure, and the Question of the State

I first went to the West Bank for research in 2007, overly aware of the geographies of occupation and heavily influenced by work that described extreme fragmentation there. I saw the wall and checkpoints and was immersed in scholarship that focused on people through the binary between the violence—overt, extreme, and pervasive—of the occupation, and the everyday micropolitics of resistance to it. But I also saw investment, accumulation, and class stratification and began to wonder about acts that are not obviously resistive, or practices framed as resistance that did not appear to be antioccupation in any familiar way. I wondered what it meant that some of the fragmented places in the West Bank seemed to feel distant from the occupation.

That year I started to look at plans for industrial zones in the West Bank, for truck-to-truck trade, and the infrastructures of an "economic peace" based on separation between labor in the West Bank and commercial markets elsewhere. But ultimately there was little I could learn about the zones—the idea has moved in and out of favor at various times, but few concrete steps were taken. However, plans and reports are still productive (Ferguson 1994). Despite the lack of progress, they were invoked; the alphabet soup of international aid organizations and governments produced documents about them, and they oriented practice, funding, investment, and intervention. Those plans and the fantasy of circumscribed free labor markets told me that inclusion and integration, however unequal and uneven, are just as important to occupation as separation.

By 2008 I had started trying to understand how racialized labor is manipulated through the occupation to benefit Israeli capitalists, and how structures of inclusion and incorporation map onto, and come to define, populations. On the West Bank side, it seemed crucial to look at what Palestinians are doing to imagine and continually produce the idea and reality of Palestine. Not simply by measuring the extent to which various projects can be counted as resistance, but by trying to understand what kinds of social and political life are emerging around and within relations and common sense of "occupation." At that time Rawabi was just entering public perception and discourse and, although ground would not be broken until spring 2010, it seemed like an ideal place to analyze imaginary and real projects for state and market building, privatization, and social reproduction. (It is still an ideal place, even if I should have foreseen the draw for others, and the problems of crafting an intervention into a field that very quickly became saturated with opinions, representations, and analysis.)

I visited Palestine nearly annually from 2007 to 2017. I lived there for fieldwork in 2009 and 2010, and I conducted about one hundred interviews in Arabic and English with key actors on the process of development from the ground up, on the new loan mechanisms that are emerging, and with a population of bureaucrats and ordinary people embedded within this broader project. I tried to understand the kinds of structural instabilities that inform distribution of space, planning, and legal ramifications and jurisdictions, while also opening a market for investors. Given the national political context, Palestinian capitalists understand investment as nationalism, at least in part. Given the political economic structure of possibility, they invest in markets that are not open but are heavily backed and insured, circumscribed, and suspended.

Urban space is made and remade; the Rawabi process fixes capital at some points in the landscape and destabilizes it at others, and the creation of the new town will reverberate throughout West Bank localities and in terms of current and future relationships between the state-in-formation and Israel. As land registration and land tenure change, emphasis is placed on individual owners buying and selling land, in contrast to historical collective family rights.[1] As the PA increasingly supports and funds privatization of large blocks of land and private development at large scale, the likelihood increases that other locales will be underfunded or defunded altogether. International organizations are giving money to the private sector through the PA, and together private developers and NGOs contribute to refocus PA priorities; documents drawn up for and by donors increasingly acquire political relevance, their principles materialized through investment and fixed capital. The PA has long been ceding public functions to the private sector, and Rawabi was—at the early stages at least—attaching itself explicitly to the state-building agenda and rhetoric.[2]

My intention here is not to make a checklist of ways in which Palestine is or is not a state, but to integrate questions of scale, capital, and state form with analyses of the relationships between the West Bank and Israel. And although occupation and resistance are central to the ways those relations are produced, they are not the sole organizing principles. Palestine is linked to the rest of the world, albeit in piecemeal and highly subject ways. The state process is a key mechanism for those links. More than just a critical shorthand or term of abuse, "neoliberalism" contains within it the capitalism, privatization, and individuation present in Palestine. Neoliberalism is an intensification of capitalism's class project; it is a process of becoming and of enabling politically sustainable accumulation (Harvey 2007). Thinking about Palestine as a state-in-formation is a way to see the transformations that had to occur for neoliberal ideology and governance to emerge. There is a push and pull between the occupation and a

> theory of political economic practices that proposes that human well-being can best be advanced by liberating individual entrepreneurial freedoms and skills within an institutional framework characterized by strong private property rights, free markets, and free trade. The role of the state is to create and preserve an institutional framework appropriate to such practices. The state has to guarantee, for example, the quality and integrity of money. But also the military, defense, police, and legal structures and functions required to secure private property rights and to guarantee, by force if need be, the proper functioning of markets. Furthermore, if markets do not exist (in areas such as land, water, education, health care, social security, or environmental pollution) then they must be created, by state action if necessary. But beyond these tasks the state should not venture. (Harvey 2007, 2)

In late 2007, the Palestinian Reform and Development Plan (PRDP) was released, and it represented the beginning of a public change in direction for the PA. It merged international ideas and energy that took shape in 2001, when Salam Fayyad was given control of the Ministry of Finance and PA capital, and it outlined a new set of government priorities. A lot has been made of the PRDP: donors and aid organizations that had some role in producing it were pleased by the government's new orientations and self-presentation. Scholars of Palestine heavily critiqued it along the lines that it was a fantasy: that the state did not, does not, and cannot exist; that it is more of the same.

Fair enough. Yet the rhetoric and the ideas contained in the PRDP and subsequent national plans—allusive as they were—are also productive. Such priorities can take shape, and orient, support, and frame practice as they circulate and manifest in projects and places. They give language to political economic and material interventions and demonstrate the extent to which practice can coalesce around ideological goals.

Given the importance of international aid and global attention to the conflict historically, ideas of priority necessarily go beyond Palestine. Capital and states are bound together, and capital looks for, requires, and produces markets. But the universalizing qualities of capitalism do not equalize, and different states are produced in the terms of and in relation to specific forms of territory and territorial imperative. And in the present global political economy, "Where geopolitics can be understood as a means of acquiring territory towards a goal of accumulating wealth, geoeconomics reverses the procedure, aiming directly at the accumulation of wealth through market control. The acquisition or control of territory is not at all irrelevant but is a tactical option rather than a strategic necessity" (Cowen and Smith 2009, 42).

The PA state project is for a neoliberal Palestine, a late capitalist state emerging in the West Bank and within a settler state's imperatives. It is a process of establishing a political form that organizes continual capitalist accumulation (Lefebvre 2009; Peck 2010). Anthropology enables an approach to ongoing and piecemeal projects as they exist both in daily life and at multiple scales. I hope that this materialist ethnography of private development and state building has helped to demystify the consequences of what people are doing in Palestine, the changes they are making to their social and material environment, and the tendrils of practices and ideas that emerge simultaneously with changing political and economic contexts. Practice and rhetoric are both productive and mutually produced, and Palestine is being reconfigured today as a unit, as a nation, and as a state in the West Bank. Phenomena, beliefs, institutions, politics, and social organization are the products of human activity, contested and elaborated.[3]

Separation and Uneven Incorporation

West Bank territory appears here in three overlapping and contrasting ways. First, it is the site of racial and ethnic definition and conflict—settler colonialism is, fundamentally, the struggle by colonists to create a land physically devoid of its indigenous inhabitants (Wolfe 2006), and by making it impossible to live as indigenous people (Kauanui 2016). Second, it is the domain of at least two unequal states, one with imprecise borders and containing multiple forms of administration over different types of people in the same place. And third, it is space produced by the interaction of capitalist and political imperatives—creating an open environment for investment, making land productive and profitable, and maintaining a Palestine subordinate to Israel.

Economy and state building are no longer about framing a captive labor market for Israel, but instead producing a semi-autonomous Palestine that minimizes Israeli maintenance (capital, personnel, political) in part by allowing more direct relationships to global capital.[4] Palestine is integrated and excluded from the Israeli economy but is a crucial part of it. Palestinians are included in the "shekelspace," the necessary circulation of currency, but not in the land market beyond the West Bank, which is open only to the Jewish people (Yiftachel 2006). The peace process is an industry that perpetuates itself rather than a project with an end goal (Massad 2006). The same is true of state building. It makes the same assumptions about peace and the day after, within the present economic environment. Today, critics argue, Palestinian capital has no general political goal other than to maximize profit and strengthen elites' position; there is a moral dimension to "the destructive role of Palestinian capital" on the national movement that converges with PA plans as "PA-style liberation" (Nakhleh 2012).

The difference, I suggest, is that "liberation" has not been forgotten; rather, it is being logically reoriented. For the PA and the private sector, "liberation" increasingly is of the universalist kind embedded in the idea of free markets. Liberation can be achieved through liberalization.

In the specific context of occupation and the general context of capitalist restructuring in Palestine, Palestinian history and present—and the sense of appropriate future outcomes—ought to be understood in terms of the colonial project and the colonial experience. The universal claims that elites make are part of the work to instantiate their status and maintain the political economic system by presenting their own aims as the general aims of society (Guha 1998)—or, as Fanon (2005) put it, the nationalist bourgeoisie under colonialism are not out simply for their own self-interest, but orient themselves toward colonizers to build something that can perpetuate that self-interest. The state-building project in Palestine is a form of elite production and stabilization that is political and economic, but also cultural and material.

The PA is a pragmatic, "realist" institution that works on and within the status quo in order to liberalize. It is a product of both the imperatives of global capital and the changing dynamics of integration and segregation from Israel and Israeli markets. And for the elite today, the anthropologist Khalil Nakhleh told me, "It is no longer a taboo to have normalized relations with Israel. It is considered savvy business." Those elites are not necessarily working against the national goals; they are working to shape the nation, the state, the economy, and the goals of each in ways that perpetuate and sustain accumulation. The extent to which the vision of liberation as liberalization can take hold through state-scale governance is an open question. But it is clear that the Palestinian nationalist bourgeoisie inside and outside of the PA, regional and global investors, liberal Israeli capitalists, NGOs, the Israeli Labor Party, profiteers such as Tony Blair, and many others are betting on it.

The State and Geographies of Capital

According to Neil Smith, although Marx saw geographical differentiation as "of secondary importance compared with the 'universalizing tendency' of capital and the consequent drive toward equalization" (1984, 128), the production of differentiated and uneven spaces is vital for capitalism's survival. If the state in the West Bank is a geography produced through and for capital relations, it could contain both an adequately functioning state in a semiclear territory and a captive and closed market under colonial rule. The kinds of contingent links that Palestine has to the outside are not malformed; they are unevenly produced.

The state is institutional and social. A geoeconomic, state-scale market is being built with a clearly defined population but without clear territory. State institutions, priorities, and laws incorporate a polity and form the context for social reproduction. They are also part of how narratives about modernity, modernization, and growth are framed. Colonialism is a productive mechanism for transforming the past into a different kind of a present. Samera Esmeir says:

> Colonial rule, knowledge, and sensibilities eradicated the past and engendered not only new ways of relating to it but also institutions constitutive of a new present open to the future. But such destructive productivity is only one part of the story, which narrates the triumph of colonialism and modernization. The other part registers, at least partially, the persistence of the past—not in the form of fixed institutions that can be immediately revived and relived but rather in the form of threads enabling the remembrance of past and consequently its reinvention. The linear understanding of time is neither the only representation of forward movement nor the sole account of backward return. (Esmeir 2012, 65)

The example of real estate development in Palestine shows the importance of the question of the state and its relationship to the global political economy. The PA state is being produced without clear boundaries and without clear sovereignty, but it is organizing accumulation and ideas about aspiration and sociality. Elites and firms working toward "the day after" in

Palestine are working against a developmental state (e.g., Chibber 2006) and toward a privatized, corporate, almost nonterritorial one. Corporations have historically emerged intertwined with the state as "immune" from the law and benefit from both its application and nonapplication (Barkan 2013). In the Palestinian case, as the state emerges, law forms around and codifies corporate practice. Capitalism is a system that implies and necessitates universality, but as Michael Blim (1997) and others have emphasized, it is far from total or preordained. Part of that narrative about the universality and linearity and naturalness of capital comes out of the practice of capitalism itself—and in ways that echo the developers' modernization narratives.

In trying to understand how the West Bank is integrated and separated from its land, its law, its neighbors, and regional and global markets, I have stressed dynamics of inclusion and distribution, of presenting, representing, and working toward certain goals; and how projects and practices at different scales resonate in relational and overlapping but not necessarily cohesive ways (Keil and Mahon 2010; Brenner 2010). I emphasize how Palestine has been unevenly incorporated rather than separated or de-developed.

Envisioning Normalcy, Producing a Future

Planning is a form of anticipation and a form of urban governance and production (Bou Akar 2018); here the entire scaffolding of the Palestinian state is basically anticipatory. The day after is not an outcome, but an organizing principle for stabilization without clear direction.

Over and over during fieldwork I was told that "there's no vision for the future" and that "Fayyad has no vision." Planning for the eventual day after, however, is that vision of the future. It is an indeterminate future premised on enhancing and formalizing the present. Indeed, now that Fayyad is out of the picture, and the PA has seen the installation, resignation, and reinstallation of Rami Hamdallah in June 2013, and at the time of writing another prime minister from the world of economic development, Mohammad Shtayyeh, there have been no major changes in policy despite his absence. There are regular cycles of violence; in late summer 2014, Palestinians in Gaza were massacred by the IDF, while the same forces protected the PA police in the West Bank from demonstrations. Demonstrations dissipated and Israel successfully reset the Hamas-Fatah "unity government" without displacing Mahmoud Abbas or strengthening the PLO at the expense of the PA.[5]

While there may be increasing threats to the status quo within the West Bank as the Fatah leadership ages out and increasingly struggles to consolidate its power, the privatization of the state has momentum through the practical vision held among the private sector, the representatives of finance capital, and NGOs. The PA has already been remade into a conduit for public and international money to private initiative. Within this system, Rawabi is not to be understood as an outside imposition, but as a political and economic project by Palestinians and an indicator of one direction Palestine is moving. Palestinian state building is proceeding within the context of Israeli settler-colonial territorial ambitions and imperatives. It is a state that frames markets, private accumulation, and the distribution of international aid at one scale, but which is subject to Israel at all others. Occupying civilians carve the landscape, and an occupying military controls the borders. This is state as market, nowhere near state as sovereign.[6] Despite what it cannot do, the new state forms the scaffolding for economies and markets emerging under its rubric, it is constantly invoked, it is perpetually emerging, and it orients the structure of interventions and projects now and in the future.

Capitalists in Palestine are often accused of normalizing relations with Israel. There are countless examples of developers talking explicitly about good relations with the Jewish diaspora and with Israel (Al Jazeera 2013) and in ways that go beyond realist and pragmatist politics (Massad 1997, 2006). Rawabi, for example, plays to its audiences worldwide. Within Palestine, it issued a strong statement against using settlement goods. But it treats it as a set of guidelines: developers told me, "We prefer Palestinian products except when the other products are better," which, given the depleted state of Palestinian industry, is a lot of the time. By virtue of their position, Masri and other members of the nationalist bourgeoisie circulate abroad as representatives of Palestine, prosperous and peaceful, and concerned with stability *rather than politics.*[7] Capital trumps politics, but it can also benefit from it, even in unlikely environments.

Through the state, Palestinian capitalists are trying to de-link big capital from the occupation and allow Palestine to more fully enter the world market. Financial normalization may change the status of "normal" as far as accumulation is concerned, and it is helping a state and economy emerge from the raw materials and the normal conditions of occupation. Everyday life is constructed around the need to live life every day: Palestinian ideas of normalcy are potentially affected and altered by changes to the wider context (L. Allen 2008, 2013). Normalization can mean class aspiration and accumulation as well as consolidation of the conditions of occupation. Taken individually, not all of these activities are so clear-cut, and it is important to emphasize that racial, political, geographic, and economic segregation are both goals and consequences of Israeli colonization. But taken together, they represent the effort to transcend division with business, to de-racialize Palestinian and Israeli capital, and to stabilize the situation without significantly altering its shape.

In Conclusion

State-scale economics is today a mechanism for stabilization in Palestine, but not for generalized political freedom for most Palestinians. It is a process of producing dynamics of unequal incorporation and distribution. I have tried to complicate the pictures of political economy and continuous state building in the West Bank, to see Palestine in the world, to understand what certain Palestinians are doing in Palestine, and how the West Bank is being set up now in ways that are constitutive of future possibility. Politics, the law, and peoples' aspirations may be changing as a result of the state-building project, just as they change and contribute to it. A new Palestinian state is emerging in the West Bank under settler colonialism. It frames open markets, but it is a truncated and circumscribed openness; uneven development is still a certain kind of development and movement. If the state-building project explicitly attempts to create, master plan, and map a middle class, the middle class also advances it. Many ordinary Palestinians are waiting for opportunities and places where they can extract a normal, stable life. Debt, the new state, and new types of housing potentially provide a new long term. Class aspiration and occupation can exist simultaneously, and laws are being reformed to create the administrative capacity for widespread change. Aspiration for the day after does not necessarily mean the desire to revolutionize the present.

I have no intention to be predictive here, but instead to describe what certain fluid classes of people are doing in and with respect to Palestine, what it might mean, and how they understand past and present to strengthen and describe the conditions on which a future might be represented and built. In doing so, I hope I can reframe the context in such a way as to present alternative pathways for ideas and work on Palestinian political aspiration; beyond class advancement or capital accumulation, but toward liberation and an actually just, emancipatory future.

In *The Condition of Postmodernity*, David Harvey describes Georges Gurvitch's typology of social times, including the dragging time academics inhabit in which "the future becomes present so late as to be outmoded as soon as it is crystallized" (Harvey 1990, 223–24). It is 2018, over a decade since the Rawabi process began, and years past the time it was to be completed. I am in my office on the gray, gothic campus of the University of Chicago, sitting below a print of a May 2003 *New Yorker* cartoon by Mick Stevens.[8] The cartoon depicts seven presumably white, well-dressed men and women sitting around a conference table, the Capitol building in Washington just visible through the window. The man at the head of the table is speaking: "Don't think of them as terrorist states. Think of them as terrorist markets." As with other *New Yorker* jokes, it is subtle and comprehensible; funny but not excessively so. It may as well be a blurb on the back of this book. In Gaza, Israeli snipers have been murdering unarmed Palestinian protestors for several weeks, while close friends in Ramallah and Birzeit report little change to the feelings of distance and insulation. This is a book about the work, the imaginative aspects and practices, and real experiential effects of the process by which Palestine is fragmented and foreclosed, as the desperate reality for many is subsumed and obscured by the vision presented by and to others.

ACKNOWLEDGMENTS

I COULD NEVER ADEQUATELY THANK, or even list, the huge number of people who helped me over the many years this book and research have taken. Succeeding even marginally at this job requires an almost impossible confluence of luck, privilege, and support that scaffolds the solitude of the work and the dislocation of constantly moving from and returning to places that have changed, if you can return at all.

I have to first express gratitude to the people I worked with at The Graduate Center, City University of New York (CUNY), Talal Asad, Michael Blim, Vincent Crapanzano, David Harvey, and Neil Smith; and Nadia Abu El-Haj (who taught my first anthropology class in 1999, for better or worse). Thanks to Julian Brash, Emily Curtin, Saygun Gokariksel, Harmony Goldberg, Kate Griffiths, Anthony Johnson, Baris Kuymulu, Martha Lincoln, Manissa Maharawal, Nada Moumtaz, Ted Powers, Jeremy Rayner, Ted Sammons, Mary Taylor, Yunus Telliel, and John Warner. Many conversations, arguments, Midtown walks, garden sits, and O'Reilly's are reflected here. Others at CUNY helped in big and small ways, including Gerald Creed, Louise Lennihan, Jeff Maskovsky, Ida Susser, Katharine Verdery, Gary Wilder, and especially Ellen DeRiso. Beyond the department, I want to thank Asher Dupuy-Spencer, Peter Frase, Jesse Goldstein, Cindy Gorn, Elizabeth Johnson, Scott Larson, Francesca Manning, Andy McKinney, Wilson Sherwin, David Spataro, Brett Story, Jake Stevens, and Owen Toews.

I am lucky to have met and been surrounded by so many brilliant and good people through this work. I have had some kind of interaction with Omar Jabary Salamanca, Sobhi Samour, and Mezna Qato nearly daily since 2007. I owe thanks to Basel Abbas, Nasser Abourahme, Ruanne Abourahme,

Lawrence Abu-Hamdan, Max Ajl, Nora Akawi, Ala Al-Azzeh, Abdullah Al-Kurd, Hazem Alnamla, Rana Barakat, Lisa Bhungalia, Andy Clarno, Beshara Doumani, Dror Etkes, Josh Friedman, Toufic Haddad, Jeff Halper, Dawood Hammoudeh, Adam Hanieh, Samir Harb, Shir Hever, Sandi Hilal, Rania Jawad, Jimmy Johnson, Raja Khalidi, Paul Kohlbry, Peter Lagerquist, Penny Mitchell, Nicola Perugini, Alessandro Petti, Lorenzo Pezzani, Tarek Radi, Vyjanthi Rao, Laura Ribero, Andrew Ross, Seth Sanders, Michal Sfard, Maida Smeir, Ron Smith, Michael Sorkin, Cindi Sousa, Sophia Stamatopoulou-Robbins, Omar Tesdell, Mandy Turner, Eyal Weizman, Alex Winder, and Khaled Ziada. Lori Allen and Amahl Bishara went out of their way to help me on my first research trip. Ziad Abu-Amr, Samia Al-Botmeh, Salah Al-Tamari, Yazid Anani, Sam Bahour, Khaled Fourani, Reema Hamami, Islah Jad, Eileen Kuttab, Khalil Nakhleh, and Lisa Taraki, all offered help and advice over time. Neve Gordon and Haim Yacobi both supported my work and helped me figure out how to stay in the country. Sherene Seikaly and Salim Tamari have both been consistently gracious over the years.

When Neil Smith passed, a group of his students came together for each other in an extremely low moment. My sincere thanks to Marnie Brady, Morgan Buck, Kathleen Dunn, Zoltan Gluck, Malav Kanuga, Steve McFarland, Laurel Mei Singh, Elizabeth Sibilia, Annie Spencer, and Stephanie Wakefield. Deb Cowen could not have been more caring and generous.

The Graduate Center, the National Science Foundation, the Palestinian American Research Center, and the Wenner-Gren Foundation all supported my research. Upon my return to New York, a fellowship at CUNY's Committee on Globalization and Social Change—and conversations with Herman Bennett, Susan Buck-Morss, and Kandice Chuh, and with Annie, David, and Gary—helped me start to figure out what material I had. CUNY, the Arab Council on Social Sciences, the University of Oxford Centre on Migration, Policy, and Society (COMPAS), the University of Chicago, and American University supported me as I wrote.

Thanks to Michael Keith, Nick Simcik-Arese, and Claudio Sopranzetti at COMPAS, and to my friends and colleagues at the University of Chicago and in the city: Fadi Bardawil, Meaghanne Barker, Nima Bassiri, Alexis Becker, Aaron Benanav, everyone at the Co-op, Joshua Craze, Alireza Doostdar, Sarah Fredericks, Diana Harper, Ghenwa Hayek, Angie Heo, John Kelly, Darryl Li, Joe Masco, Deb Neibel, Moishe Postone, Jim Sparrow, Jake Warner, Chloe Watlington, Lisa Wedeen, and Dan Wyche. Everyone at American University and in Washington—Ori Burton, C. Anne Claus, Amanda Huron and Mike Andre, Manissa, Sam Menefee-Libey, Adrienne Pine, Dan Sayers, David Vine, Rachel Watkins, and Jeanie Wogaman—has been welcoming and supportive as this process ends and another begins.

Previous rehearsals of some of these arguments appeared in the *New Left Review*, the *Jerusalem Quarterly*, and Stefano Jacoviello and Tomasso Sbriccoli's edited volume. I am grateful to all involved, and once again to Nicola, with whom I worked on material that went into the settler chapters. Parts of this book would not exist without specific people. I owe much to an unnamed interlocutor who showed me what to look for during fieldwork. The staff at Geomolg, Ahmad Barclay at Palestine Open Maps, Samir, Paul, and Haim were instrumental in helping me gather and make sense of the data for the maps that Meagan A. Snow made. Eyal introduced me to Carmel Pomerantz, who petitioned the court on my behalf and gathered the filings in the Rawabi/Regavim case. Guy Eytan translated those filings from Hebrew; another translator did the filings from Yesh Din. Léo Lambert generously allowed me to use his photos. Thanks to everyone who spoke with me in and around Rawabi, in the ministries, in the development and finance worlds, and elsewhere—named and unnamed.

Max, Peter, Joe, Mezna, Sherene, and Sophia all read large parts of the manuscript as it progressed and helped it along immeasurably. Thera Webb went through the very first version, Ida Audeh did more recently, and Nada fixed the transliterations.

At Duke University Press, utmost thanks to Ken Wissoker for his support and guidance, to Jade Brooks for bringing me in, to Joshua Gutterman Tranen for his enthusiasm and work near the end, to Lisa Lawley and Shazia Aminfor editing; as well as Cathy Hannabach for indexing. I am also thankful for the helpful and diligent comments—of all varieties, really—from my two anonymous reviewers.

This kind of work sometimes feels inescapable, so it is especially important for me to name some of the people who reminded me to do other things. I could not have managed without friendship and support from Tim Aher, Mio Alter, Mike Berg, Pat Berran, Sarah Cassidy, Danielle Choi, Matt Coe, Talya Cooper, Sarah Geis, Guy Greenberg, Geoff Guy, Nick Kukla, Nina Lalli, Eric Lee, Nick Kukla, Beverly Liang, Andrew Lindner, Mona Mady, Peter McArthur, Milosz Meller, Stephanie Pope, Chris Terry, and Emily Winter. Pete Corrie, Alex Curtin, Nick Curtin, Josh Egnew, Bjorn Johnson, Sean O'Keefe, Eric Owens, Jeremy Scott, Jed Smith, and J. B. Townshend, helped me maintain a reasonable standard of life elsewhere. I absolutely could not have done this without my best friend and constant companion, Ginger. It is too bad she will never read this (because she is a dog).

My family has always been supportive of my work and habit of returning to Palestine. Thanks to my parents and sisters, Maha, Mohamed, Aseel, and Haneen.

Everyone always ends these things by asserting their final responsibility for the text. On the one hand, I know people disagree with things I say here, and obviously the book ends up with my name on it, on the hook for its shortcomings. On the other, I hope my responsibility is to others (and theirs to me), to my colleagues and friends and peers, to those who preceded me and to the next batch of people doing this kind of work, and to inflecting common sense on Palestine toward a real and just future.

Finally, I want to return to the beginning of this process. Without Neil Smith as my adviser during the first seven years of graduate school, this project would never really have gotten started. I miss him and wish he were here to talk, to push, and to keep me accountable to the people and things and ideas that actually matter. I owe him a lot, and although it was not always straightforward, I am hugely indebted for his teaching, support, and friendship. Annie told me she feels he is alive in us in profound ways. I hope I have made some headway there. But it is also only because of Michael Blim's personal, intellectual, and practical help throughout graduate school, and his care and willingness those last two years to take on the responsibility to see me through, that this project ever got finished.

NOTES

Introduction

1 The description can be vague, but useful accounts include Samara 2000; Hanieh 2002; Raja Khalidi and Samour 2011; and Haddad 2016.

2 Pasternak and Dafnos (2018) focus on the ways settler states secure capacities for circulation and how indigenous people can disrupt them. In Israel, where there are no real pockets of indigenous jurisdiction within the state, this is the flip side. The continuous privatization in the West Bank operates to solidify the context for investment and circulation, insulated from disruptive intervention.

3 In 2018, *Fortune Magazine* listed him as number 38 of the "World's 50 Greatest Leaders," a "doer . . . stepping up to meet today's challenges." He shares the list with various CEOs and politicians, the #MeToo Movement, the students of Marjorie Stoneman Douglas High School, and Reese Witherspoon (Fortune Editors 2018).

4 Rawabi's municipal structure has made the reality of the present situation visible in ways developers may not have anticipated. The preliminary results of the 2017 Palestinian census show a population of just 710 (State of Palestine, Palestinian Central Bureau of Statistics 2018), many of whom I know to have been employees renting directly from the firm. One such renter I interviewed was a young foreign student. Recruited from overseas, she lived there on a three-month internship. Her primary experience of residence in shared company housing was isolation from Ramallah. She experienced a subtle kind of security monitoring, where guards prevented her and her female colleagues from walking the streets at night or told them to "sit properly" rather than recline in public. She described a place that was empty during the day, where there was only one supermarket. It was a place she had to leave in order to socialize. Her airfare was covered and her wages, as an intern, were an extremely generous USD700 a month. Rawabi's central shopping area, the Q Center (named for Qatar), is brightly lit, clean, half occupied, and very often empty of shoppers.

Young employees mill about circulating, socializing, and acting as promoters and tour guides. Not yet a city, it is a plan materialized, a model. It is preliminary and partial proof of concept and a demonstration of how people could become incorporated.

5 The land market is of course still an unsettled issue: in March 2017, Israel closed the Palestinian office that tracks land sales to Jewish Israelis, seizing the computers and arresting staff. Three days later, computers were returned, but six months after that, Israelis broke up a conference on the topic (Hasson 2017; Lieber 2017). Such closures and repression of information happen constantly in Israel, but the clear takeaway is that it does not benefit the regime to limit land sales; the more lucrative strategy is to maintain open markets that operate within systems of racial exclusion. Moreover, land has a market character, and housing can incorporate people and produce consensus about markets and ideology. The Israeli system of political control over the West Bank is cohesive and coherent but not uniform: material, ideological work needs to be done to transform its attributes into a common sense.

6 The contemporary critical literature tends to presuppose separation from Israel and to judge the successes or failures of Fayyadism by the extent to which it has achieved some stated goals of national development or liberation (see, e.g., Tilley 2015; Dana 2015; Tartir 2015). I believe the framework of uneven incorporation—in some ways a contemporary outcome of Walter Rodney's (1982) underdevelopment thesis and its forms of structural dependence that here produce stability and market relations rather than strictly exploitative modes of production—captures what happens at a wider scale. It presents privatization neither as an anomaly nor an outside imposition, but as part of a historical and worldwide process.

7 Even as the state-building and private development period in the West Bank emerges from the peace process and is, I believe, a continuation of its logic, ideas of development and land improvement have been a fundamental aspect of capitalism since it emerged (Wood 2002; Robinson 2000; Williams 1975). Moreover, within a system of colonial domination in Historic Palestine, Brenna Bhandar (2018) shows how such logics of improvement enabled property by title and culminated in a practical and juridical system of racial, colonial, private landholding. Today, state sovereignty often means market sovereignty, and a kind of poststate and nonstate authority is emerging in Palestine through economic practice and jurisdiction. The Middle East has been a central problem for global politics since before the Cold War. This is the turn toward markets and management, the late capitalist inflection.

8 Social scientists have long understood how the idea of separation between the economy and the state is fundamental to how both are conceived and operate. A false and productive assumption, it organizes relations between polity, the conditions of possibility and intervention, and the contexts in which social life takes place. In the contemporary global economic division of labor characterized by uneven geographical development, national production within states has be-

come less relevant than forms of circulation. David Harvey proposes relinking the state and economy as a "state-finance nexus," an attempt to describe

> the confluence of state and financial power that confounds the analytic tendency to see state and capital as clearly separable from each other. This does not mean that state and capital constituted then or now are an identity, but that there are structures of governance (such as power of the coinage of the realm in the past and central banks and treasure departments today) where the state management of capital creation and monetary flows becomes integral to, rather than separable from, the circulation of capital. The reverse relation also holds as taxes or borrowings flow into the coffers of the state and as state functions also become monetized, commodified and ultimately privatized. (Harvey 2011, 48)

Within the geographies formed through and in relation to the dynamics and imperatives of capitalism, each state has a particular form of the state-finance nexus similar to what I have described in terms of practical interventions to shape future interventions. This is an active process, and as the case of new development in Palestine demonstrates clearly, money is made not just out of production and labor, but through the creation of geographies. One manifestation Harvey analyzes is how rising prices and rents are difficult to sustain over time because fewer and fewer people can afford them. Elsewhere this might mean gentrification. In Palestine, the array of processes and politically informed investment means new forms of debt and political intervention reformulated as market stability and as state governance.

9 This is perhaps why some of the clearest scholars and practitioners of a legal approach such as Noura Erakat (2019) take it to be partial, an opening. The worldwide Boycott, Divestment, and Sanctions (BDS) movement to pressure Israel until it complies with international law is built out of the discourse on rights, but as a movement toward wider decolonial and anti-settler-colonial praxis. By critically embracing universalism and universal rights, they work to subvert the initial problem, context, and local situation. In doing so, they bind together and question both the statist approach in the West Bank and the Israeli settler-colonial regime. Erakat lucidly articulates the legal history and context of Israeli rule over Palestine that I also discuss in the settler chapters, and theorizes the consequences and stakes for utilizing it.

10 One of the most troubling questions for legal scholars of Israel/Palestine is how it feeds back into the state through law. Different bodies of law and practice incorporate and assume citizens, subjects, and polities. In his work on the legal dynamics of exclusion within Israel, Mazen Masri (2017) begins with the question, "Who is 'the people'" that ought to be the basis for sovereignty? He winds that question through the contradictory and overlapping ideas of a state defined as ethnically Jewish as well as generally democratic. And he shows that Palestinians are legally excluded from participation and full citizenship. Who is a part of this West Bank state? And what do territory and the ongoing fluvial processes of inclusion and exclusion have to do with it?

11 Developers and proponents of privatization in the West Bank often discuss standards of living among Palestinians as political questions related to occupation. Are they free participants in an open market? Does the presence of wealth contradict the occupation? Can economic growth circumvent occupation? Yet such questions presuppose separation and ignore the multiple ways the West Bank is embedded in a much wider settler capitalist geography. Even the availability of credit for Palestinians is part of the fabric of licit and illicit Israeli political economy: capital circulates in Palestinian banks in part because Israelis use them to launder money (Khoury 2018).

12 Now generalized worldwide through what Nancy Kwak calls "consensus language," the ideal of home ownership emerged as an "interconnected set of ideals and practical needs brought together ideas about democracy—whether through a widespread access to a consumer economy, a more diffuse sense of equality, or anticommunist dogma—with a very specific, 'modern' version of debt-driven, state-regulated ownership that gave at least the illusion of growing affluence and security" (2015, 2). Kwak observes, "The appearance of consensus could help governments court international aid and navigate domestic political pressures while wooing foreign investors and seeking competitive advantage in a global marketplace" (212). Through development projects, it quickly became clear that "low-income homeownership was advantageous for almost everyone except the new homeowners themselves: politicians could claim to be helping the poor without building public housing. The middle class in formation benefitted from their own second-tier investments while enjoying the moral satisfaction of their own, 'earned' position in the social hierarchy. Bankers and investors thrived" (206).

   In Palestine as in the cases Kwak describes, local implementation is a question of negotiation, priority, and ability; and ownership is part of the story of the development of capital. The case of housing development in Palestine demonstrates how global logical consensus has been translated into local vernacular. Home ownership is a specific historical formation with differing emphasis on property, modern form, or investment in different places. Here, as a continuation of the peace process and after the global housing crisis, home ownership is coherent within political imperatives to simultaneously expand and de-intensify the occupation.

13 As for the land, national planning now operates to benefit development by consolidating land under clear title and opening it to the market. Sure enough, the Ministry of Planning and International Cooperation was subsumed into the ministries of Finance and of Local Government in 2014—another victory of market over state.

Chapter One. The Site

1 See https://machsomwatch.org/en/reports/checkpoints/22032017/morning/55130.
2 A Rawabi employee described instances where, for example, the owner was under eighteen and could not sell or was abroad and could not be found. She

said the ratio of what they were able to buy versus what they were granted via eminent domain was something like 49:1. When I accidentally referred to land "expropriation," she said, "No, no, it is acquisition, not expropriation. Expropriation is what colonies do."

3   Sam Bahour (2012), a Palestinian businessman and critic, asks similar questions and says developers' focus on the economic parts of the future amounts to participation in an "economic hallucination."

4   A former employee told me that Masri demanded a huge planning zone to prevent villagers, "not the good kind of people," from building next to Rawabi. Land dealers I interviewed in 2015 told me the company owns much of the land in that area and beyond it, through various types of land deals, obscured by layers of holding companies, and so on.

5   And by early 2018, the landmark "Rawabi junction" was the site of a settler attack on Palestinians (Wafa: Palestinian News and Info Agency 2018).

Chapter Two. Developers and Designers

1   See www.portlandtrust.org.

2   This is a sore subject: people were brought onto the project, some kind of dispute happened, and they left. Several scholars, researchers, and planners removed their names from Al-Reehan or Rawabi research. I asked numerous people about what happened, but they either would not talk about it or were coy—"I will tell you if [someone else] tells you first." The point is that some people found the unspecified methods and outcomes distasteful.

3   On this point, the developers agree with Regavim, the settler organization I discuss in chapters 9 and 10, which argues that Israel is facing an Arab housing crisis that can be solved by building in greater density (Arutz Sheva Staff 2019a). In this and in many other ways, the shared physical and ideological landscape produces solutions to political problems that result in shrinking capacities for Arab Palestinians to live as Arab Palestinians.

4   See Abu El-Haj (2001) and Weizman (2007) for a discussion of the ways that stone-cladding projects the image of timelessness.

5   Safdie has thought about social housing for displaced Palestinians since 1967, when he actively worked toward it with the Baron de Rothschild. His is a liberal universalist vision for the whole of Palestine and the West Bank, based on a need to reform an oppressive state toward a true liberal multiculturalism (Safdie 1973). He is against the Israeli settlement movement in the West Bank and Gaza, and has not accepted commissions there. As for the controversy around the idea that Rawabi is a "Palestinian settlement," Palestine is not so static that a widespread building typology can be understood simply as an imposition. Rather, the way that the project was conceived and designed tells us not only that Palestine is part of the world and world economy, but that this is the form of building coherent within the context of today's privatizing Palestine.

6   See http://www.aecom.com/Where+We+Are/Asia/Urban+Development /_carousel/Long+Hung+Commune,+Ho+Chi+Minh+City,+Vietnam. Accessed April 27, 2010.

7   See Talal Asad's elegantly devastating review of the Israeli British anthropologist Abner Cohen for a discussion of the ways the political, historical, and political economic contexts around the *hamula* were productively misunderstood, rendering it as an unchanging and static, indigenous and premodern form of family organization. It was the "ideological resolution of a Zionist problem . . . a mode of control and an imputed identity for the only political existence allowed to Arab villagers in Israel" (1975, 274).

8   This is pervasive in Palestinian politics. Sophia Stamatopoulou-Robbins (2018) describes environmental planning for the future and the trouble establishing fixity when so much is uncertain.

Chapter Three. Image, Process, and Precedent

1   Before groundbreaking it became public that Massar was working with the Jewish National Fund (JNF) to plant trees and to "green" the area. Hugely controversial from all angles, developers were forced to refuse the offer under pressure. One Rawabi employee told me that they simply did not know what the JNF was. This seems far-fetched. But it does point toward some of the ways that Rawabi employees position themselves toward Israel—the company had a web form for people to buy trees to be planted in Palestine. The JNF donated three thousand trees. Why would anyone object? the employee asked. "You can't discriminate if people want to donate" for the environment. It turned out to be such a "huge mistake" that he joked that it was "a mistake to even bring it up with" me.

2   Bishara answered Erdan's question with another: "Why don't you just go fuck yourself?" (Frenkel 2006). As of 2020, Erdan has been named Israel's ambassador both to the UN and to the United States.

3   This was one of those times anthropological method makes a researcher's life easier: we can write about not getting an interview just as easily as getting one.

4   Moreover, in Palestine, NGOs are critical producers of research and knowledge in and about the conflicts and contexts. The NGO Al-Marsad, which monitors various security agreements, has referenced it as a case study, mostly in an objective and noncritical register (Marsad 2016, 2017) or in straightforward reporting (Marsad 2010, 2013). Other NGOs such as Ma'an Development Center and Badil do not, at the time of writing, have any reports on Rawabi publicly available in English or Arabic. In its rundown of the news, the Institute for Palestine Studies also seems to see Rawabi as a national-scale project worth tracking, and has translated Hebrew news commentary on Rawabi, particularly around the 2010 settler demonstrations I discuss in chapter 9. When an NGO report manages to rise to the level of public debate, as Bisan's did, developers work to limit its reach and potential circulation.

5   This was in an email a colleague in a very radical architecture department forwarded to me.

6   I grew up around Washington, DC, and, along with dozens of members of the
    Palestinian community at the time, I was there too. I was an awkward teen with
    a bad skaterish haircut, and my mother still has the blurry photo of me and
    Arafat on the corkboard in her kitchen.

7   It feels impossible to parse Masri's beliefs from his political optimism and his
    opportunism. At the 2018 Aspen Ideas festival, he said, "We had a terrible 8
    years during Obama's presidency. So anything vis-à-vis the Palestinian-Israeli
    issue is not terrible anymore for the Palestinians. Obama's administration was
    not positive to the Palestinians. He talked a lot about the Palestinians but then
    he became enemies with Israel and that doesn't do us any good. So I am hoping
    the friendship President Trump has built with Prime Minister Netanyahu, and
    more importantly with the Israeli people, will benefit us" (Haaretz Jewish In-
    sider Staff 2018). In this schema and certainly in terms of market stability, good
    for Israel is good for the Palestinians.

8   To be fair, the geographer Lisa Bhungalia, who studies USAID and develop-
    ment in Palestine, told me that high overhead percentages, even this high, are
    not uncommon.

9   One rumor had it the chief accountant is paid $1,200/month while Masri's
    driver makes $2,000/month, something that had incensed two former employ-
    ees I interviewed.

10 By comparison, the Palestine Investment Fund makes a point of presenting
    itself as a private developer operating in the public interest, and much more of
    its information is publicly available.

Chapter Four. Public Urban Planning

1   I keep returning to Max Weber's (1992) famous descriptions of the ways anach-
    ronistic beliefs, ethics, laws, and practices can be left behind yet remain relevant
    as organizing principles, or perhaps as apparitions. Just as previous planners may
    have chosen to create racist, punitive laws and practices, we are forced to comply
    despite all the new laws, images of openness, freedom, and self-rule. Vestigial, they
    nevertheless have purchase. They are out-of-date but somehow still valid.

2   And so "planning" itself becomes a different kind of an exercise. Around the
    time of my longest fieldwork stint in 2010, there was a movement among plan-
    ning NGOs to promote a "day after" that often entirely skipped over present
    material and political conditions. In part because of the skepticism of planning
    as imposed modernization, plans begin in a future when the occupation will be
    a nonissue. One think tank generated a lot of work on Jerusalem and Ramallah
    and migration based on housing cost. Planners talked about how migration of
    middle- and upper-class "yuppies" to Ramallah leaves Jerusalem with "the poor
    population" that cannot sustain the Jerusalem Arab "urban economy"—as
    though these are solely market phenomena.

3   This is an early example of the idea that Palestinian building ought to be mov-
    ing inward and upward, given imposed constraints. The idea is practical, about

density but most of all about preventing Palestinian people and life from expanding freely or organically.

Chapter Five. Housing Shortage and National Priority

1   At the time of my research, PADICO was chaired by Palestine's billionaire, Munib al-Masri, a distant relative of Bashar Masri and the man who was put in charge of the Fatah/Hamas political reconciliation portfolio. Bashar Masri himself was elected chair in 2019.
2   This is not at all unique to Palestine; Nancy Kwak (2015) demonstrates how this process is bound with international development and has a long history as a form of postwar global political intervention. The logics Kwak describes can be seen throughout these studies, government policy documents, and World Bank reports.
3   The Aspen Institute is a "non-partisan" economic development NGO founded by Walter Isaacson, author of a recent Steve Jobs biography; it has a large board of trustees that at the time of my research included Henry Louis Gates, Elaine Pagels, Condoleezza Rice, Queen Noor of Jordan, philanthropist Margot Pritzker, and a Koch brother. Lifetime members include Henry Kissinger and Madeleine Albright.
4   By 2013, according to the United States Government Accountability Office (2013), no funds had been disbursed to buyers, yet the processes AMAL jump-started continue, state reform progresses, and investments generate profit. It is unclear to me how that USD500 million materialized.

Chapter Six. Public-Private Partnership

1   However, some Palestinians see the rollback of central government in favor of local control as an opportunity for counter-PA electoral politics. But elections are often postponed, and when they do happen, as in spring 2017, voters fail to be inspired to turn out.
2   And it is about creating narrow independence within the occupation. In July 2014 horrific incursions into the West Bank, ostensibly in response to the kidnapping and murder of three Israeli settlers, did not destabilize the government as much as allow Israel to set back the clock on Fatah-Hamas reconciliation. Israel might want to dismantle the unity government, but it probably needs the PA.
3   Again and again, people in government claimed to be "with Rawabi" but mostly insofar as it had been defined as part of the national interest or a condition of their employment.
4   See Shehadeh (1982) for a detailed outline of the legal categories and historical legal precedent defining and governing state land, public good, and so on.
5   The PIF is private and more or less separate from the PA and has been bringing foreign investments back to Palestine since it was founded in 2003. This arose

due to anxiety about protecting PA capital from a Rhode Island civil court case filed in 2000. The PA was found liable for damages resulting from a 1996 Hamas attack that killed two settlers, Yaron and Efrat Ungar, an American citizen and his Israeli wife; the court froze the PA's assets in 2004. That judgment was overturned in 2010, and the two sides reached an undisclosed settlement in 2011 (Stockman 2005; Mulvaney 2011).

6   And Gaza has "national" but not "regional" planning. It is, a primary national planner at the time told me, "a big mess."

7   There is also a method issue here: if the context is purposely confusing, it becomes nearly impossible to piece together how various laws and practices fit together. But it may not be entirely relevant, if the point is that practical confusion aligns with deregulation.

8   In contrast to the astonishing speed with which this all happened, the official Israeli restrictions on investment were a convoluted mess of a bureaucratic process, like something out of Terry Gilliam's *Brazil*. Why was Rawabi different, and what did it do differently?

9   And they believe they are succeeding. At the time I was trying, with great difficulty, to arrange a meeting with Masri, I was also trying to arrange to sit down with the prime minister. The latter meeting probably would have happened had our travel schedules not repeatedly clashed. I mentioned this to a Massar employee, who laughed and said, "Bashar is probably busier than the PM!"

Chapter Seven. Buyers and Villagers

1   Numan says this meeting took place in 2005, well before the development firm was established or the project was announced. Following the time line I pieced together in an earlier chapter, these were probably researchers from the Portland Trust, and whatever findings they made probably accrued to give authority to the wider development agenda. I also have been told by land dealers that Masri and others were actively buying land in the area as early as 2004, but nothing was happening in public view at that time.

2   For example, "unless better options are unavailable," Massar was at the time of my interviews considering directly contracting to NetVision, the main Israeli IT firm, for a line running to Rawabi from the nearby settlement Ateret. Or, as one Massar employee told me, the company treats its obligation to boycott Israeli settlement goods as a set of best practices, not unbreakable principles. In a lawsuit I focus on in chapter 9, Rawabi describes itself as "motivated by economic reasons and has no political agenda . . . [and] can happily state that their actions advance collaborations with Israeli companies" and general economic growth (H.C., 3355/14, Regavim v. Minister of Defense et al. [unpublished]).

3   There are, however, relevant external impositions. Moretti and Pestre (2015) have provided a quantitative analysis of years of World Bank documents and show a change over time in two contrasting paradigms of discourse. Early

documents show that the World Bank concentrated on lending but are written in a specific, technical language. From the early 1990s onward, finance, management, and governance become the central words and ideas. The changes are due to exogenous elements, and the causal chain is "loans." Next come debts, and the subsequent necessity to support private lenders. Through this ideological shift, there emerges a "growing indifference to space and time" and how these forms of intervention look locally. But the forms of global capital and technocratic intervention certainly do exist within a context, and here, one of military occupation. That growing indifference among lenders is part of how these interventions are normalized. Thus, the idea that Rawabi is somehow an "American imposition" is both correct and insufficient if the broader relations and forms of integration are taken into account.

4 The same is true of prisons. In Israel, as in the United States and elsewhere, representative infrastructure is hidden from the public. But political imprisonment is a widespread experience, and prisons themselves function as social and educational institutions, influencing politics and lives beyond their walls. In Palestine, where huge numbers of people have been detained (650,000 between 1967 and 2005, according to Saree Makdisi [2008]), each brings their experience back into the public and punitive engagement with the legal system is sociological fact. The public sector in the form of the PA supports prisoners and their families, and prison strikes have massive social resonance (as in summer 2017). Public and private are mixed in ways that complicate questions of public works and visibility, and of public and private generally (Hajjar 2005). Moreover, the shrinking public sphere enables collectivity at smaller scales, which may take the form of individual aspiration just as much as a political commons.

5 When the interim council was formed in summer 2013, it was made up of eleven people with private development, NGO, and PA backgrounds, but when the city reaches a threshold of five thousand residents, elections will be held. Part of the anxiety is about whether village councils will be a part of that process.

6 He continued, "Look at you, from the States. Names don't change. The name of Yazur," the village where my family originated, "didn't change for you even though there are no Palestinians anymore and it's owned entirely by Jewish Israelis."

7 This is not only fundamental to the emergence of capitalism as primitive accumulation, but persists in settler-colonial relations through recognition (Coulthard 2014), and in the circuit of capital as global division of labor that exists in the real world as forms of unevenness (N. Smith 1984) or "accumulation by dispossession" (Harvey 2003).

8 A colleague has provided a huge amount of data from 'Abwayn on a CD-ROM, but the files were corrupted, and I do not cite it here. The 'Abwayn interviews reiterate a few of the important points: that the land sale and seizure process was not believed to have happened fairly, that Rawabi created a wave of insecu-

rity, and that there is no real reason for Rawabi to be where it is as far as either housing scarcity or service provision are concerned.

Chapter Eight. Critique, Capital, and the Landscape

1 The currency union with Israel is useful as metaphor. The Paris Protocol creates the ephemera of integration while presenting real obstacles to growth in the Palestinian economy. There is integration with Israel at one scale, but as far as industry or economic practice is concerned, Israel owns frequencies and aquifers and whatever resources exist, dictates who can travel, holds taxes and imports, places settlements and roads on private Palestinian land, and so on. It is a rather small opportunity for control, but a large one for accumulation in service of political stability.

2 As I suggested earlier, developers actively use the international press to exert pressure on the PA, NGOs, and USAID for funding.

3 Basically, any contemporary popular left-leaning discussion of Palestine outside of Palestine—from film reviews, to academic travelogues, to political speech—will focus less on wider geopolitical and geoeconomic contexts of the Israeli occupation than on the brutalization of humble, steadfast villagers by a modern occupying army. I do not mean to suggest there are not villagers or that the occupation is not brutal. But this binary, and the centrality of victimhood, often obscures class difference and what Palestinians are doing to shape Palestine. It is clear that these ideas are fundamental to the narrative and to organizing outside of Palestine, but internally, flattening the Palestinian experience may enable specific forms of aspirational capitalist modernity to gain traction. After all, village life, poverty, and military repression are unpleasant. With the emergence of Rawabi, developers ask, are they potentially a thing of the past?

4 Sayigh (1979) is a notable corrective.

5 The historical forms of integration have been debated by economic historians— Samih Farsoun charts a history from subsistence economy to global market integration; Roger Owen and Charles Issawi stress the importance of trade with Europe; and Beshara Doumani focuses on the regional dynamics of indigenous agricultural specialization and commercialization more broadly (Farsoun and Hawatmeh 1997; Owen 1993; Issawi 2010; Doumani 1995). Omar Tesdell (2019) demonstrates how Palestine was conceived as an object of scientific intervention during the early colonial period and how this led to the emergence of industrial agriculture. Political forms are also economic—in 1967 Israel benefitted from tremendous amounts of foreign aid, as part of its war effort and otherwise, and Zachary Lockman (1996) argues that labor replacement was a crucial attribute of the Zionist project. Oslo was an economic agreement, and Arab laborers and goods have had different levels of market penetration based on changing political facts over time; Shir Hever (2010) extends this analysis to Israel's separation from the West Bank in the period since then. This has meant increased separation because of the wall, through Israeli importation of

guest workers from Asia, the permit regime, and plans for industrial zones and truck-to-truck trade that would eliminate Arab labor from Israel and maintain the Occupied Territories as a captive market for goods. The larger point is that subsistence, market integration, and trade beyond Palestine are parts of its history fundamental to an understanding of its politics.

6 This raises difficult questions about the consequences for liberation politics in a context of ongoing erasure. Many Palestinians would disagree with this part of Frantz Fanon's project, but he argues very clearly about the need to be disalienated from the past: "In no way do I have to dedicate myself to reviving a black civilization unjustly ignored. I will not make myself the man of any past. I do not want to sing the past to the detriment of my present and my future" (Fanon 2008, 201). There is not, Aimé Césaire (2001) says, a unified proletariat to be cultivated or to identify with. Césaire is clear that political movements should not be backward-looking: there is a desire to attach an authentic core to the peasant, but this has strange effects on struggle and solidarity. Even finding the ability to imagine real change might mean upending the current regime.

7 Canaan's work is a meticulous and totally decontextualized work of salvage anthropology. Writing in 1933 as a rebellion was forming, he saw an immediate need to keep the past in the present *in the face of political change*. Palestinians were living artifacts—"It is interesting to note that the various civilized nations which have governed Palestine and introduced their specific cultures, were unable to impose their methods and ideas upon the inhabitants" (1933, iii). And so Canaan's monograph on Palestinian architecture would be widely appreciated and "of some help to the Biblical student and archaeologists, to the architects of Palestine, and to the Arabist" (iii). Canaan sheds an indirect light on the past, and on the biblical history of the Holy Land. This kind of work can—and should—be appreciated. But when critics of Rawabi invoke traditional ways of life, they are invoking "tradition" without mentioning that that specific tradition means things like the way that Palestinian doors represent the house, which represents the cervix, which also represents the anus. That it encompasses things like the "superstitions common to all inhabitants of the Holy Land" who live in huts, tents, and housing with indoor livestock. No one argues seriously for a return to this, and no one ought to argue that these descriptions were historically precise, or directly relevant for the future.

8 Geographical consolidation and indebtedness—something like settler capitalism—have long been vital techniques for settler colonists. Here's Thomas Jefferson in 1803 to William Henry Harrison, governor in the Indian Territory and later United States president:

> We wish to draw them to agriculture, to spinning & weaving. The latter branches they take up with great readiness, because they fall to the women, who gain by quitting the labours of the field for those which are exercised within doors. when they withdraw themselves to the culture of a small piece of land, they will perceive how useless to them are their extensive forests, and will be willing to pare them off from time to time in exchange for nec-

essaries for their farms & families. to promote this disposition to exchange lands which they have to spare & we want, for necessaries, which we have to spare & they want, we shall push our trading houses, and be glad to see the good & influential individuals among them run in debt, because we observe that when these debts get beyond what the individuals can pay, they become willing to lop th[em off] by a cession of lands. at our trading houses too we mean to sell so low as merely to repay us cost and charges so as neither to lessen or enlarge our capital. this is what private traders cannot do, for they must gain; they will consequently retire from the competition, & we shall thus get clear of this pest without giving offence or umbrage to the Indians. in this way our settlements will gradually circumscribe & approach the Indians, & they will in time either incorporate with us as citizens of the US. or remove beyond the Missisipi [sic]. the former is certainly the termination of their history most happy for themselves. but in the whole course of this, it is essential to cultivate their love. as to their fear, we presume that our strength & their weakness is now so visible that they must see we have only to shut our hand to crush them, & that all our liberalities to them proceed from motives of pure humanity only. should any tribe be fool-hardy enough to take up the hatchet at any time, the seizing the whole country of that tribe & driving them across the Mississippi, as the only condition of peace, would be an example to others, and a furtherance of our final consolidation. (US National Archives 1803)

Chapter Nine. Settlers and the Land

1 See Merry (2006) on the ways human rights are translated into local vernacular, and the disconnect between transnational reform and situated iterations and conceptions of justice.

2 An issue that remains confusing to me is the extent to which the drone and satellite photography are useful as evidence. In the filings I received, the scans are terrible and do not transmit much information. If the originals are blurry, the metaphor about planning and operationalizing the idea of planning to solidify one side's claim is clear. And if not, the sophistication with which they use the system to monitor and disable legal work in the landscape is clear.

3 Simone de Beauvoir (2012) had another context in mind, but her formulation describes this attribute of the law well: "Laws may change, but they keep their prestige."

4 Amona is still there and settlers are still fighting back against the state. It is a closed military zone, yet settlers periodically settle, supported by state-funded NGOs, until the state evacuates the settlement. It seems to happen nearly annually, and the Israeli government continues to play all angles (Levinson 2011; Lazaroff and Hoffman 2019; Berger 2019a, 2019b, 2019c).

5 Jeff Halper of the Israeli Committee Against House Demolitions distinguishes between two types of West Bank settlers: "ideological" settlers in outposts and

"economic" settlers in suburban commuter developments such as Maale Ad-umim. This chapter refers mainly to ideological settlers and outposts, although it is an open question whether the multiple forms of settlement differ much in their consequences for Israeli territorial control or the geographic imperatives.

6 Not all settlers are content to reform Israel; messianic groups work toward the construction of a Third Temple on the ruins of the Dome of the Rock that will lead to the ultimate dissolution of the state. Those groups and that particular cosmology and temporality are parallel, but not directly related, to practices by organizations like Regavim and others on the ultra-nationalist right.

7 And this is the place where liberal Zionist arguments usually go sideways. The issue is not that Israel's liberalism goes unfulfilled because of fringe elements in the coalition; racial/national/ethnic categories are central to the character of the state, state administration, and inclusion and exclusion. Those groups are intrinsic to Israeli liberalism and enabled in ongoing ways by the legal catego-ries and geographies they produce in the West Bank, Gaza, and inside Israel.

8 Race and ideology are not the only things that are obscured in the settlement enterprise or representations of it. Zionist historical geographer Yossi Katz has worked to revise the history of capitalist enterprise in Palestine during the sec-ond wave of Zionist immigration, 1904–1914. He notes there has always been capitalist intention in the Zionist project, but it gets written out of political history. "Private enterprise was downgraded due to the stigma and image (in my opinion, erroneous) that private capital in general lacked an ideological foundation, and that its activity stemmed exclusively from a profit motive" (1994, 11).

9 This openly discriminatory law is insufficient for Regavim, which asked in 2019, "Is the Regulation Law being used to protect Arab buildings?" (Arutz Sheva Staff 2019b)

Chapter Ten. The Law, Mirroring, and the State

1 And this seems to be supported by Berger (2018).

2 Needless to say, in this right-wing and sometimes messianic framework, Pal-estinian suffering does not compare with historical Jewish suffering, which not only is held to be exceptional, but can be *redeemed* by the settlement project.

3 The house is the "Red Castle" located in the West Bank town of Battir on the line between Areas B and C. It was the subject of a research project led by Nicola Perugini in association with the Decolonizing Architecture collective. See http://www.decolonizing.ps/site/battir-5/ for more information on the proj-ect and on a touring exhibition that emerged from it.

4 And this false equivalence is not just articulated in the courts. Housing and land rights become another site where Israeli state discrimination and violence against Palestinians is visible. The open market is seen as acting in discrimina-tory ways, and the fear of Palestinians utilizing an actually open market is acute for Israeli rightists. The idea that the deck is stacked against Jewish people is

a way to (a) mask the actual, intrinsic, and structural discrimination against Palestinians; and (b) reform the liberal—legal, economic—framework so as to more efficiently discriminate. And although the land market in Palestine functioned to disadvantage Palestinians and force sales to Jewish Israelis (Mousa 2006), that market nevertheless is a target for rightists. Privatization and "ethnosecurity discourses" are formed in relation to one another in Israel, in the present geoeconomic environment (Yacobi 2012), and they supplement racial privilege.

5 There is no shortage of examples that demonstrate the way the Palestinian state is incorporated into Israeli legal control; here are two that point toward the difficulties in making assumptions about what law is or should be doing. According to Yesh Din, it sued Israeli quarries operating in the West Bank for violating the prohibitions under the law of belligerent occupation that prevent an occupying power profiting from occupied resources. After Yesh Din submitted its petition, the state made two concessions: it pledged not to open any new quarries and to pay restitution of $7.5 million a year to the local government. That government? The Israeli Civil Administration. The Israeli Supreme Court ruled that as a remedy for illegal Israeli state extraction of Palestinian resources in the West Bank, the Israeli state could pay restitution to its own occupying military there. Another is an earlier attempt to pass a law that would allow the Knesset to overturn judicial rulings, thus threatening judicial review (Lis and Bar-Zohar 2012; Scheindlin 2012). This law was proposed specifically to try to limit the "activist" court from acting against Jewish settlers. It would upend the relationship between the branches of government, and it illuminates law as a terrain of constant struggle over how to encompass, minimize, or legalize the contradictions that emerge as a result of Israel's settlement and colonial projects.

6 The legal historian Assaf Meyadani (a conservative as far as his treatment of Oslo as an intra-Israeli decision, use of settler language like "Judea and Samaria," and jarringly infrequent mentions of Palestinians) believes that the contests in the court are central to the reform process in Israel. In terms of politics and presentation the book is difficult, but it demonstrates that, across the political spectrum, the court is understood as occupying a position where it has to appeal somehow to the law, or to legal principles of objectivity, but that it is nevertheless easily subject to pressure by both the state and civilians (Meydani 2011).

7 For example, a 2018 opinion piece in *Haaretz* describes the tragic death of an unborn baby in a drive-by shooting carried out by Palestinians against Israeli settlers, and how it was immediately and cynically operationalized by "settler real estate activists" to enable land expansion (Michael 2018). As a response to a series of horrible events, activists shaped violence into legal activity, materialized into land disputes.

Conclusion

1 What Sam Bahour (2012) has described as "Americanization," the individuation of Palestinians against collective goals.

2 What are the relationships between privatization, the private sector, and states emerging from colonialism? Jean and John Comaroff put it this way:

> The means and ends of the liberal democratic state are refracted, deflected, and dispersed into the murkier reaches of the private sector, sometimes in ways unimagined by even the most enterprising of capitalists, sometimes without appearing to be doing very much at all to disturb the established order of things. . . . Vastly lucrative returns also inhere in actively sustaining zones of ambiguity between the presence and absence of the law: returns made from controlling uncertainty, terror, even life itself; from privatizing public contracts and resources; from 'discretionary' policing and 'launder-ing' of various kinds. From amassing value, that is, by exploiting the new aporias of jurisdiction opened up under neoliberal conditions. (Comaroff and Comaroff 2009, 5)

3 Erich Fromm describes Marx's historical materialism in a way that resonates: if, for Montesquieu and others, "Man is formed by his practice of life," what Marx added was that he "analyzed in detail what these institutions are, or rather, that the institutions themselves were to be understood as part of the whole system of production which characterizes a given society" (Fromm 2013, 31–32).

4 Salim Tamari disagrees and has wondered aloud if it is less about producing semi-autonomy than about laying the foundation for EU trusteeship.

5 The political divisions and differences between the different parts of the West Bank and Gaza experiences are huge by design, and they can be continuously felt. In December 2009 I attended a demonstration and candlelight vigil in the Manara, the old central circle of Ramallah, marking the first anniversary of Israel's war on Gaza. There were barely forty people by the time I arrived, and probably fewer than one hundred in total. Demonstrators were dispirited by the low turnout, and the police presence was disproportionate. At one point a police officer tried to move people onto the sidewalk. Exasperated, he turned to an American who did not speak Arabic and said, "What are you doing anyway? This isn't Bil'in," a village where weekly nonviolent demonstrations against the separation wall have been routinely met by Israeli live fire since 2005, and vil-lagers face constant harassment, "this is Ramallah!" It is impossible to imagine even the mirage of separation from either occupation or from Palestine could be spoken about in this way in Gaza, or in Bil'in itself.

6 Sometimes there is a dark humor to it. One example that has stuck with me for years: in 2009 I saw the Israeli military pull over a Palestinian police car for speeding.

7 It is this conception of cooperation as above politics that has left the company open to critique from antinormalization and Boycott, Divestment, and Sanc-tions activists: one of the company's more explicit attempts to circumvent its

context occurred when it worked with the Zionist Jewish National Fund (JNF), yet claimed not to know what the fund was when it became publicly known and controversial among Palestinians. According to young boycott activists, Masri refused to repudiate his connection to the JNF when confronted. Massar hired Israeli lobbyist Dov Weissglass to help influence the Israeli political and economic elite. It has made explicit reference to influence from a settlement. Its main investor, Qatari Diar, acquired a small stake in a Dutch transportation firm that has been a primary target of boycott activists. And so on.

8   I later discovered the Dutch political economist P. W. Zuidhof found the cartoon similarly useful and opened his dissertation with it. The man at the head of the table, Zuidhof says, is "using one of the creative tools of the consultant or policy advisor, he proposes to alter the way one conceives of the problem, so as to be able to imagine new and resourceful solutions" (2012, 1).

REFERENCES

Abourahme, Nasser. 2019. "Beneath the Concrete." Unpublished manuscript.

Abrams, Phillip. 1988. "Notes on the Difficulty of Studying the State." In *The Anthropology of the State: A Reader*, edited by Aradhana Sharma and Akhil Gupta, 112–30. Oxford: Blackwell.

Abu El-Haj, Nadia. 2001. *Facts on the Ground: Archaeological Practice and Territorial Self-Fashioning in Israeli Society*. Chicago: University of Chicago Press.

Abunimah, Ali. 2011. "Rawabi Developer Masri Helps Deepen Israel's Grip on West Bank." *The Electronic Intifada*, January 6. http://electronicintifada.net/content/rawabi-developer-masri-helps-deepen-israels-grip-west-bank/9170.

Abunimah, Ali. 2012. "Boycott Committee: Palestinian 'Rawabi' Tycoon Bashar Masri 'Must End All Normalization Activities with Israel.'" *The Electronic Intifada*, September 10. https://electronicintifada.net/blogs/ali-abunimah/boycott-committee-palestinian-rawabi-tycoon-bashar-masri-must-end-all.

Achcar, Gilbert. 2018. "Marx wa al-sharq al-awsat [Marx and the Middle East]." *Bidayat Magazine*. https://www.bidayatmag.com/archive/2019/01.

Aglietta, Michel. 2016. *A Theory of Capitalist Regulation: The US Experience*. London: Verso.

Al Jazeera. 2013. "The Promised City." *Al Jazeera's Witness*, May 16. http://www.aljazeera.com/programmes/witness/2013/05/2013514104857113718.html.

Allen, Judith. 1990. "Does Feminism Need a Theory of 'the State'?" In *Playing the State: Australian Feminist Interventions*, edited by Sophie Watson, 21–37. London: Verso.

Allen, Lori. 2008. "Getting by the Occupation: How Violence Became Normal during the Second Palestinian Intifada." *Cultural Anthropology: Journal of the Society for Cultural Anthropology* 23 (3): 453–87.

Allen, Lori. 2013. *The Rise and Fall of Human Rights: Cynicism and Politics in Occupied Palestine*. Stanford, CA: Stanford University Press.

Althusser, Louis. 2006. "Ideology and Ideological State Apparatuses (Notes to-wards an Investigation)." In *The Anthropology of the State: A Reader*, edited by Aradhana Sharma and Akhil Gupta, 86–111. Oxford: Blackwell.

AME Info. 2013. "New Municipal Council Holds First Meeting in Rawabi." July 1, ameinfo.com. Archived at https://www.rawabi.ps/en/news/1524672029.

Anagnost, Ann. 1997. *National Past-Times: Narrative, Representation, and Power in Modern China*. Durham, NC: Duke University Press.

Anderson, Charles. 2013. "From Petition to Confrontation: The Palestinian National Movement and the Rise of Mass Politics, 1929–1939." PhD dissertation, New York University.

Anderson, Charles. 2015. "Will the Real Palestinian Peasantry Please Sit Down? Towards a New History of British Rule in Palestine, 1917–1936." 10. LSE Middle East Center Paper Series. London: London School of Economics.

Anderson, Charles. 2017. "State Formation from Below and the Great Revolt in Palestine." *Journal of Palestine Studies* 47 (1): 39–55. https://doi.org/10.1525 /jps.2017.47.1.39.

Anderson, Charles. 2018. "The British Mandate and the Crisis of Palestinian Land-lessness, 1929–1936." *Middle Eastern Studies* 54 (2): 171–215. https://doi.org/10 .1080/00263206.2017.1372427.

Anderson, Perry. 2013. *Lineages of the Absolutist State*. London: Verso.

The Applied Research Institute-Jerusalem. 2012a. "Palestinian Localities Study: 'Abwein Town Profile." http://vprofile.arij.org/ramallah/pdfs/vprofile /Abwein_tp_en.pdf.

The Applied Research Institute-Jerusalem. 2012b. "Palestinian Localities Study: 'Ajjul Town Profile." http://vprofile.arij.org/ramallah/pdfs/vprofile/Ajjul _Profile_en.pdf.

The Applied Research Institute-Jerusalem. 2012c. "Palestinian Localities Study: 'Atara Town Profile." http://vprofile.arij.org/ramallah/pdfs/vprofile/Atara _tp_en.pdf.

Arendt, Hannah. 2006. *Eichmann in Jerusalem: A Report on the Banality of Evil*. New York: Penguin.

Arutz Sheva Staff. 2017a. "Regavim Applauds Interior Committee Passage of 'Kamenetz Bill.'" Israel National News, February 4. http://www.israelnational news.com/News/News.aspx/227619.

Arutz Sheva Staff. 2017b. "The Supreme Court Has Become a Threat to Democracy." Israel National News, February 12. http://www.israelnationalnews.com /News/News.aspx/224861.

Arutz Sheva Staff. 2017c. "Regavim: Civil Administration 'Needs Reorganization.'" Israel National News, August 24. http://www.israelnationalnews.com/News /Flash.aspx/396404.

Arutz Sheva Staff. 2017d. "Jewish Residents Suffer as Samaria Arabs Illegally Burn Trash." Israel National News, August 27. http://www.israelnationalnews.com /News/News.aspx/234600.

Arutz Sheva Staff. 2018. "Enabling Arab Shooting Victims to Reach Out for Help."

Israel National News, July 27. http://www.israelnationalnews.com/News /News.aspx/249645.

Arutz Sheva Staff. 2019a. "Arab Sector Housing Crisis Is Real—but Solvable." Israel National News, May 14. http://www.israelnationalnews.com/News/News .aspx/263122.

Arutz Sheva Staff. 2019b. "Is Regulation Law Being Used to Protect Illegal Arab Buildings?" Israel National News, September 19. http://www.israelnational news.com/News/News.aspx/268950.

Asad, Talal. 1975. "Anthropological Texts and Ideological Problems: An Analysis of Cohen on Arab Villages in Israel." *Economy and Society* 4 (3): 251–82. https:// doi.org/10.1080/03085147500000014.

Asad, Talal. 2000. "What Do Human Rights Do? An Anthropological Enquiry." *Theory and Event* 4 (4).

Asad, Talal. 2003. *Formations of the Secular: Christianity, Islam, Modernity.* Stanford, CA: Stanford University Press.

Bahour, Sam. 2012. "Palestine's Economic Hallucination." *This Week in Palestine* no. 165, January. http://www.twip-archive.com/archive/details.php?id =3596&ed=202&edid=202.

Banko, Lauren. 2019. "'As Bad and Precarious as a Death Sentence': Deportation, the Loss of Homes and the Loss of Livelihoods during the Palestine Mandate." Paper presented at Palestinian Homes and Houses: Subjectivities and Materialities, the Sixth Annual New Directions in Palestinian Studies Workshop. Brown University, Providence, RI, March 15–16.

Barkan, Joshua. 2013. *Corporate Sovereignty: Law and Government Under Capitalism.* Minneapolis: University of Minnesota Press.

Baruch, Hezki. 2017. "The Supreme Court Doesn't Respect the Law." Israel National News, August 17. http://www.israelnationalnews.com/News/News.aspx/234065.

Baruch, Uzi. 2017. "Arab Infiltration Thwarted at Binyamin Region Community." Israel National News, August 20. http://www.israelnationalnews.com/News /News.aspx/234152.

Beauvoir, Simone de. 2012. *The Second Sex.* New York: Knopf Doubleday.

Benari, Elad. 2012. "Regavim Petitions Against Illegal Arab Outpost." Israel National News, April 4. http://www.israelnationalnews.com/News/News .aspx/154478.

Ben-Naftali, Orna, and Yuval Shany. 2005. "Living in Denial: The Application of Human Rights in the Occupied Territories." SSRN Scholarly Paper. Rochester, NY: Social Science Research Network. http://papers.ssrn.com/abstract =712002.

Ben-Porat, Ido. 2016. "PA 'Intel Base' Overlooking Sensitive IDF Base." Israel National News, March 11. http://www.israelnationalnews.com/News/News .aspx/209265.

Berger, Yotam. 2017a. "Israel Expands Remapping Effort in Bid to Claim More West Bank Land." *Haaretz*, January 30. http://www.haaretz.com/israel-news /.premium-1.768311.

Berger, Yotam. 2017b. "Israeli Court Freezes West Bank 'Land Grab' Law." *Haaretz*, August 18. http://www.haaretz.com/israel-news/.premium-1.807616.

Berger, Yotam. 2017c. "Israel to High Court: Law Seizing Palestinian Land Is Humane Response to 'Distress' of Thousands of Settlers." *Haaretz*, August 22. http://www.haaretz.com/israel-news/.premium-1.808317?=&ts=_1503681324314.

Berger, Yotam. 2018. "How Israeli Taxpayers Are Funding a Right-Wing NGO Dedicated to Getting Palestinians Evicted." *Haaretz*, January 19. https://www.haaretz.com/israel-news/israeli-right-wing-ngo-regavim-gets-millions-of-shekels-in-public-fund-1.5744933.

Berger, Yotam. 2019a. "Israel Again Evacuates Illegal West Bank Outpost of Amona; Dozens Wounded." *Haaretz*, January 3. https://www.haaretz.com/israel-news/.premium-israeli-army-begins-demolition-of-illegal-outpost-in-amona-1.6806109.

Berger, Yotam. 2019b. "Israeli Taxpayers Help Foot the Bill for Settlers' Return to Amona Outpost." *Haaretz*, January 3. https://www.haaretz.com/israel-news/.premium-taxpayers-help-foot-the-bill-for-settlers-return-to-amona-outpost-1.6805973.

Berger, Yotam. 2019c. "Israel Lets Settlers Spend Passover at Evacuated Outpost but Forbids Entry to Palestinian Land Owners." *Haaretz*, April 28. https://www.haaretz.com/israel-news/.premium-israel-lets-settlers-into-evacuated-outpost-but-forbids-entry-to-palestinians-1.7172705.

Bhandar, Brenna. 2018. *Colonial Lives of Property: Law, Land, and Racial Regimes of Ownership*. Durham, NC: Duke University Press.

Bhattacharya, Tithi, and Lise Vogel. 2017. *Social Reproduction Theory: Remapping Class, Recentering Oppression*. London: Pluto.

Bidayat Magazine. 2018. "Marx fi al-qarn al-thalith, ayn kan ʿala haqq [Marx in the Third Century: Where Was He Right?]." https://www.bidayatmag.com/archive/2019/01.

Bisan Center for Research and Development. 2014. "Rawabi: Normalization and Political, Economic, Psychological, and Architectural Extortion . . . with Nothing to Do within Development." Bisan Center for Research and Development. Ramallah, Palestine.

Blim, Michael. 1997. "Can NOT-Capitalism Lie at the End of History, or Is Capitalism's History Drawing to an End?" *Critique of Anthropology* 17 (4): 351–63. https://doi.org/10.1177/0308275X9701700403.

Booth, William. 2017. "A $1.4 Billion Gamble on a New Future for Palestinians." *Washington Post*, May 25. https://www.washingtonpost.com/graphics/world/occupied/palestinian-metropolis-rawabi-rises-in-west-bank-as-israeli-occupation-turns-50.

Bou Akar, Hiba. 2018. *For the War Yet to Come: Planning Beirut's Frontiers*. Stanford, CA: Stanford University Press.

Boyer, Robert. 1990. *The Regulation School: A Critical Introduction*. New York: Columbia University Press.

Boyer, Robert, and Daniel Drache. 2005. *States Against Markets: The Limits of Globalization*. New York: Routledge.

Brenner, Neil. 2010. "A Thousand Leaves: Notes on the Geographies of Uneven Spatial Development." In *Leviathan Undone? Towards a Political Economy of Scale*, edited by Roger Keil and Rianne Mahon, 27–50. Vancouver, Canada: University of British Columbia Press.

Brinn, David. 2017. "Coldplay Arrives in Israel to Scout Possible Concert Locations." *Jerusalem Post*, February 24. http://www.jpost.com/Israel-News /Culture/Its-official-Coldplay-is-coming-to-Israel-482528.

Brown, Wendy. 2006. "Finding the Man in the State." In *The Anthropology of the State: A Reader*, edited by Aradhana Sharma and Akhil Gupta, 187–210. Oxford: Blackwell.

Brown, Wendy. 2015. *Undoing the Demos: Neoliberalism's Stealth Revolution*. Brooklyn, NY: Zone Books.

Canaan, Taufik. 1933. *The Palestinian Arab House: Its Architecture and Folklore*. Jerusalem: Syrian Orphanage Press.

Carrington, Daisy. 2013. "New City Offers Vision of Better Life in West Bank." cnn, July 4. http://www.cnn.com/2013/07/04/world/meast/rawabi -palestinian-project/index.html.

Césaire, Aimé. 2001. *Discourse on Colonialism*. Translated by Joan Pinkham. New York: Monthly Review.

Chaidez, Alexandra A. 2018. "hks Launches Fellowship for Palestinian Students." *The Crimson*, April 25. http://www.thecrimson.com/article/2018/4/25/hks -palestinian-fellowship.

Chibber, Vivek. 2006. *Locked in Place: State-Building and Late Industrialization in India*. Princeton, NJ: Princeton University Press.

Clarno, Andy. 2017. *Neoliberal Apartheid: Palestine/Israel and South Africa after 1994*. Chicago: University of Chicago Press.

Comaroff, Jean, and John L. Comaroff, eds. 2009. *Law and Disorder in the Postcolony*. Chicago: University of Chicago Press.

Cook, Jonathan. 2013. "Court Nixes Push for 'Israeli Nationality.'" Al Jazeera, October 18. http://www.aljazeera.com/indepth/features/2013/10/court-nixes -push-israeli-nationality-20131017115755321289.html.

Coon, Anthony. 1992. *Town Planning under Military Occupation: An Examination of the Law and Practice of Town Planning in the Occupied West Bank*. Aldershot, UK: Dartmouth Publishing.

Coulthard, Glen. 2014. *Red Skin, White Masks: Rejecting the Colonial Politics of Recognition*. Minneapolis: University of Minnesota Press.

Cowen, Deborah, and Neil Smith. 2009. "After Geopolitics? From the Geopolitical Social to Geoeconomics." *Antipode* 41 (1): 22–48. https://doi.org/10.1111/j .1467-8330.2008.00654.x.

Cuen, Leigh. 2017. "How Fintech Plays into the Israeli-Palestinian Conflict." ib *Times*, September 23. http://www.ibtimes.com/how-fintech-plays-israeli -palestinian-conflict-2592984.

Dana, Tariq. 2014. "The Palestinian Capitalists That Have Gone Too Far." Al-Shabaka Policy Brief. Al-Shabaka: The Palestinian Policy Network. http://bit.ly/plCptl.

Dana, Tariq. 2015. "The Symbiosis between Palestinian 'Fayyadism' and Israeli 'Economic Peace': The Political Economy of Capitalist Peace in the Context of Colonisation." *Conflict, Security and Development* 15 (5): 455–77. https://doi.org/10.1080/14678802.2015.1100013.

Doumani, Beshara. 1995. *Rediscovering Palestine: Merchants and Peasants in Jabal Nablus, 1700–1900*. Berkeley: University of California Press.

Duara, Prasenjit. 1995. *Rescuing History from the Nation: Questioning Narratives of Modern China*. Chicago: University of Chicago Press.

Elden, Stuart. 2009. *Terror and Territory: The Spatial Extent of Sovereignty*. Minneapolis: University of Minnesota Press.

Erakat, Noura. 2019. *Justice for Some: Law and the Question of Palestine*. Stanford, CA: Stanford University Press.

Esmeir, Samera. 2012. *Juridical Humanity: A Colonial History*. Stanford, CA: Stanford University Press.

Evyatar, Ilan. 2016. "More Rawabis, Not More Walls." *Jerusalem Post*, January 28. https://www.jpost.com/Opinion/More-Rawabis-not-more-walls-443193.

Fakher Eldin, Munir. 2008. "Communities of Owners: Land Law, Governance, and Politics in Palestine 1858–1948." PhD dissertation, New York University.

Fanon, Frantz. 2005. *The Wretched of the Earth*. New York: Grove Press.

Fanon, Frantz. 2008. *Black Skin, White Masks*. New York: Grove Press.

Farsakh, Leila. 2005. *Palestinian Labour Migration to Israel: Labour, Land and Occupation*. New York: Routledge.

Farsoun, Samih K., and Christina Zacharia Hawatmeh. 1997. *Palestine and the Palestinians: A Social and Political History*. Boulder, Colorado: Westview.

Fayyad, Salam. 2008. "We Are Throwing a Party, and the Whole World Is Invited." Palestine Investment Conference. http://www.pic-palestine.ps/2008/salam.php.

Fendel, Hilel. 2016. "Saving the Land of Israel via Drone." Israel National News, June 12. http://www.israelnationalnews.com/News/News.aspx/221293.

Ferguson, James. 1994. *The Anti-Politics Machine: Development, Depoliticization, and Bureaucratic Power in Lesotho*. Minneapolis: University of Minnesota Press.

Fischbach, Michael R. 2003. *Records of Dispossession: Palestinian Refugee Property and the Arab-Israeli Conflict*. New York: Columbia University Press.

Ford, Lisa. 2010. *Settler Sovereignty: Jurisdiction and Indigenous People in America and Australia, 1788–1836*. Cambridge: Harvard University Press.

Fortune Editors. 2018. "The World's 50 Greatest Leaders." *Fortune Magazine*, April 19. http://fortune.com/longform/worlds-greatest-leaders-2018.

Frenkel, Sheera Claire. 2006. "Bishara Flings Obscenities at Erdan." *Jerusalem Post*, December 5. https://www.jpost.com/Israel/Bishara-flings-obscenities-at-Erdan.

Friedman, Thomas. 2009. "Green Shoots in Palestine." *New York Times*, August 4. https://www.nytimes.com/2009/08/05/opinion/05friedman.html

Fromm, Erich. 2013. *Marx's Concept of Man*. London: Bloomsbury Academic.

Gasper, Michael Ezekiel. 2009. *The Power of Representation: Publics, Peasants, and Islam in Egypt*. Stanford, CA: Stanford University Press.

Gavish, Dov. 2005. *The Survey of Palestine Under the British Mandate, 1920–1948*. Routledge Studies in Middle Eastern History. London: Routledge Curzon.

Gearan, Anne, and William Booth. 2013. "Kerry Announces $4 Billion Economic Development Proposal for West Bank." *Washington Post*, May 26. https://www.washingtonpost.com/world/africa/kerry-says-us-drone-program-strict-fair/2013/05/26/80058422-c615-11e2-9cd9-3b9a22a4000a_story.html.

Gilmore, Ruth Wilson. 2007. *Golden Gulag: Prisons, Surplus, Crisis, and Opposition in Globalizing California*. Berkeley: University of California Press.

Goedeken, Susan Christine. 2009. "Made to Measure? Fitting a Development Project to the Occupied Palestinian Territories." MA thesis, Beirut, Lebanon: American University of Beirut.

Goldman, Emma. 2016. "Meet the NGO Writing Israeli Policy in the West Bank." Matzav Blog, August 15. http://www.matzavblog.com/2016/08/meet-ngo-writing-israeli-policy-west-bank.

Gordon, Neve. 2008. *Israel's Occupation*. Berkeley: University of California Press.

Graeber, David. 2011. *Debt: The First 5,000 Years*. New York: Melville House.

Gross, Ayel. 2013. "Court Rejection of Israeli Nationality Highlights Flaws of Jewish Democracy." *Haaretz*, October 10. http://www.haaretz.com/opinion/.premium-1.550336.

Grossman, Shmulik. 2010. "Settlers Try to Stop New Palestinian City." *Ynet*, March 3. http://www.ynetnews.com/articles/0,7340,L-3870243,00.html.

Guha, Ranajit. 1998. *Dominance without Hegemony: History and Power in Colonial India*. Cambridge, MA: Harvard University Press.

Haaretz. 2017. "Coldplay Denies Scheduling Show in Israel, Palestine: 'We're Only Here to Learn.'" *Haaretz*, February 25. http://www.haaretz.com/israel-news/culture/leisure/1.773767.

Haaretz Jewish Insider Staff. 2018. "Jewish Insider's Daily Kickoff: June 27, 2018." *Haaretz*, June 27. https://www.haaretz.com/us-news/jewish-insider-s-daily-kickoff-june-27-2018-1.6219789.

Haddad, Toufic. 2016. *Palestine Ltd: Neoliberalism and Nationalism in the Occupied Territory*. London: I. B. Tauris.

Haila, Anne. 2015. *Urban Land Rent: Singapore as a Property State*. Malden, MA: Wiley-Blackwell.

Hajjar, Lisa. 2005. *Courting Conflict the Israeli Military Court System in the West Bank and Gaza*. Berkeley: University of California Press.

Hamdan, Lubna. 2018. "Palestine: Business beyond the Wall." Arabian Business Global, January 6. http://www.arabianbusiness.com/politics-economics/386973-palestine-business-beyond-the-wall.

Hanieh, Adam. 2002. "Class, Economy, and the Second Intifada." *Monthly Review* 54 (5). https://doi.org/10.14452/MR-054-05-2002-09_3.

Hanieh, Adam. 2003. "From State-Led Growth to Globalization: The Evolution of Israeli Capitalism." *Journal of Palestine Studies* 32 (4): 5–21. https://doi.org /10.1525/jps.2003.32.4.5.

Hanieh, Adam. 2008. "Palestine in the Middle East: Opposing Neoliberalism and US Power." Monthly Review Online. http://www.monthlyreview.org/mrzine /hanieh190708a.html.

Hanieh, Adam. 2013a. *Lineages of Revolt: Issues of Contemporary Capitalism in the Middle East.* Chicago: Haymarket Books.

Hanieh, Adam. 2013b. "The Oslo Illusion." *Jacobin.* https://www.jacobinmag.com /2013/04/the-oslo-illusion.

Harker, Christopher. 2014a. "The Only Way Is Up? Ordinary Topologies of Ramallah." *International Journal of Urban and Regional Research* 38 (1): 318–35. https://doi.org/10.1111/1468-2427.12094.

Harker, Christopher. 2014b. "Debt and Obligation in Contemporary Ramallah." *Jadaliyya,* October 19. http://www.jadaliyya.com/Details/31373/Debt-and -Obligation-in-Contemporary-Ramallah.

Harker, Christopher. 2017. "Debt Space: Topologies, Ecologies and Ramallah, Palestine." *Environment and Planning D: Society and Space* 35 (4): 600–19. https://doi.org/10.1177/0263775816686973.

Harkov, Lahav. 2016. "Israeli NGO's pro-Brexit Campaign Joins Debate among British Expats." *Jerusalem Post*, May 10. http://www.jpost.com/Israel-News /Israeli-NGOs-pro-Brexit-campaign-joins-debate-among-British-expats -453583.

Harvey, David. 1990. *The Condition of Postmodernity: An Enquiry into the Origins of Cultural Change.* Oxford: Blackwell.

Harvey, David. 2003. *The New Imperialism.* Oxford: Oxford University Press.

Harvey, David. 2007. *A Brief History of Neoliberalism.* Oxford: Oxford University Press.

Harvey, David. 2011. *The Enigma of Capital and the Crises of Capitalism.* Oxford: Oxford University Press.

Hasson, Nir. 2017. "Jerusalem Mapping Office Allowed to Reopen Days After It Was Shuttered for 'Tracking Palestinian Land Sales to Jews.'" *Haaretz*, March 17. https://www.haaretz.com/israel-news/.premium-jerusalem-mapping -office-reopened-days-after-shuttered-by-police-1.5450029.

Hasten, Josh. 2017. "How the 'Blue Liners' Forced the Regulation Law's Passing." *Jerusalem Post*, February 13. http://www.jpost.com/Opinion/How-the-Blue -Liners-forced-the-Regulation-Laws-passing-481435.

H.C. (High Court), 3355/14, Regavim v. Minister of Defense et al. (not published). H.C.

H.C., 4475/09, Village Council of Dayr Istiya et al. v. Minister of Defense et al. (not published). H.C.

H. C., 6068/12, Regavim v. Minister of Defense et al. (not published). H.C.

H. C., 7121/12, Regavim v. Minister of Defense et al. (not published). H.C.

Hever, Shir. 2010. *The Political Economy of Israel's Occupation*. London: Pluto.

Hibou, Beatrice. 2004. "From Privatising the Economy to Privatising the State: An Analysis of the Continual Formation of the State." In *Privatizing the State*, edited by Beatrice Hibou, 1–46. New York: Columbia University Press.

Hilal, Jamil. 2006. *Al-Tabaqa al-Wusta al-Filistiniyya: Bahth Fi Fawda al-Hawiyya Wa al-Marja'iyya Wa al-Thaqafa [The Palestinian Middle Class: Study into the Confusion of Identity, Authority, and Culture]*. Beirut, Lebanon: Institute for Palestine Studies.

Hilal, Jamil. 2014. "Palestinian Class Formation Under Settler Colonialism." Paper presented at Political Economy and the Economy of the Political, the First Annual New Directions in Palestinian Studies Workshop. Brown University, Providence, RI, February 28–March 1.

Hilal, Jamil, and Abaher El-Sakka. 2015. "A Reading on the Socio Urban Changes in Ramallah and Kufur Aqab." Birzeit, Palestine: Center for Development Studies and Rosa Luxemburg Stiftung.

Hilal, Sandi, and Alessandro Petti. 2018. *Permanent Temporariness*. Stockholm: Art and Theory Publishing.

Howard, Caroline. 2017. "Can Social Entrepreneurs Create A New City Of Palestinian Opportunity?" *Forbes*, April 6. https://www.forbes.com/sites /carolinehoward/2017/04/06/can-entrepreneurs-create-a-new-city-of -palestinian-economic-opportunity.

Hull, Matthew S. 2012. *Government of Paper: The Materiality of Bureaucracy in Urban Pakistan*. Berkeley: University of California Press.

Ibrahim, Anas. 2017. "Rawabi Al-Madina: Qalaq Khisa' Wa Tamahin . . . Wa Ashya' Ukhra [The City of Rawabi: Castration Anxiety, Complicity . . . and Other Things]." Ultra Palestine, July 10. https://ultrapal.ultrasawt.com روابي-المدينة-قلق-خصاء-وتماه-وأشياء-أخرى/أنس-حسونة/قول/.

Independent Evaluation Group, World Bank. 2016. "Housing Finance: World Bank Group Support for Housing Finance, An IEG Learning Product." Washington, DC: International Bank for Reconstruction and Development and the World Bank.

Issawi, Charles. 2010. *An Economic History of the Middle East and North Africa*. London: Routledge.

Jabary Salamanca, Omar. 2014. "Hooked on Electricity: The Charged Political Economy of Electrification in the Palestinian West Bank." Unpublished manuscript.

Jacobs, Harrison. 2018. "Bashar Al-Masri: Activists Boycotting Israel Have Made a Huge Mistake." *Business Insider*, October 22. https://www.businessinsider .com/masri-activists-boycotting-israel-2018–10.

Jessop, Bob. 2014. "Poulantzas's State, Power, Socialism as a Modern Classic." *Bob Jessop* (blog), March 27. https://bobjessop.wordpress.com/2014/03/27 /poulantzass-state-power-socialism-as-a-modern-classic.

Jessop, Bob. 2016. *The State: Past, Present, Future*. Cambridge, MA: Polity.

Kadri, Ali. 2014. *Arab Development Denied: Dynamics of Accumulation by Wars of Encroachment*. London: Anthem.

Karmi, Ghada. 2015. *Return: A Palestinian Memoir*. London: Verso.

Kattan, Victor. 2009. *From Coexistence to Conquest: International Law and the Origins of the Arab-Israeli Conflict 1891–1949*. London: Pluto.

Katz, Cindi. 2001. "Vagabond Capitalism and the Necessity of Social Reproduction." *Antipode* 33 (4): 709–28. https://doi.org/10.1111/1467-8330.00207.

Katz, Yossi. 1994. *The "Business" of Settlement: Private Entrepreneurship in the Jewish Settlement of Palestine, 1900–1914*. Jerusalem: Magnes Press, Hebrew University.

Kauanui, J. Kēhaulani. 2016. "'A Structure, Not an Event': Settler Colonialism and Enduring Indigeneity." *Lateral* 5 (1). https://doi.org/10.25158/L5.1.7.

Keil, Roger, and Rianne Mahon, eds. 2010. *Leviathan Undone? Towards a Political Economy of Scale*. Vancouver, Canada: University of British Columbia Press.

Khalidi, Raja. 2015. "Hawl Taʿaththur Madinat Rawabi Fi Al-Daffa [Regarding the Troubles the of City of Rawabi in the West Bank]." *As-Safir Al-Arabi*, September 24. http://assafirarabi.com/ar/3782.

Khalidi, Raja, and Sobhi Samour. 2011. "Neoliberalism as Liberation: The Statehood Program and the Remaking of the Palestinian National Movement." *Journal of Palestine Studies* 40 (2): 6–25.

Khalidi, Rashid. 1997. *Palestinian Identity: The Construction of Modern National Consciousness*. New York: Columbia University Press.

Khan, Mushtaq H. 2004. *State Formation in Palestine: Viability and Governance during a Social Transformation*. London: Routledge Curzon.

Khoury, Jack. 2018. "Standard of Living in West Bank Dropping for First Time in Years, World Bank Warns." *Haaretz*, March 15. https://www.haaretz.com /middle-east-news/.premium-world-bank-report-standard-of-living-in-the -west-bank-is-dropping-1.5908617.

Kirk, Mimi. 2016. "The First Palestinian Planned City Is Nothing If Not Divisive." *CityLab*, July 18. http://www.citylab.com/politics/2016/07/the-first -palestinian-planned-city/491492.

Kligman, Gail. 1992. "The Politics of Reproduction in Ceausescu's Romania: A Case Study in Political Culture." *Eastern European Politics and Societies* 6 (3): 364–418. https://doi.org/10.1177/0888325492006003010.

Kohlbry, Paul. 2018. "Owning the Homeland: Property, Markets, and Land Defense in the West Bank." *Journal of Palestine Studies* 47 (4): 30–45. https:// doi.org/10.1525/jps.2018.47.4.30.

Kohlbry, Paul. 2019. "Plots and Deeds: Property and Formations of Land Defense in the West Bank." PhD dissertation, Johns Hopkins University.

Kretzmer, David. 2002. *The Occupation of Justice: The Supreme Court of Israel and the Occupied Territories*. Albany: State University of New York Press.

Kuttab, Eileen. 2010. "Empowerment as Resistance: Conceptualizing Palestinian Women's Empowerment." *Development* 53 (2): 247–53. https://doi.org/10 .1057/dev.2010.22.

Kutub, Nadia. 2014. "Rawabi Tutalib Bi-Malyun Dular Taʿwidat Min Markaz

Bisan Li'l-Abhath Wa al-Inma' [Rawabi Demands One Million Dollars in Compensation from the Bisan Center for Research and Development]." *Al Hadath,* December 24. http://www.alhadath.ps/article.php?id=83dcc9y 8641737Y83dcc9.

Kwak, Nancy H. 2015. *A World of Homeowners: American Power and the Politics of Housing Aid.* Chicago: University of Chicago Press.

Latour, Bruno. 2005. *Reassembling the Social: An Introduction to Actor-Network-Theory.* Oxford: Oxford University Press.

Lazaroff, Tovah. 2016. "Israeli NGO Seeks Demolition of Unauthorized Road in Palestinian City of Rawabi." *Jerusalem Post,* February 2. http://www.jpost.com/Arab-Israeli-Conflict/Israeli-NGO-seeks-demolition-of-illegal-West-Bank-road-in-Palestinian-city-443644.

Lazaroff, Tovah. 2017. "Analysis: Moving from Occupation to Normalization in the West Bank." *Jerusalem Post,* August 23. http://www.jpost.com/Israel-News/Is-an-Israeli-legal-revolution-brewing-in-the-West-Bank-503175.

Lazaroff, Tovah, and Maayan Hoffman. 2019. "Border Police Evacuate Site of Former Amona Outpost, Violence Erupts." *Jerusalem Post,* January 3. https://www.jpost.com/Israel-News/Border-police-evacuating-site-of-former-Amona-outpost-violence-erupts-576209.

Lefebvre, Henri. 2003. *The Urban Revolution.* Minneapolis: University of Minnesota Press.

Lefebvre, Henri. 2009. *State, Space, World: Selected Essays.* Edited by Neil Brenner and Stuart Elden. Minneapolis: University of Minnesota Press.

Levinson, Chaim. 2011. "Illegal West Bank Outpost to Be Razed by End of 2012, Barak Decides." *Haaretz,* November 1. http://www.haaretz.com/print-edition/news/illegal-west-bank-outpost-to-be-razed-by-end-of-2012-barak-decides-1.393032.

Levinson, Chaim. 2016. "Almost All West Bank Land Deals for Illegal Settlements Forged, Investigation Finds." *Haaretz,* February 1. http://www.haaretz.com/israel-news/.premium-1.700794?=&ts=_1502476222267.

Lieber, Dov. 2017. "Police Shutter PA Conference in Jerusalem about Land Sales to Jews." *Times of Israel,* October 25. https://www.timesofisrael.com/police-shutter-pa-conference-in-jerusalem-about-land-sales-to-jews.

Lis, Jonathan, and Ophir Bar-Zohar. 2012. "Knesset Speaker Backs Bill to Overturn Laws Struck Down by Israel's Supreme Court." *Haaretz,* April 8. http://www.haaretz.com/news/national/knesset-speaker-backs-bill-to-overturn-laws-struck-down-by-israel-s-supreme-court-1.423266.

Lockman, Zachary. 1996. *Comrades and Enemies: Arab and Jewish Workers in Palestine, 1906–1948.* Berkeley: University of California Press.

Losurdo, Domenico. 2011. *Liberalism: A Counter-History.* Translated by Gregory Elliott. London: Verso.

Luxemburg, Rosa. 2003. *The Accumulation of Capital.* London: Routledge.

Maan News. 2011. "PCBS: 84% of Palestinians Are Homeowners." Maan News Agency, April 4. http://www.maannews.net/eng/ViewDetails.aspx?ID=375503.

Maan News. 2015. "Baʿd Al-Rawabi: Hal Tuwafiq Israʾil ʿala Binaʾ Madina Jadida Biʾl-Daffa? [After Rawabi: Will Israel Approve the Building of a New City in the West Bank?]." Maan News Agency, September 11. http://www.maannews .net/Content.aspx?ID=808283.

Madden, David J, and Peter Marcuse. 2016. *In Defense of Housing: The Politics of Crisis*. London: Verso.

Makdisi, Saree. 2008. *Palestine Inside Out: An Everyday Occupation*. New York: W. W. Norton.

Mansour, George. 2012. "The Arab Worker under the Palestine Mandate (1937)." *Settler Colonial Studies* 2 (1): 190–205. https://doi.org/10.1080/22014 73X.2012.10648832.

Marsad. 2010. "Wafd Filistini Yabhath fi Washintun Naql al-Manatiq B wa C liʾl-Siyada al-Filistiniyya wa Mustawtinun Yaqtahimun Mashruʿ ʿal-Rawabiʾ 1-faslih ʿan Ramallah [A Palestinian Delegation in Washington Investigates Transferring Zones B and C to Palestinian Sovereignty, and Settlers Invade the 'Rawabi' Project to Separate it from Ramallah]." Marsad Palestine, April 1. https://www.marsad.ps/ar/2010/04/01 /وفد-فلسطيني-يبحث-في-واشنطن-نقل-المناطق-b.

Marsad. 2013. "Baladiyyat Rawabi Taʿqid Ijtimaʿaha al-Awwal bi-Hudur Wazir al-Hukm al-Mahalli [The Municipality of Rawabi Holds its First Meeting with the Presence of the Minister of Local Government]." Marsad Palestine, July 24. https://www.marsad.ps/ar/2013/07/24 /بلدية-رواي-تعقد-اجتماعها-الأول-بحضور.

Marsad. 2016. "Occupation, Inc. How Settlement Businesses Contribute to Israel's Violations of Palestinian Rights." Marsad Palestine, January 19. https://www .marsad.ps/en/2016/01/19/occupation-inc-how-settlement-businesses -contribute-to-israels-violations-of-palestinian-rights.

Marsad. 2017. "Renewing Cooperation on Water: What Hope for the Two State Solution?" Marsad Palestine, January 26. https://www.marsad.ps/en/2017 /01/26/renewing-cooperation-water-hope-two-state-solution.

Martin, Richard. 2009. "Palestine: Public Private Partnerships in the Housing Sector, Final Report." DFID and World Bank. London and Washington, DC.

Marx, Karl. 1990. *Capital Volume I: A Critique of Political Economy*. Translated by Ben Fowkes. New York: Penguin Classics.

Masri, Mazen. 2017. *The Dynamics of Exclusionary Constitutionalism: Israel as a Jewish and Democratic State*. Oxford and Portland, OR: Hart Publishing.

Massad, Joseph A. 1997. "Political Realists or Comprador Intelligentsia: Palestinian Intellectuals and the National Struggle." *Middle East Critique* 6 (11): 21–35. https://doi.org/10.1080/10669929708720108.

Massad, Joseph A. 2006. *The Persistence of the Palestinian Question: Essays on Zionism and the Palestinians*. London: Routledge.

Mathew, Johan. 2016. *Margins of the Market: Trafficking and Capitalism across the Arabian Sea*. Berkeley: University of California Press.

McMullen, Jane. 2015. "The Billion Dollar Gamble." BBC's *Our World*, February 7. http://www.bbc.co.uk/programmes/b052qxwv.

Merry, Sally Engle. 2006. *Human Rights and Gender Violence: Translating International Law into Local Justice*. Chicago: University of Chicago Press.

Meydani, Assaf. 2011. *The Israeli Supreme Court and the Human Rights Revolution: Courts as Agenda Setters*. Cambridge: Cambridge University Press.

Mezzadra, Sandro, and Brett Neilson. 2013. *Border as Method, or, the Multiplication of Labor*. Durham, NC: Duke University Press.

Michael, B. 2018. "Co-Opting a Fetus for Their Land Grab." *Haaretz*, December 12. https://www.haaretz.com/opinion/.premium-co-opting-a -fetus-for-their-land-grab-1.6740875.

Ministry of Planning and International Cooperation (MOPIC). 1998. "The Regional Plan for the West Bank Governorate." Ministry of National Planning and International Cooperation. Ramallah, Palestine.

Mironova, Oksana, and Samuel Stein. 2018. "Where Does Public Land Come From? Municipalization and Privatization Debates." Metropolitiques.eu, March 6. https://www.metropolitiques.eu/Where-Does-Public-Land-Come -From-Municipalization-and-Privatization-Debates.html.

Mitchell, Timothy. 1999. "Society, Economy, and the State Effect." In *State/Culture: State-Formation after the Cultural Turn*, edited by George Steinmetz, 76–97. Ithaca, NY: Cornell University Press.

Mitchell, Timothy. 2002. *Rule of Experts: Egypt, Techno-Politics, Modernity*. Berkeley: University of California Press.

Mitter, Sreemati. 2020. "Bankrupt: Financial Life in Late Mandate Palestine." *International Journal of Middle East Studies* 52 (2): 289–310. https://doi .org/10.1017/S0020743819001120.

Monni, Michele. 2017. "Mideast: Rawabi, the New Palestinian City in West Bank." ANSAmed, June 20. http://www.ansamed.info/ansamed/en/news/nations /israel/2016/06/20/mideast-rawabi-the-new-palestinian-city-in-west-bank _88b45e6e-fe37-4356-9d8d-6f9149f69130.html.

Moretti, Franco, and Dominique Pestre. 2015. "Bankspeak." *New Left Review*, no. 92 (April): 75–99.

Mousa, Riyad. 2006. "The Dispossession of the Peasantry: Colonial Policies, Settler Capitalism, and Rural Change in Palestine, 1918–1948." PhD dissertation, University of Utah.

Moyn, Samuel. 2018. *Not Enough: Human Rights in an Unequal World*. Cambridge: Belknap.

Mulvaney, Katie. 2011. "Federal Magistrate Judge Plans to Retire." *The Providence Journal*, December 31.

Nakba Files. 2016. "An Israeli Guide to Annexation." *The Nakba Files*, June 23. http://nakbafiles.org/2016/06/23/israel-and-annexations-a-guide.

Nakhleh, Khalil. 2012. *Globalized Palestine: The National Sell-out of a Homeland*. New Jersey: The Red Sea Press.

Norris, Jacob. 2013. *Land of Progress: Palestine in the Age of Colonial Development, 1905–1948*. Oxford: Oxford University Press.

Norris, Jacob. 2019. "Mobile Homes: Bethlehem Merchants and the Refashioning of Palestinian Homes in the Late Ottoman Period." Paper presented at Palestinian Homes and Houses: Subjectivities and Materialities, the Sixth Annual New Directions in Palestinian Studies Workshop. Brown University, Providence, RI, March 15–16.

Owen, Roger. 1993. *The Middle East in the World Economy, 1800–1914*. London: I. B. Tauris.

Palestine Today. 2018. "Nushata' Facebook Sakhitun 'ala Hafl Ghina'i fi Madinat Rawabi [Facebook Activsts Angry at Music Concert in the City of Rawabi]." Palestine Today. October 1. https://paltoday.ps/ar/post/332387 نشطاء-الفيسبوك-ساخطون-على-حفل-غنائي-في-مدينة-رواني/.

Palestinian National Authority. 2010. "Palestinian National Plan 2011–2013: Housing Sector Strategic Plan Summary." Ramallah, Palestine.

Palestinian National Authority, Palestinian Central Bureau of Statistics. 2009. "Census Final Results, Population, Housing, and Establishment Census 2007: Population Report, West Bank." Ramallah, Palestine. http://www.pcbs.gov.ps/Downloads/book1530.pdf.

Pasternak, Shiri. 2017. *Grounded Authority: The Algonquins of Barriere Lake against the State*. Minneapolis: University of Minnesota Press.

Pasternak, Shiri, and Tia Dafnos. 2018. "How Does a Settler State Secure the Circuitry of Capital?" *Environment and Planning D: Society and Space* 36 (4): 739–57. https://doi.org/10.1177/0263775817713209.

PBS. 2013. "Rawabi: A Planned Palestinian City for the West Bank." PBS *NewsHour*, September 28. https://www.pbs.org/newshour/show/a-planned-palestinian -city-for-the-west-bank.

Peck, Jamie. 2010. *Constructions of Neoliberal Reason*. Oxford: Oxford University Press.

Peck, Jamie, and Adam Tickell. 2002. "Neoliberalizing Space." *Antipode* 34 (3): 380–404. https://doi.org/10.1111/1467-8330.00247.

Perugini, Nicola, and Neve Gordon. 2015. *The Human Right to Dominate*. Oxford: Oxford University Press.

Perugini, Nicola, and Kareem Rabie. 2012. "The Human Right to the Colony." In *Shifting Borders: European Perspectives on Creolisation*, edited by Tommaso Sbriccoli and Stefano Jacoviello, 35–56. Newcastle upon Tyne: Cambridge Scholars Publishing.

Petersburg, Ofer. 2011. "Tel Aviv to Get Its Own 'Times Square.'" *Ynet*, October 19. http://www.ynetnews.com/articles/0,7340,L-4131801,00.html.

Polanyi, Karl. 2012. *The Great Transformation: The Political and Economic Origins of Our Time*. Boston: Beacon.

Poulantzas, Nicos. 1980. *State, Power, Socialism*. London: Verso.

Rabie, Kareem. 2018. "Remaking Ramallah." *New Left Review*, no. 111 (June): 42–60.

Ramallah News. 2017. "Al-Masri: Rawabi Buniyat Li'l-Filistiniyyin Wa Lan Yaskun Fiha Ayy Isra'iliyy [al-Masri: 'Rawabi Was Built for Palestinians and No Israeli Will Live There]." Ramallah News, January 15. http://ramallah.news /post/72753.

Rawabi Owners' Union. 2017. "Bayan sadir ʿan ittihad al-mullak fi madinat Rawabi [Statement issued by the City of Rawabi Owner's Union]." *Al Iqtisadi*, July 20. http://www.aliqtisadi.ps/article/45963 /بيان-صادر-عن-إتحاد-الملاك-في-مدينة-رواي.

Razack, Sherene. 2002. *Race, Space, and the Law: Unmapping a White Settler Society*. Toronto: Between the Lines.

Regavim. 2010. "On the Perversion of Justice: Is Israel's Supreme Court Indeed the Last Refuge of the Citizen?" Regavim: The National Land Protection Trust. Jerusalem.

Regavim. 2017. "Summer Summary Newsletter," September 12. Regavim: The National Land Protection Trust. Jerusalem.

Robinson, Cedric J. 2000. *Black Marxism: The Making of the Black Radical Tradition*. Chapel Hill: University of North Carolina Press.

Rodney, Walter. 1982. *How Europe Underdeveloped Africa*. Washington, DC: Howard University Press.

Roitman, Janet. 2013. *Anti-Crisis*. Durham, NC: Duke University Press.

Rosove, Rabbi John. 2013. "Rawabi's Success Will Signal the Success of a Two-State Solution." *Israel Journal Part VII* (blog), October 31. http://www.jewish journal.com/rabbijohnrosovesblog/item/rawabis_success_will_signal_the _success_of_a_two_state_solution_israel_jour.

Ross, Andrew. 2019. *Stone Men: The Palestinians Who Built Israel*. London: Verso.

Roy, Sara. 1999. "De-Development Revisited: Palestinian Economy and Society Since Oslo." *Journal of Palestine Studies* 28 (3): 64–82.

Rudee, Eliana. 2018. "Could Trees Be the Greatest Threat to Israel?" Breaking Israel News, April 11. https://www.breakingisraelnews.com/105679/whats -the-greatest-threat-to-the-future-of-israel-trees.

Safdie, Moshe. 1973. *Beyond Habitat*. Cambridge: MIT Press.

Said, Edward W. 1993. *Culture and Imperialism*. New York: Knopf.

Samara, Adel. 2000. "Globalization, the Palestinian Economy, and the 'Peace Process.'" *Journal of Palestine Studies* 29 (2): 20–34.

Sayigh, Rosemary. 1979. *The Palestinians: From Peasants to Revolutionaries*. London: Zed Press.

Scheindlin, Dahlia. 2012. "New Bill Would Let the Knesset Crush the Court." +972 Magazine, April 8. http://972mag.com/ new-bill-would-let-the-knesset-crush-the-court/40668.

Schölch, Alexander. 1993. *Palestine in Transformation, 1856–1882: Studies in Social, Economic, and Political Development*. Washington, DC: Institute for Palestine Studies.

Searle, Llerena Guiu. 2016. *Landscapes of Accumulation: Real Estate and the Neoliberal Imagination in Contemporary India*. Chicago: University of Chicago Press.

Segal, Rafi, and Eyal Weizman, eds. 2003. *A Civilian Occupation: The Politics of Israeli Architecture*. London: Verso.

Segel, Arthur, Sarika Agarawal, Nimrod Brandt, Daniel Kuhagen, and Thomas Reithinger. 2014. "Rawabi." HBS Case Collection No. 9-214-008. Boston: Harvard Business School Publishing.

Seikaly, Sherene. 2015. *Men of Capital: Scarcity and Economy in Mandate Palestine.* Stanford, CA: Stanford University Press.

Selim, Samah. 2004. *The Novel and the Rural Imaginary in Egypt, 1880–1985.* New York: Routledge Curzon.

Shehadeh, Raja. 1982. "The Land Law of Palestine: An Analysis of the Definition of State Lands." *Journal of Palestine Studies* 11 (2): 82–99. https://doi.org/10.2307/2536271.

Shehadeh, Raja. 2012. *Occupation Diaries.* New York: OR Books.

Sherwood, Harriet. 2013. "Rawabi Rises: New West Bank City Symbolises Palestine's Potential." *The Guardian*, August 8. http://www.theguardian.com/world/2013/aug/08/rawabi-west-bank-city-palestine.

Simpson, Audra. 2014. *Mohawk Interruptus: Political Life across the Borders of Settler States.* Durham, NC: Duke University Press.

Smith, Barbara Jean. 1993. *The Roots of Separatism in Palestine: British Economic Policy, 1920–1929.* Syracuse, NY: Syracuse University Press.

Smith, Neil. 1984. *Uneven Development: Nature, Capital, and the Production of Space.* New York: Blackwell.

Smith, Neil. 2002. "New Globalism, New Urbanism: Gentrification as Global Urban Strategy." *Antipode* 34 (3): 427–50. https://doi.org/10.1111/1467-8330.00249.

Smith, Neil. 2003. *American Empire: Roosevelt's Geographer and the Prelude to Globalization.* Berkeley: University of California Press.

Smith, Pamela Ann. 1984. *Palestine and the Palestinians 1876–1983.* New York: St. Martin's.

Smith, Pamela Ann. 1986. "The Exile Bourgeoisie of Palestine." *Middle East Research and Information Project*, no. 142 (September): 23–27. https://doi.org/10.2307/3011986.

Soja, Edward W. 1996. *Thirdspace: Journeys to Los Angeles and Other Real-and-Imagined Places.* Malden, MA: Blackwell.

Sones, Mordechai. 2018a. "'Camel Law' Passes First Reading in Knesset." Israel National News, February 20. http://www.israelnationalnews.com/News/News.aspx/242195.

Sones, Mordechai. 2018b. "Arab Tractor Documented Breaking into IDF Territory." Israel National News, December 16. http://www.israelnationalnews.com/News/News.aspx/256237.

Stamatopoulou-Robbins, Sophia. 2018. "An Uncertain Climate in Risky Times: How Occupation Became like the Rain in Post-Oslo Palestine." *International Journal of Middle East Studies* 50 (03): 383–404. https://doi.org/10.1017/S0020743818000818.

State of Palestine, Palestinian Central Bureau of Statistics. 2018. "Preliminary Results of the Population, Housing and Establishments Census 2017." Ramallah, Palestine. http://www.pcbs.gov.ps/Downloads/book2364-1.pdf.

Stockman, Farah. 2005. "Palestinian Authority's US Assets Are Frozen." *The Boston Globe*, August 30. http://www.boston.com/news/world/middleeast/articles/2005/08/30/palestinian_authoritys_us_assets_are_frozen/?page=full.

Sultany, Nimer. 2002. "The Perfect Crime: The Supreme Court, the Occupied Territories and al-Aqsa Intifada." *Adalah's Review* 3: 49–57.

Sultany, Nimer. 2014. "Activism and Legitimation in Israel's Jurisprudence of Occupation." *Social and Legal Studies* 23 (3): 315–39. https://doi.org/10.1177/0964663914521449.

Surani, Ghazi. 2009. *Al-Tahawwulat al-Ijtimaʿiyya Wa al-Tabaqiyya Fi al-Diffa al-Gharibyya Wa Qitaʿ Ghazza [Social and Class Transformation in the West Bank and Gaza]*, 3rd ed. Ramallah, Palestine.

Swedenburg, Ted. 1990. "The Palestinian Peasant as National Signifier." *Anthropological Quarterly* 63 (1): 18–30.

Tamari, Salim. 1983. "The Dislocation and Re-Constitution of a Peasantry: The Social Economy of Agrarian Palestine in the Central Highlands and the Jordan Valley, 1960–1980." PhD dissertation, University of Manchester.

Tamari, Salim. 1988. "Soul of the Nation: The Fallah in the Eyes of the Urban Intelligentsia." *Review of Middle East Studies* 5: 74–83.

Tamari, Salim. 2004. "Lepers, Lunatics and Saints: The Nativist Ethnography of Tawfiq Canaan and His Jerusalem Circle." *Jerusalem Quarterly* 20: 24–43.

Tamari, Salim. 2008. *Mountain against the Sea: Essays on Palestinian Society and Culture*. Berkeley: University of California Press.

Taraki, Lisa. 1990. "The Development of Political Consciousness among Palestinians in the Occupied Territories, 1967–1987." In *Intifada: Palestine at the Crossroads*, edited by Jamal R Nassar and Roger Heacock, 53–72. New York: Praeger.

Taraki, Lisa. 2008a. "Enclave Micropolis: The Paradoxical Case of Ramallah/al-Bireh." *Journal of Palestine Studies* 37 (4): 6–20. https://doi.org/10.1525/jps.2008.37.4.6.

Taraki, Lisa. 2008b. "Urban Modernity on the Periphery: A New Middle Class Reinvents the Palestinian City." *Social Text* 26 (2): 61–81. https://doi.org/10.1215/01642472-2007-029.

Tartir, Alaa. 2015. "Securitised Development and Palestinian Authoritarianism Under Fayyadism." *Conflict, Security and Development* 15 (5): 479–502. https://doi.org/10.1080/14678802.2015.1100016.

Tesdell, Omar. 2019. "Shadow Spaces: Territory, Sovereignty, and the Question of Palestinian Cultivation." Unpublished manuscript.

Thawaba, Salem. 2019. "Building and Planning Regulations under Israeli Colonial Power: A Critical Study from Palestine." *Planning Perspectives* 34 (1): 133–46. https://doi.org/10.1080/02665433.2018.1543611.

Tilley, Virginia. 2015. "After Oslo, a Paradigm Shift? Redefining 'Peoples', Sovereignty and Justice in Israel-Palestine." *Conflict, Security and Development* 15 (5): 425–53. https://doi.org/10.1080/14678802.2015.1100017.

Tilly, Charles. 1990. *Coercion, Capital, and European States, AD 990–1990*. Cambridge, MA: Blackwell.

Trouillot, Michel-Rolph. 2003. *Global Transformations: Anthropology and the Modern World*. New York: Palgrave Macmillan.

Turner, Mandy. 2011. "Creating 'Partners for Peace': The Palestinian Authority and the International Statebuilding Agenda." *Journal of Intervention and Statebuilding* 5 (1): 1–21. https://doi.org/10.1080/17502977.2011.541777.

Turner, Mandy. 2012. "Completing the Circle: Peacebuilding as Colonial Practice in the Occupied Palestinian Territory." *International Peacekeeping* 19 (4): 492–507. https://doi.org/10.1080/13533312.2012.709774.

Turner, Mandy, and Omar Shweiki, eds. 2014. *Decolonizing Palestinian Political Economy: De-Development and Beyond*. London: Palgrave Macmillan.

UCI. 2013. The Businessman Eng. Khaled Sabawi in an Interview with *Al-Quds Newspaper*. August 5. http://www.uci.ps/index.php?TemplateId=4&id=35&ParentId=4&Lang=en.

Ultra Palestine. 2017. "Sunduq Ra's Al-Mal al-Isra'iliyy al-Mughamir Fi Rawabi [The Israeli Venture Capital Fund in Rawabi]." Ultra Palestine, December 14. https://ultrapal.ultrasawt.com
.صندوق-رأس-المال-الإسرائيلي-المغامر-في-روابي/الترا-فلسطين/راصد/

Ultra Palestine. 2018a. "Azmat Akadimiyyat Rawabi Tatafaqam . . . Shakawa Min Qam' Wa Idhlal [The Crisis of the Rawabi Academy Worsens: Complaints about Repression and Humiliation]." Ultra Palestine, July 28. https://ultrapal.ultrasawt.com
.أزمة-أكاديمية-روابي-تتفاقم-شكاوى-من-قمع-وإذلال/الترا-فلسطين/تقارير/أخبار/

Ultra Palestine. 2018b. "Wafd Isra'ili Fi Diayafat Rawabi [Israeli Delegation Hosted in Rawabi]." Ultra Palestine, August 26. https://ultrapal.ultrasawt.com
.وفد-إسرائيلي-في-ضيافة-روابي/الترا-فلسطين/تقارير/أخبار/

Ultra Palestine. 2018c. "Fidiyu | Mujaddadan: Junud Isra'iliyyun Fi Madinat Rawabi [Video | Again: Israeli Soliders in the City of Rawabi]." Ultra Palestine, September 6. https://ultrapal.ultrasawt.com
.فيديو-مجددًا-جنود-إسرائيليون-في-مدينة-روابي/الترا-فلسطين/راصد/

UN-Habitat. 2009. "UN-Habitat Program Document 2010–2011: Occupied Palestinian Territory." Nairobi: United Nations Human Settlements Programme, Regional Office for Africa and the Arab States.

United States Government Accountability Office. 2013. "Foreign Assistance: U.S. Programs Involving the Palestine Investment Fund." Report to Congressional Requesters GAO-13-537. United States Government Accountability Office.

U.S. National Archives. 1803. "Founders Online: From Thomas Jefferson to William Henry Harrison, 27 February 1803." http://founders.archives.gov/documents/Jefferson/01-39-02-0500.

Voice of America. 2013. "US Unveils $75 Million for Palestinian Economy." Voice of America, November 6. https://www.voanews.com/world-news/middle-east-dont-use/us-unveils-75-million-palestinian-economy.

Wafa: Palestinian News and Info Agency. 2018. "Israeli Settler Shoots Palestinian Northwest of Ramallah." Wafa: Palestinian News and Info Agency, February 2. http://english.wafa.ps/page.aspx?id=2JYDvra96313596588a2JYDvr.

Wainer, David. 2018. "New in the West Bank: A Credit Boom Waiting for a Real Economy." Bloomberg, January 2. https://www.bloomberg.com/news /articles/2018–01–03/new-in-the-west-bank-a-credit-boom-waiting-for-a -real-economy.

Waldoks, Ehud Zion. 2010. "Erdan Threatens to Block Building of New Palestinian City." *The Jerusalem Post*, June 10. http://www.jpost.com/Israel /Erdan-threatens-to-block-building-of-new-Palestinian-city.

Watson, Sophie, ed. 1990. *Playing the State: Australian Feminist Interventions*. London: Verso.

Weber, Max. 1992. *The Protestant Ethic and the Spirit of Capitalism*. New York: Routledge.

Weizman, Eyal. 2007. *Hollow Land: Israel's Architecture of Occupation*. New York: Verso.

Wilder, Gary. 2005. *The French Imperial Nation-State: Negritude and Colonial Humanism between the Two World Wars*. Chicago: The University of Chicago Press.

Wilder, Gary. 2014. *Freedom Time: Negritude, Decolonization, and the Future of the World*. Durham, NC: Duke University Press.

Williams, Raymond. 1975. *The Country and the City*. Oxford: Oxford University Press.

Wolfe, Patrick. 2006. "Settler Colonialism and the Elimination of the Native." *Journal of Genocide Research* 8 (4): 387–409. https://doi.org/10.1080 /14623520601056240.

Wood, Ellen Meiksins. 2002. *The Origin of Capitalism: A Longer View*. New York: Verso.

World Bank. 1993. *Housing: Enabling Markets to Work*. A World Bank Policy Paper. Washington, DC: World Bank. https://doi.org/10.1596/0-8213-2434-9.

World Bank. 2018. "Doing Business 2018: Reforming to Create Jobs." Washington, DC: World Bank. https://www.doingbusiness.org/content/dam/doing Business/media/Annual-Reports/English/DB2018-Full-Report.pdf.

World Bank. 2020. "Supporting Institutional Reform Agenda of the Palestinian Authority." Washington, DC: World Bank. https://www.worldbank.org/en /programs/palestinian-recovery-and-development-program-trust-fund#2.

Yacobi, Haim. 2012. "God, Globalization, and Geopolitics: On West Jerusalem's Gated Communities." *Environment and Planning A: Economy and Space* 44 (11): 2705–20. https://doi.org/10.1068/a44612.

Yehya, Abbad. 2012. "Rawabi: Israeli Model for 'Neo-Palestinian' City." Al Akhbar English, June 1. http://english.al-akhbar.com/content/rawabi-israeli -model-"neo-palestinian"-city.

Yiftachel, Oren. 2006. *Ethnocracy: Land and Identity Politics in Israel/Palestine*. Philadelphia: University of Pennsylvania Press.

Zawya. 2013. "New Municipal Council Holds First Meeting in Rawabi." Zawya, June 30. http://www.zawya.com/story/New_Municipal_Council_Holds _First_Meeting_in_Rawabi-ZAWYA20130630142349.

Zeid, Maali, and Salem Thawaba. 2018. "Planning under a Colonial Regime in Palestine: Counter Planning/Decolonizing the West Bank." *Land Use Policy* 71 (February): 11–23. https://doi.org/10.1016/j.landusepol.2017.11.048.

Zhang, Li. 2010. *In Search of Paradise: Middle-Class Living in a Chinese Metropolis.* Ithaca, NY: Cornell University Press.

Zuidhof, P. W. 2012. "Imagining Markets: The Discursive Politics of Neoliberalism." PhD dissertation, Erasmus University. https://repub.eur.nl/pub/31134.

INDEX

Page numbers in italics refer to figures.

Aspen Institute, 224n3; and Aspen Ideas festival, 223n7; and Middle East Investment Initiative, 102

Ateret, 40–42, *127*, 143, 163, *168*, 225n2

'Attara, 154, 161, 163; checkpoint, 37, 126; relationship with Rawabi, 40–42, 64, 114, 140–46

autochthony, 52, 155, 158, 161. *See also* indigenous people

'Awda, Zaki, 141

Badil, 222n4

Bahour, Sam, 221n3, 232n1

Balfour Declaration, 173

Ban Ki-Moon, 199

Bank of Palestine, 146

Barak, Ehud, 184

Baron de Rothschild, 221n5

Battir, 230n3

Baydar, 58

Bayti Real Estate Investment Company, 62, 73, 124, 144; and Economic Growth Strategy, 125

Beauvoir, Simone de, 229n3

Beilin, Yossi, 142

Ben-Ami, Jeremy, 76

Bethlehem, 8, 79–80

Bhandar, Brenna, 218n7

Bhungalia, Lisa, 223n8

Bil'in, 232n5

Binyamin Regional Settlement Council, 175–76, 183

Birthright Israel, 142

Birzeit, 32, 37, 39, 124, 158, 163, 212

Birzeit University, 37, 59, 73

Bisan Center for Research and Development, 74, 152–53, 222n4

Bishara, Azmi, 70, 222n2

Blair, Tony, 8, 56, 70, 124, 142, 208

Blim, Michael, 209

blue line plans. *See* special outline plans

Bou Akar, Hiba, 6–7, 82

Boycott, Divestment, and Sanctions (BDS) movement, 76, 219n9, 232n7

Brexit, 179

British Mandatory law, 164, 171

"Building the State of Palestine: A Success Story," 85

Canaan, Taufik, 158, 228n7

Central Planning Department (CPD), 90–91

Césaire, Aimé, 228n6

checkpoints, 37, 39, 76, 126, 137, 203

Chemonics International, 77

citizenship, 164, 219n10, 228n8; Israeli, 136, 165, 172, 177–78, 182, 193

Clarno, Andy, 18

class, 5, 20, 35, 70, 131, 184, 220n12, 227n3; aspirations, 4, 29, 32, 43, 62, 71, 80, 107, 147, 210–11; capitalist class, 10, 27, 85; class stratification, 11, 26, 137, 158–59, 201, 203; debt and, 33; housing and, 8, 23–27, 42, 56, 94–95, 111, 117, 150–52, 223n2; neoliberalism and, 205; Palestinian identity and, 155–60; planning and, 7, 81, 87; Rawabi and, 11–12, 134, 137–41, 146–48; spatialization of, 9, 25, 31; working class, 24, 156. *See also* fallah; middle class

Cohen, Abner, 222n7

Cohen, Ronald, 59

Coldplay, 72, 199

colonialism, 3, 61, 154–61, 174, 179–80, 227n5; capitalism and, 22, 27, 207–8, 232n2; colonial law, 83, 170–71; occupation and, 6, 31, 33; planning and, 85, 89–90, 139; Rawabi and, 62, 151–52, 220n2; resistance to, 4, 201–2, 219n9. *See also* settler colonialism

Comaroff, Jean and John, 232n2

Coon, Anthony, 32, 88–92

Cooperative Housing Foundation (CHF), 102–3, 133

copy/paste petitions. *See* mirror petitions

credit, 11, 29, 87, 220n11. *See also* debt; lenders; loans; mortgages

Dafnos, Tia, 217n2

Dajani, Amir, 55–56, 60, 65

Dana, Tariq, 24

Dayr Istiya, 186

Gramsci, Antonio, 21

Great Britain, 7, 56, 57, 72, 126, 160, 222n7; role in Zionism, 14–15, *121*, 173. *See also* Mandatory Palestine

GROW for a Greener Palestine, 124

Gurvitch, Georges, 211

Gush Emunim, 171

Habitat '67, 60

Haddad, Toufic, 23–24, 26

Haifa, 33, 155

Halper, Jeff, 229n5

Hamas, 17, 71, 109, 209, 224n1, 224n2, 224n5

Hamdallah, Rami, 209

Hanieh, Adam, 23–24, 56

Harb, Samir, 16

Harrison, William Henry, 228n8

Harvard. *See* John F. Kennedy School of Government

Harvey, David, 20, 22, 211, 218n8

Hever, Shir, 227n5

Higher Planning Council (HPC), 37, 86, 95, 116, 120, 123

Hilal, Jamil, 24–25, 139–40

Hilal, Sandi, 29, 141

Historic Palestine, 4–5, 7, 14, 31, 186, 218n7

Hjouj, Azzam, 87

Holocaust, 60, 175

home buyers, 107, 113, 143, 146–47, 224n4; class and, 26, 95, 111, 150; first-time, 32, 42; loans and, 97–104; Rawabi attracting, 131–37

"Home-stretch to Freedom" (document), 104

housing shortage, 33, 56, 62, 93–104, 109, 125, 148

Hroub, Hani, 114

Huleileh, Samir, 57, 60

Hull, Matthew, 106–7

humanitarianism, 8, 45, 74, 91, 101, 130, 173

human rights, 82, 151, 172, 181, 189, 195–96, 229n1; Israeli settlement and, 34, 71, 164, 165–66, 173–78, 184–86

ideological state apparatuses, 21

indigenous people, 12, 22, 164, 178, 196, 206, 217n2, 227n5. *See also* autochthony

Institute for Palestine Studies, 222n4

Interim Agreement on the West Bank and Gaza Strip, 84

internal migration, 33

International Criminal Court, 197

International Humanitarian Law, 91

international law, 164–67, 171–74, 181–82, 188, 219n9. *See also* Geneva Conventions; human rights

International Monetary Fund (IMF), 17, 106, 109

Isaacson, Walter, 224n3

Islamabad, 106

Israel Declaration of Independence, 193

Israel Defense Forces (IDF), 153, 171, 176, 187, 209; Central Command, 186

Israeli Civil Administration, 39, 180, 182, 186, 231n5; control of Palestinian planning, 65–66, 84, 89, 124, 127, 167–68, 185; Regavim's work with, 177, 179, 183

Israeli civil law, 34, 88, 91, 119, 164–65, 170, 176–77, 180

Israeli Committee Against House Demolitions, 229n5

Israeli High Court of Justice, 170–72, 181, 187, 194–95, 197

Israeli military law, 88, 119, 162, 164, 177

Israeli Supreme Court, 164, 170–71, 180–81, 191, 194, 231n5

Issawi, Charles, 227n5

istimlak, 41, 56, 116–17, 143–45, 168. *See also* eminent domain

Jaffa, 155

Jefferson, Thomas, 228n8

Jerusalem/al-Quds, 17, 52–53, 82, 153; East, 3, 6, 85; map of, 2; urbanism in, 33, 155, 223n2; West, 176

Jessop, Bob, 19

Jewish National Fund (JNF), 52, 125, 178, 222n1, 232n7. *See also* tree planting programs

John F. Kennedy School of Government

(Harvard): Rawabi Fellowship for
Leaders from Palestine, 199
Joint Water Committee, 65
Jordan, 2, 40, 45, 116, 119
Jordanian law, 162, 164; *istimlak*, 41, 56,
116–17, 143–45, 168; *maliyya*, 145; planning and, 88–91, 105, 111, 116, 119–20,
122
Jordanian Law no. 79, 105
J Street, 75–76
Judea and Samaria, 176, 181–82, 186,
189–91, 194–95, 231n6
jurisdiction, 41, 84, 162, 204, 217n2, 232n2;
development and, 79, 86, 88, 106, 108,
111, 115–16; housing and, 21–22; as
occupation tool, 34, 82–83, 164–69,
172–73, 177–78, 181, 189, 196–97; sovereignty and, 91–92, 218n7; state building
and, 19–20, 23

Kadri, Ali, 26
Kafr Thulth, 186
Karmi, Ghada, 201
Katz, Cindi, 25
Katz, Yossi, 14, 230n8
Kerry, John, 75, 110
Kfayr, 91
Khalidi, Raja, 26, 74, 79, 107, 152–53
Khoury, Rami, 103, 146
Knesset, 70, 166, 176–77, 181, 231n5; right-wing members, 163, 180, 199
Kohlbry, Paul, 29
Kwak, Nancy, 220n12, 224n2

land markets, 14, 87, 90, 114, 146, 160–62,
207, 218, 230n4
land tenure/titling, 10, 13, 27, 82, 166, 186;
development and, 32, 101–4, 118–21,
121, 161, 204; land markets and, 14, 156,
220n13; *maliyya*, 145; tabu, 145
Latour, Bruno, 106
Law by Decree (2016), 59
Lebanon, 2, 7, 119
Le Corbusier, 30
Lefebvre, Henri, 13–14, 16
lenders, 11, 13, 99, 101–3, 106, 118–19, 139,

147, 225n3. *See also* credit; debt; loans;
mortgages
liberalism, 54, 139, 141–42, 172, 199;
development and, 60, 68; human rights
and, 164, 166–67; liberal democracy,
34, 177, 232n2; multiculturalism, 221n5;
Rawabi and, 28, 71–73, 76; settler colonialism and, 180, 183, 193, 195–97,
230n4; Zionism and, 76, 176–77,
230n7
loans, 10, 29, 51, 97–103, 118, 134, 147, 204,
225n3; international aid and, 11, 23. *See
also* credit; lenders; mortgages
Lockman, Zachary, 227n5
London Investment Conference, 124

Maale Adumim, 229n5
Ma'an Development Center, 222n4
Makdisi, Saree, 226n4
maliyya, 145
Mandatory Palestine, 7, 24, 89, 91, 173;
British Mandatory law, 164, 171; Zionism in, 14–15, 156
market creation, 14–15, 21, 99, 138, 146–48
"Marshall Plan" for Palestine, 75
Martin, Richard, 58, 106, 109, 133
Marx, Karl, 20, 26, 162, 208, 232n3
Marxism, 27
Masri, Bashar, 8, 23, 27–28, 45, 47, 61, 125,
210, 225n1; Bayti Real Estate Investment Company and, 144–45; employees, 57, 135–36, 221n4, 223n9, 225n9;
Jewish National Fund and, 232n7; on
jobs, 45; PADICO and, 224n1; political
beliefs, 223n7; Portland Trust and, 58,
60; role in Rawabi, 67–78, 88, 111, 113,
153
Masri, Mazen, 219n10
Masri, Munib al-, 224n1
Massar International, 74, 103, 225n2,
232n7; employees, 55, 68, 77, 225n9;
Jewish National Fund and, 222n1; role
in Rawabi, 55, 57–58, 61–62, 68, 71,
77–78, 115, 123–26; suit against Bisan, 74
Mekharot, 65
Mellanox Technologies, 76

Palestine Development and Investment Company (PADICO), 45, 57, 93–94, 224n1

Palestine Investment Conference (PIC), 1, 3, 8, 124

Palestine Investment Fund (PPIF), 57–58, 94–95, 97–98, 101–4, 118, 147, 223n10, 224n5

Palestine Liberation Organization (PLO), 17, 84, 129, 209

"Palestine Moving Forward" (document), 104

Palestine Real Estate Investment Company (PRICO), 57–58

Palestinian Central Bureau of Statistics, 93–94, 140

Palestinian Land Authority, 89, 116–17, 119

Palestinian law, 88, 164

Palestinian Legislative Council, 17, 84

Palestinian National Authority (PA), 1, 30, 116, 209, 224n5, 224nn1–2, 226nn4–5; aid and, 130; capacity of, 56, 110, 113, 115, 128, 136; capitalism and, 24, 54, 74, 80, 203, 207–8; creation of, 17, 149; development and, 10–11, 33, 75, 105, 138, 159, 227n2; eminent domain and, 41, 143; as employer, 10, 46, 129; housing and, 101–4, 133; law and, 23, 32, 83, 88–92, 119, 162; Masri and, 27–28, 111; planning and, 82–87, 124; PRDP and, 205; public-private partnerships and, 106–11, 161, 204, 210; Ramallah and, 5, 113–15, 134; Rawabi and, 45, 55–56, 64–66, 69–70, 117, 123–28, 141–43, 151, 168; Regavim and, 169, 179; state building and, 39, 206; taxes and, 58–59; wages, 139–40. *See also* Ministry of Finance (MOF); Ministry of Local Government (MOLG); Ministry of Planning and International Cooperation (MOPIC); Ministry of Public Works and Housing (MOPWH)

Palestinian Reform and Development Plan (PRDP), 55–56, 85–86, 104–6, 110, 112, 125, 138, 205

Palestinian Water Authority, 65

PalGaz, 78

Paris Protocol (Protocol on Economic Relations), 59, 227n1

Pasternak, Shiri, 22, 217n2

Peace Now, 180–81, 195; Settlement Watch Project, 183

Perugini, Nicola, 34, 176, 183, 230n3

Pestre, Dominique, 225n3

Petti, Alessandro, 29, 141

planning laws, 58, 88, 90, 105, 117

Polanyi, Karl, 18

Portland Trust, 57–60, 69, 94, 97–98, 103–4, 124, 133, 144

postcolonialism, 160, 201

privatization, 4, 19, 79, 107, 156, 217n2, 218n6, 230n4; critiques of, 28–29, 33, 159; debt and, 11, 98; enabling conditions for, 17, 150; housing and, 58–59, 93, 103–4, 112, 118, 138–39; international aid and, 32, 101; Palestinian identity and, 145–46, 221n5; planning and, 7, 81, 85; of public infrastructure, 128; Rawabi and, 136–40, 143, 162, 204–5; state and, 111, 167, 209–10, 218n8, 232n2; supporters of, 17, 58, 98, 104, 129, 220n11. *See also* neoliberalism

public good, 115–16, 119

public-private partnerships, 1, 31, 105–30, 138

"Putting Citizens First" (document), 104

Qatar, 144–45, 217n4; role in Rawabi, 8, 41–42, 62, 65, 70, 78–79, 124–25, 151

Qatari Diar, 124, 232n7

Q Center, 217n4

Quartet, the, 56, 80, 124

Rabin, Yitzhak, 76, 187

race, 12, 34–35, 186, 206, 211, 218n5, 218n7, 230n4; in Israeli Declaration of Independence, 193; planning and, 90, 223n1; racialized class, 156, 159; racialized labor, 203; in Zionism, 14–15, 156, 165, 230n7, 230n8

Rafidi, George, 45–46, 55, 70

Ramallah, 8, 37, 39, 43, 77, 79, 212, 232n5; growth of, 3–5, 16, 32, 38, 140, 152, 201; housing in, 95–96, 133–34, 217n4, 223n2; maps of, 2; planning and, 85, 87, 115; Rawabi and, 51, 55, 61, 63, 112–13, 131, 139, 151

Rawabi bylaw, 46, 62, 87–88, 111, 116

Rawabi Owners' Union, 153

Razack, Sherene, 178

Red Castle, 230n3

Regavim, The National Land Protection Trust, 33; Israeli settler colonialism and, 34, 163–64, 166–72, 176–97, 221n3, 230n6, 230n9; "On the Perversion of Justice," 191

Regional Outline Planning Scheme Jerusalem District, 89

Regional Settlement Councils, 184

Regulation Law (2017), 180–81, 230n9

Regulation School, 20

renters, 58, 86, 94, 96, 112, 116, 133–34, 138, 202, 217n4, 218n8

return (economic), 8, 26, 79–80, 118, 136, 232n2

return (political), 8, 60, 80, 85, 195; class and, 12, 31; Ramallah and, 5, 201; right of, 11, 17

Revolt of 1936–1939, 157

Rodney, Walter, 218n6

Ross, Andrew, 28, 45

RTI International, 67–69, 124–25

Rubenstein, Amnon, 82

rumors/gossip, 28, 78–79, 142, 144, 153, 223n9

ruralism, 14, 140; Palestinian identity and, 12, 39, 138, 140–41, 145, 149, 154–59; planning and, 86, 91; urbanism and, 13, 96, 149–51, 157, 160–61

Sabawi, Khaled al-, 65

Safdie, Moshe, 60–61, 74, 221n5

Said, Edward, 160

Samach, Raffie, 58–62, 139

Samaria Development Plan, 89

Samaria District Regional Outline Planning Scheme, 89

Samaria Regional Council, 186

Samour, Sobhi, 79

Sayyid, Afif al-, 105, 108, 114, 143

Schölch, Alexander, 13

second intifada, 94, 163

Seikaly, Sherene, 15

settler colonialism, 6, 24, 92, 162–63, 166, 219n9, 228n8; capitalism and, 27, 226n7; democracy and, 34, 176–77, 193–97; human rights and, 175, 184; law and, 177–78, 196–98, 231n5; liberalism and, 180, 183, 193, 195–97, 230n4; race and, 14–15, 71, 91, 164–65, 172, 177–78, 180–81, 196, 206, 218n7; state and, 31, 210–11; Zionism and, 12–15, 33, 140, 156–58, 165, 173, 184. See also colonialism

Sfard, Michal, 181, 196

Shahin, Nisreen, 57–59, 133

Shamgar, Meir, 190; Shamgar report, 187

Sharon, Ariel, 174

Shawa, Hashim, 146–47

Shehadeh, Raja, 151–52, 224n4

Shtayyeh, Mohammad, 209

Simpson, Audra, 92

Siraj Fund Management Company, 78

Smith, Neil, 18, 30, 162, 208

social reproduction, 13–14, 16, 19, 21, 25, 29, 31, 138, 140, 201, 204, 208

South Hebron Hills, 185–86

sovereignty, 6, 17, 57, 83, 85, 126, 202; embedded, 92; jurisdiction and, 22–23, 91, 196–97; law and, 21, 34, 182, 219n10; state and, 18–19, 30–31, 104, 165, 208, 210, 218n7

special outline plans (blue line plans), 87–91, 171, 179

Stamatopoulou-Robbins, Sophia, 222n8

"State Building to Sovereignty" (document), 104

State Investigative Commission: Shamgar report, 187

state-scale economics, 7, 11, 16, 25, 30, 57, 81, 202, 208, 211

state mode of production, 16, 25

state-scale planning, 5, 16, 82, 86, 113–14

* 9 7 8 1 4 7 8 0 1 4 0 9 6 *